CW00953068

UNDENIABLE

Also by Cameron Hanes

Endure: How to Work Hard, Outlast, and Keep Hammering

UNDENIABLE

HOW TO REACH THE TOP
AND STAY THERE

CAMERON
HANES

MACMILLAN
BUSINESS

First published 2025 by St. Martin's Press,
an imprint of St. Martin's Publishing Group

This edition first published in the UK 2025 by Macmillan Business
an imprint of Pan Macmillan
The Smithson, 6 Briset Street, London EC1M 5NR
EU representative: Macmillan Publishers Ireland Ltd, 1st Floor,
The Liffey Trust Centre, 117–126 Sheriff Street Upper,
Dublin 1, D01 YC43
Associated companies throughout the world
www.panmacmillan.com

ISBN 978-1-0350-7912-4 HB
ISBN 978-1-0350-7913-1 TPB

9 8 7 6 5 4 3 2 1

A CIP catalogue record for this book is available from the British Library.

Interior design by Peter Romeo, Wooly Head Design
Printed and bound by CPI Group (UK) Ltd, Croydon, CR0 4YY

Visit **www.panmacmillan.com** to read more about all our books
and to buy them. You will also find features, author interviews and
news of any author events, and you can sign up for e-newsletters
so that you're always first to hear about our new releases.

CONTENTS

"THERE'S NO REST FOR ME IN THIS WORLD.
PERHAPS IN THE NEXT."

—*T. Shelby*

FOREWORD

Human motivation is a peculiar thing. We all come into this world with the same circuits—the same biological machinery that creates an ability for us to pursue goals, to do hard things. It is ancient stuff: these neurons and brain circuits that place our mind and body into a state of wanting, and in some cases *needing*, to move toward a goal. All animals have these circuits, and they always look pretty much the same. In fact, it doesn't matter if you're looking at the brain of a dog, a horse, a raccoon, or a person. They're identical and they all leverage the same chemical—dopamine, as a sort of currency for determining the value of our efforts.

Humans are special, however, because we have an expanded patch of real estate in the front of our brain—our prefrontal cortex, that lets us apply new rules, *our* rules, to basic drives. In other words, our prefrontal cortex gives us the opportunity to get motivated by the *idea* of something, not just by our emotions or biological drives. We can be motivated by the idea of serving family, our country, to earn self-respect, by fear, by love, or by a higher calling. That makes us truly special, but it also means that there truly are no excuses. A failure to motivate to get things done is a failure to honor our God-given uniqueness as a species.

I don't know if Cameron Hanes ever sat back and thought about any of that. Probably not. But what I do know is that Cam honors and embodies that gift every single day, and I know of no other human as hardworking, or consistent with his efforts across as many domains of life, as Cam is.

Cam's is a wild story. A boy growing up in a broken home in a small Oregon town outside another small Oregon town becomes an athlete and a drinker, just like his father was. And in an almost predictable way, both of them experience a series of near-fatal accidents, potentially irreversible detours, and increasingly deterministic circumstances.

Why predictable? Well, because those circuits for motivation—they have another unique feature in humans too. Humans are the only species that uses the motivation-generating circuitry to become addicted to behaviors or substances that can lead to our demise. So, if ever there was a double-edged blade in our wiring, it is that the same brain circuits that can drive us to do phenomenally hard and positively generative things can destroy us.

Whether consciously or not, Cam Hanes internalized that reality. He took the life he had been handed—the lack of stability in his childhood home, his internal frustration about the world he was born into, and he made the decision to lean into his love of bowhunting, to get sober from alcohol, to get married and to embrace the joys and challenges raising three children. By any measure, he took the right road.

But love is a special motivator. It's not just an idea. It's an idea fused to an emotion that doesn't just leverage dopamine, it generates it. Cam used his love of bowhunting to embrace daily shooting practice. Soon he realized he could venture deeper into the woods, stalk more efficiently and carry out larger game if he trained harder, and harder, and longer. Soon Cam's runs became daily half- or full marathons. That's right, a full or half-marathon every day before a full day's work, followed by shooting practice, lifting weights in the garage, tending to his home business, and all while being a devoted husband and father.

Eventually the mighty Joe Rogan learned of Cam's training and hunting prowess, and the rest is history. The whole world now knows who Cameron Hanes is and his "Keep Hammering" mantra is as direct and impactful as Nike's "Just Do It," but frankly, more so because "Keep Hammering" is an everyday thing. Running, lifting, shooting, no matter what. No 21-days-to-this or New Year's resolutions to that. No flashy commercials. Keep Hammering is, just as it sounds, unrelenting.

No one can stay unrelentingly driven unless they have a readily accessible set of motivators to pull from. I mean, c'mon, this the USA—and there are countless stories of people rising from anonymity or challenges to significant levels of recognition, then succumbing to the excesses or slowly fading away. Not Cam. What truly sets Cameron Hanes apart and why he is such a shining example of human motivation, is that he wasn't handed a path, an academic staircase, or a military road to follow. To be sure, those are respectable trajectories, but he had no roadmap. He looked at what he had, and he looked inward, into the understanding that motivation is not just a choice but a series of choices. Then made the one choice—to lean into his loves, and to let that serve as the organizational and driving force for all the rest. Cam loves to share his love of hunting—so he teaches it online, and to the guests and listeners of his podcast. He loves being a provider, so he hunts, and he shares the meat he kills. He loves to run, so he runs, and shares his love of running. And on, and on, and on.

Everything about Cam and everything he does is steeped in that love and I do believe that God offers special powers to those that embrace life through that portal. After all, we all share the same circuitry. It's not just a question of what we do with it. It matters what we use as fuel.

So, as we marvel at the head-shake-inducing battles Cam endures: 100-mile races on badly broken feet, a super-human training schedule and unbreaking devotion to his wife and kids, we feel Cam's love. We feel it as his fuel. God offered us Cam Hanes as an example of what's possible to achieve, but also how to achieve it. The question then becomes, what do we do with that feeling? How do we harness and apply it toward creating our own best life, our own right road?

Undeniable shows you how.

Andrew D. Huberman, Ph.D.

PROLOGUE: REACHING THE TOP

My world used to be 20 miles big. When I was a teenager, I lived in a small logging community 20 miles outside of Springfield, Oregon. A big trip would be to go to town—where the "flatlanders" lived—to get pizza or see a movie or hang out in a bar. Growing up, I was a guy with my head down, always looking at the ground, never really finding a reason to look up and have dreams. Those 20 miles represented my life's universe.

Chances are, you know what happened next. By now, you probably know my origin story: how a guy going nowhere got brought into the world of bowhunting by a high school friend named Roy Roth. Things started to happen, and all of a sudden my gaze began to go up. I started looking farther: To places like the mountains way over in eastern Oregon. The Eagle Cap Wilderness. The wilderness was a lot more than 20 miles. To me, that was a whole other world. Soon it became *my* world.

The bigger the world became, the stronger my mission inside it grew. On my quest to become the best bowhunter I could be, I soon realized how many others were on similar quests in their lives. I found so many connections in this big world of ours. One day I received a tweet with an invitation to come to Los Angeles and talk about bowhunting and fitness with Joe Rogan, and I discovered that my quest was a lot bigger than I thought it was. Suddenly I found myself looking toward the mountains—toward any mountain in sight—and wondering what was on the other side of them.

That's how it always starts. It begins with this person who has no real reason to dream. No reason to be confident and nothing to be excited about. A head down and a heart desolate. But then something happens. Little changes start to take place.

One person believing in you gives you motivation.

One person doubting you gives you fuel.

One passion gives you purpose.

One victory gives you confidence to keep going.

It all starts with that small journey. And as I always say, if I did it, *anyone can.*

I shared my story in *Endure,* and it's been gratifying to see the response from readers. If that book is my origin story, then this is the next installment of my journey. The invitation to share my passion of this unique endeavor called bowhunting with Joe Rogan and the rest of the world opened many doors. All of a sudden this bowhunter from a logging town began to find himself meeting and training with incredible individuals from all over the world: Olympians and fighters and runners and intellectuals. I said a few years ago in my book *Endure* that I could fill an entire book full of the outliers I've met and what I've learned from them. *Undeniable* is that book.

I might owe Rogan for the inspiration behind the title. During one visit, I was sharing how I was able to train with all of these different outliers and how that allowed me to pick their brains and see what made them tick. I was able to run alongside the best of the best, and *that* is how you progress. Anybody who has ever risen to heights in their field has always learned from the greats and has always strived to add tools to their toolbox. Now I was able to immerse myself amongst winners to try to learn more from their mindset.

"It's like that expression 'Be undeniable,'" Joe said. "There's a certain level that you can achieve in life. You can say all you want about Michael Jordan. That motherfucker's undeniable. He's one of the greatest basketball players that's ever walked the face of the planet Earth, if not the best. That's just an undeniable person. And it's very few people that get to that undeniable place. And if you really want to have no excuses in life, you're going to have to be undeniable, and you're going to have haters. You're going to have haters. But those haters can all *suck* it, because they're just lying to themselves."

I've always taken a lot of inspiration from those undeniable people like Jordan and Kobe Bryant. I will always remember something the great Hall of Famer Allen Iverson shared about Kobe, who he had often faced as an opponent. He said that when the other players would go out to the club, Kobe would go to the gym.

"That was just him," Iverson said. "That was 'Mamba.' He was younger than me, but I actually looked up to him and his greatness."[1]

That was why there was only one Kobe. He was simply working harder than his competitors. That's what sets those who are undeniable from the rest.

What drives me every day and it has for decades is asking myself the following questions:

How can I become the best I can be?

What can I do today to become better than I was yesterday?

And how can I be better tomorrow than I am today?

That's why I study outliers, men and women who are experts in their field. They can be track athletes, mixed martial arts (MMA) fighters, scientists, or experts in any discipline. There's something about all these people that makes them truly exceptional, so I examine those people, and I try to use what I learned from them to earn an edge over what I had the previous day. That's why I created my podcast called the *Keep Hammering Collective*. It's a chance to bring together winners and successful people and learn from their journeys. We get to hear about their successes and failures, but mostly we can hear how they've obtained their winning mindset. But before I pick their brains, I share my routine with these outliers. Each one is introduced to my daily Lift Run Shoot.

I know I have to put in the work every day to be the best I can be, so Lift Run Shoot has been a big part of it. It can be in any order—it doesn't matter. My ultimate goal every day is to hurt. Unless I'm outdoing everybody, I'm not offering my best. Running is to build endurance throughout those long hunts. Lifting is to build strength for packing the animal out after the kill, and as we know strength is never a weakness. And lastly, shooting my bow accurately is what makes those other two happen. No matter how fit you are, if you can't hit the animal you want to hit, you don't have to worry about your endurance or strength.

Outliers who visit share this Lift Run Shoot experience with me, and then we sit down to talk for the podcast. What better way is there to get to know someone before an interview than suffering together?

I want to talk to these outliers and hear how they became successful. These people have done extraordinary things with their lives. My hope with my podcast and now this book is to glean things for others to take and use to elevate their own lives.

Sometimes I sit back and wonder how a bowhunter from that small logging town in Oregon is now training with all of these incredible outliers who have risen to the top of their fields. But the truth is I like people who put themselves in a position to become undeniable at what they do. Some people out there might not like me, and they might say all sorts of things about me, but they cannot deny the work I put in and the results to show for it. You can judge and say whatever the fuck you want, but when the goal and tunnel-vision focus is on becoming undeniable, hollow criticism from the cheap seats doesn't hold much weight.

Just like I wrote in *Endure,* I hate giving advice. I don't have a blueprint. But I will listen to those outliers who will share their wisdom and show their roadmap to success. I am always learning and trying to improve. Along those lines, my intent with this book is to share some of that wisdom with you.

Do you want to be elite, or do you want to be normal? If you want to be elite, you're going to have to step out of what normal people do, ignore how they think, and dismiss how they approach things.

You need to study from the masters. Then you need take those nuggets and apply them to your own life.

When you do that, who knows what's possible?

CHAPTER 1

CHOOSE YOUR SUFFERING

RESILIENCE:

The capability of a strained body to recover its size and shape after deformation caused especially by compressive stress

"SUCCESS IS A FUNCTION OF PERSISTENCE
AND DOGGEDNESS AND THE WILLINGNESS TO
WORK HARD FOR TWENTY-TWO MINUTES TO
MAKE SENSE OF SOMETHING THAT
MOST PEOPLE WOULD GIVE UP ON AFTER
THIRTY SECONDS."

—*Malcolm Gladwell, journalist and author,*
Outliers: The Story of Success

Nobody wants to get into a race to the death with David Goggins. I learned that the first time he came out to my town in 2018 to do what would become the first-ever Lift Run Shoot experience I shared with an outlier. We had a big Saturday planned that consisted of a 50K that would be followed by shooting bows, lifting weights, and then watching Ultimate Fighting Championship (UFC). Since he came in the day before, we decided to take a run up Mount Pisgah. That's when I saw the two sides of the man. There is the stoic David who you might share a cup of coffee with, then there's Goggins who you throw raw meat at.

I normally take guests to Mount Pisgah, where we can share a run together. I can usually tell pretty quickly how good a runner somebody is in the first few hundred yards. As we took off up the backside of the hill, I thought to myself, *Damn he's got a long stride!* At the time, he was living in Nashville, so I assumed that since there were no hills there, this was going to be the equalizer. But the farther up the mountain we got, his stride never changed. Normally when you're running uphill, you shorten your stride—because if you don't, you're going to gas out—but Goggins's stride never seemed to change.

This is gonna be rough.

He never faded in our run to the top of the mountain. After we finished, he remained calm and serious. I had grown used to Goggins, the badass who spoke to followers on social media, but David was cool to hang out with. I appreciated being able to train with somebody who was going to push me. And this was just our warm-up for the Frozen Trail Run 50K the next morning.

David Goggins has provided an incredible amount of inspiration, not just for me, but my family in general. For example, my son, Truett, who has been the Guinness Book of World Records holder of pull-ups in a day, got the idea to chase that title solely because David previously held it.

Photo by Ryan Loco

The following day was cold and rainy. Miles into the race, everybody was soaking wet. By mile 22, something started happening with Goggins's feet. He had to untie his shoes and take them off, something that's never a good sign 22 miles into a 32-mile 50K ultramarathon. Your feet get torn up in long races: toes can be bleeding, toenails are torn off. This is what happens. I wasn't sure what was going on, but I decided to keep chugging along. I assumed that David would get it figured out and would catch up with me. But I couldn't help having doubts.

Maybe I won't see him again?

But . . . no. Sure as shit, he caught back up with me and my brother, Taylor Spike, who was also running the race. By the time he reached us, he was running in a different groove. Just as we were going up this last grade to do one more summit in the race, my calf began to lock up so I couldn't run it. As I started to power hike up the hill, that's when Goggins took off. When I reached the top of the mountain, 30 miles into the race with only a couple left to go, I asked a cameraman who was up there how Goggins looked.

"Well, he had his shirt off"—remember, it was cold and rainy—and he was saying, "They don't fucking know me! They don't know me, son!'"

"Who was he saying that to?" I asked the cameraman.

"Nobody. There was nobody up there."

Goggins got *better* the farther he ran. He crushed the second half of that race. I saw David turn into Goggins firsthand, and it was real. When shit got hard, he got into this different zone. He became better and tougher. All I could think was, *This guy is different.* And I loved it.

The same thing happened when we were lifting weights later that day. We had been doing as many reps as we could on the incline bench, true burnout sets, however many it took to get 100 reps, and this was after doing 600 total reps already during this weightlifting session. My younger son, Truett, who was 21 at the time, was working out with us as well. My trainer, Eric McCormack, was running us through the workout, so, on the last set, McCormack was standing behind Goggins, urging him on. I had been able to get in only 15 or maybe just 13 for my last set, but David switched to Goggins mode and pushed it. It was insane to watch. McCormack was calling off the numbers—"Nineteen! Twenty! Twenty-one!"—all while Goggins began to shout, "They don't know me, son!" and "Who's gonna carry the boats and the logs?" Most people get fatigued, but once again he showed us how he was actually getting stronger.

Say whatever you want about David, but when he morphs into Goggins, look out. He's a whole different person; someone who's unstoppable. Someone who is truly undeniable.

We all look for inspiration, for people to follow and emulate. Goggins is one of those people who I love the most. Good, hardworking people who embrace suffering. I fall in love with their spirit. Goggins is one of those guys that I know is never going to waver. You always know what you're going to get with him. He understands what it takes to be undeniable.

"It's a lot more than mind over matter," Goggins wrote in his book *Can't Hurt Me: Master Your Mind and Defy the Odds.* "It takes relentless self-discipline to schedule suffering into your day, every day."

I am always looking to learn more about my breaking point and ability. I am drawn to challenges where success often hinges on one's ability to deal with pain, to endure suffering. Bowhunting the country I love, the rugged mountains, is tough. Do it long enough and there will be many days that you'll question why you subject yourself to such misery.

Sometimes I wonder if I am drawn to endeavors like bowhunting or extreme endurance running because I like the challenge or because I am good at suffering. I think it is because of the latter. I've been doing it a long time.

My mom and dad divorced when I was four going on five. He was a star athlete; she was a cheerleader. Theirs is not the first such union to fail. Young adults having kids is never easy. I've never blamed them or used the fact that I came from a "broken home" as a crutch. Just the opposite, in fact. Their divorce did hurt me and my younger brother, Pete, though. I think this was when I first learned to excel at suffering. I remember wanting nothing more than my mom and dad to be back together. Not having my dad around made my heart ache. He was like a god to me. And while I didn't see him nearly as much as I wanted to after the split, his legend motivated me.

Kids many times put their parents on pedestals, but parents are not perfect. They screw up, and their kids are exposed to their flaws. That never really happened with my dad. He set the standard, was infallible and omnipresent. No one could ever compete. My mom remarried, and, of course, I hated my stepdad because he wasn't Bob Hanes. There was drama in the house, and eventually I went to live with my dad. Suffering followed me.

Living with Dad was tough because I dearly missed my brother Pete, who opted to stay with Mom. Pete didn't have the same connection with Dad because he was so young when our parents divorced. With Dad busy starting a new business and me missing Pete, I moved back with my mom. One good thing came out of it. My stepdad, trying to extend an olive branch of sorts, took me and Pete rifle hunting. I was 15, and Pete was 12. Right out of the gate, I was a good, successful hunter and an accurate shot. I went out by myself a lot, as while my stepdad got me started in the field, I still wasn't that excited to hang out with him; accepting my stepdad felt like it meant I was disrespecting my real dad.

I kept filling tags until I was 19, when my buddy Roy Roth got me started in bowhunting. The timing was perfect. I needed the challenge of bowhunting. Rifle hunting wasn't offering it.

At first, I was in over my head. My very first morning out with my bow, I had a big 6x7 bull elk come stomping into range, bugling the entire way. I was knelt down, shaking. My arms felt tingly, like they were asleep, and I wondered how I would ever get my bow pulled back. Even if I did, I had doubts that my tiny arrow could down the amazing beast that stood before me. I got my bow back and completely missed that big bull elk on the first shot, then somehow got another shot before he spooked and blew that shot too.

Learning from that mistake and many thereafter, I eventually found success that very first year after 18 straight days of elk hunting when I arrowed a spike bull elk. The next year, in my second season bowhunting in the woods near my hometown, I arrowed a 5-point bull elk, a black bear, and a Pope & Young blacktail buck.

It wasn't long before I knew it was time to take this passion of bowhunting to the next level. I had my sights set on Oregon's largest roadless wilderness area, the Eagle Cap. Roy and I headed toward the middle to the most remote area I could find on my topo map. We were 400 miles away from home; away from the only area we had ever hunted. Just as I had hoped, the Eagle Cap Wilderness was tougher than anything I had experienced. Not only was the hunting hard, but the country was overwhelming, and the conditions were extreme. It was a true test. I missed the comforts of home. I missed my loved ones. Being away hurt, and I was suffering. But that feeling was familiar.

The ache and the pain. The misery. I embraced it.

I thought of my family and my dad a lot in the mountains. Absence makes the heart grow fonder, they say. I think they are right. The irony was that I loved the hunt, and my father never hunted. He never bought one hunting license in his entire life, and, in fact, he didn't get why anyone would hunt. Regardless of this, he was always proud of my accomplishments. But those accomplishments came from those early days of suffering in the wilderness.

Shared suffering builds bonds. I first discovered this with Roy Roth. Before he ever invited me to start bowhunting, I already knew something about suffering, but my misery came from hating my life and never feeling happy. The only suffering my body felt came from being lonely or the morning after a long night of drinking. I never realized that one day I would welcome suffering and, actually, that I would *thrive* on suffering. The wilderness offered a different sort of misery. This was the kind that helped you grow and made you stronger.

Roy understood this well. It came from venturing into the rugged and treacherous wilderness. Of course, not everybody would view this kind of suffering as a positive thing. Most people wouldn't want anything to do with it. So, when Roy moved to Alaska in the early 1990s, just as I was all in on backcountry bowhunting, I had to learn to suffer by myself.

The pain felt wonderful.

You find out what type of person somebody is when they put a fucking rock on their back. That's why I love the Lift Run Shoot experience.

My fourth guest to visit was Chris Williamson. Even though I had been following him for a while and loving the content he was putting on his *Modern Wisdom* podcast, I was able to get to know him more and to dive deeper into this theme of suffering while showing him my daily routine. In some ways, Williamson's childhood resembled my own. He was an only child living in a northeast town of England called Stockton-on-Tees. As someone really unpopular and bullied at school, he grew up convinced that he was flawed and chronically meant to be alone. I understood this feeling. But this drove him to become the man he has become today.

"Most of the high performers that I know about are coming from a place of insufficiency," Chris told me. "They're trying to prove something to that parent, that teacher, that bully, that group of friends or whoever from their childhood that they actually are worthy of love or praise or acceptance or admiration."

When he first got to a university, Williamson wanted to have an excuse to party for free, so he became a club promoter and became very good at it. He and his business partner built a successful business. In his late 20s, he became widely known to the British public

The first "intellectual" I ever interviewed was Chris Williamson. I was stressed out because that's not my forte, but it turned out to be one of my most popular podcasts, and his "unchosen suffering" take from the discussion went viral when he ended up on a reality dating show called *Love Island*. To Chris, this big reality TV dating show was the pinnacle of the party-boy world championships. But suddenly he found that he didn't like his life.

"I thought, *Is this really all that I've got to offer the world?* You know: me in tiny swim shorts prancing about on TV. Not that that's not nothing, but it just felt like there was something else missing. And even though I loved the work that I'd done, it felt like being a crab that kind of was outgrowing his shell somehow."

Williamson found meaning and purpose after two of his friends invited him on their podcast, and he discovered that he really enjoyed it. He thought, *If I do this on my own, I can do this as much as I want.* So, in 2018 he started his own podcast. Five years later when we spoke, *Modern Wisdom* had 600 episodes.

When Williamson came to visit, he admitted that he hadn't run in a long time but rather only did little jogging warm-ups in between lifting. For a while, he did CrossFit. After picking him up at the airport, I took him to shoot some arrows at The Bow Rack, the archery pro shop in Springfield, Oregon, that opened in 1971. After that I drove by the house I grew up in and the first place I used to hunt. I wanted to give him the perspective I had when I was in my early 20s.

"I thought if I could have a little mobile home like that," I said, motioning to a trailer we were driving by at the time, "and a decent truck that I could count on getting me to work—if that was my setup right there, I thought I'd be set. My own little place and a truck. That was going to be my life. That was the goal."

"What's the goal now?" Chris asked me.

"I don't know. I feel like I'm playing with house money. Since a trailer and truck was my goal, and I have more than that, I can't lose. I already won, no matter what happens. I should never have made it out of this small town and don't really know how I did."

I elaborated on my attitude of feeling like I didn't deserve everything I had, like the house I owned or the life I was leading. I told Chris I felt like somebody was going to figure that out, and everything was going to go away in a snap.

"There are people out here who work their ass off who will never have what I have, so why should *I* have it?" I explained.

Chris told me this was a feeling that he really struggled with himself, a feeling that he was only now starting to get past.

"I think it's a by-product of coming up in a super-working-class background, where you associate the amount of money that you deserve—or the recognition or whatever—

not only with the amount of work that you put in but the amount of suffering associated with that work. And this sort of Puritan work ethic—it's what my country is very good at. So, you can imagine these priests in the Middle Ages, and the sun's beating down on their back, and their hoeing the ground in the garden. But they're not doing it necessarily for what the work achieves. It's the work itself. It's in service of God. Right? That's that Puritan work ethic. It's almost like self-flagellation. They're making themselves hurt because the sacrifice is their tribute."

After shooting arrows, we took a warm-up run up Mount Pisgah before grabbing the 72-pound rock in my truck. The clouds had settled over the 1,060-foot-tall mountain, so we jogged in a thick fog for about 7 miles before heading back to the truck to pick up the rock. We took turns hauling it up the mountain. Chris learned something that everybody who comes learns eventually:

There is no good way to carry a giant rock up a mountain.

As we were nearing the top of Pisgah, I took over carrying the rock and went ahead while Chris continued walking and caught his breath. The guys were there filming him, so they captured his thoughts.

"I respect Cam," he said. "I admire him a lot. I've got to learn a lot from him today. There's not much else I could do right now that would fulfill me more than this. I mean, it could be a bit warmer, I guess. But again, we're gonna have some elk chili later on, and it's going to taste a lot better because we've done this. And also, man, I work hard, right? I put myself through difficult things, especially cognitively. But I can't push myself this hard without a reason to do it. Performance without a purpose is one hell of a skill to have. No one there cheering you on. No race to prepare for. No finish line. No glory. No nothing. Yet he still performs. He still pushes hard. And I suck at that. I find it very, very hard to put myself into the place that Cam's put me in today without a Cam there."

After taking turns with the rock until reaching the cloudy summit, all that was left was to lift, then we would have earned our suffering for the day. It turned out that this would be one of the themes of our discussion the following day when we spoke about taking that rock up the mountain.

"Why I like doing it is because when someone suffers, there's never a more honest time," I said. "When you're suffering, you can't fake it. That's one reason why the Mob has used torture: they're going to find out the truth about a person. The military makes their men suffer because they want to find out who's weak and who's the best. Because you cannot lie when you're suffering."

I asked Chris whether he thought suffering was the ultimate truth teller, the ultimate truth serum? He said it definitely opens people up, and he proceeded to the concept of chosen and unchosen suffering from David Goggins's latest book, *Never Finished*. Unchosen suffering is going to happen in life: like your parents passing away, and relationships breaking down, and your body failing you. Things are going to happen that you have no control over, Chris said, and the only way that you can prepare yourself for unchosen suffering is with chosen suffering.

"You can elect to put yourself into a position to become a stronger alloy of whatever the metal is that you're made of," Chris stated. "And by purposefully choosing difficult things, you will arm yourself against that situation . . . Every single person that I know that is incredibly successful in a balanced way and has a good perspective on it elects to do very hard things regularly. It humbles them. It reminds them that they're just mortal. And it also means that if the entire mainstream media apparatus tries to come down on top of you—let's say just as a hypothetical—you can deal with it because you know that you've dealt with a thousand disgusting kettlebell workouts followed by a cold tub."

The other concept Williamson spoke about was also from Goggins's latest book: performance without a purpose.

Launching arrows with Chris Williamson

"I found that very interesting because a lot of the time people need an excuse to perform. They need a race to be working toward a goal, a holiday, a photo shoot, a wedding. And that is what drives them forward. And, you know, that's not nothing. That's an incredibly powerful, potent motivator. But if you can manage to perform without that, that's *real* power. Because it means that not only are you going to choose your suffering, but you're going to continue to hit close to your maximum performance with no finish line, no crowd celebrating your completion, no glory. No nothing. And that's why you carrying this fucking pointless rock uphill with marker pen on it that reads 'Poser,' with no one there. That's why that's impressive."

As we talked about Goggins, I said I believed he was the master of self-motivation. Williamson shared how the two of us were similar in regard to motivating ourselves.

"The desire to prove other people wrong is a fucking potent fuel, but it is toxic," he said. "I do think that as much as proving other people wrong is great and useful and can get you a good amount of the way there, I do wonder how much peace you find with that. And I asked Goggins that as well. 'Have you found peace?' And he said, 'When you go to war with yourself, you find an awful lot of peace.' So maybe the only way out is through stuff like this."

Williamson expressed how he wished that the Gogginses of the world—those people who were daily doing these sorts of things of going to war with themselves—could go to bed with a little peace, knowing they had made a sacrifice trying to inspire others. But then he wondered if having a little bit more inner peace would mean those people would be less motivated and disciplined.

Hearing that word *peace* made me think of something else a lot of people say, how the key is *balance*.

"If you're 'balanced,' you're probably not doing shit to stand out," I said. "A lot of people are balanced. They go run a mile, they have a cookie. Very balanced. You rewarded your effort. The people I know who are the best at what they do are not balanced. And I don't know about how peace relates to that. I feel a peace in the mountains and sleep great. At home, I have a hard time sleeping, because I'm like, 'I should be putting in miles, doing work. I'm wasting time sleeping.'"

To me, sacrificing more means that at the end of the day you feel exhausted. At the end of the Lift Run Shoot with Chris, I went to bed feeling like it had been a good day. A good day of training where I loved the fellowship and where I felt pretty good. I was at peace with the effort, I told him, but I didn't necessarily feel "balanced."

"You are in the top 0.1 percentile of people that do hard things, showing suffering on a daily basis that inspires a lot of other people," Chris said, adding that many people might admire that but wouldn't want to live that life.

Williamson compared that sort of suffering to a scout for an army going out on their own.

"They're suffering with wilderness and loneliness and foraging for food and all the rest of it for the troops. What they bring back is the information that makes the rest of the army better. And that's a fucking noble purpose. That's an incredibly noble purpose."

The way Chris sees this is that people can't take only a part of someone's life. They can't look at someone like Goggins or myself and say that they like our approach to training but don't want to deal with sleeping four hours a night or don't want to feel like they should be out there getting in miles. Yes, they might want my motivation for training, but they didn't want to deal with my permanent discontent when I wasn't putting in work.

"This isn't an outfit; this is a onesie," Chris stated. "You have to take every single bit. You have to take the bad childhood. You have to take the loneliness at the age of thirteen. You have to take the regret for four decades about the decision to leave your father and move back to live with your mom and brother. Every single bit of you has contributed to make the person that you are. It's like alchemy. Like taking something which is toxic or bad or useless and turning it into something which is positive. That is where the magic lies."

The Eagle Cap Wilderness was the most wild and intimidating place I ever stepped foot in. It was a big, unforgiving country where every kill is earned with blood, sweat, and tears.

Roy was still living in Oregon when we scraped up enough money to hunt Eagle Cap. The first time we went, we got our butts kicked, but we still loved everything about seeing big, unforgiving elk country and embracing the challenge. We went the first week of the season, in the last week in August, which isn't the best time to hunt elk, since they hadn't started to rut yet. We needed a break on the elk but didn't get one that first trip, so we decided we had to get back somehow.

On the third week of the season, Roy and I made it back to Eagle Cap, and that's when I killed my first wilderness bull—a spike bull. It was 22 miles to the trailhead, and we had two llamas to assist us. A spike bull doesn't yield a ton of meat, so it wasn't too heavy weight-wise, but it was still 22 miles. This wasn't the giant trophy I was going for, but the bull was still a big mark of success for me. It meant a lot to go back there and hunt a country that people larger than life—heroes of mine—had hunted. Roy didn't kill, but he had opportunities; it's just a tough hunt. Regardless, my friend was excited for me. We felt like we had done something monumental. This was our introduction to the brutal challenges of the wilderness.

Then Roy moved his family up to Alaska and started building his legacy as both a contractor and a hunter while I remained in Oregon. I tried to find people to share that wilderness experience with, but it was a hard time. It's not for everybody. You either love it and can't think about anything else or you hate it. There's not much in between. That sprawling remote country and the feeling of insignificance it brings is too much for some people.

It made me feel alive.

For the next 12 years, I ventured into the Eagle Cap Wilderness. Most of the time, I was by myself; I stopped wasting the energy trying to convince somebody to join me. I couldn't afford to squander it, as it took all I had to withstand those unrelenting mountains.

I did have a friend named South Cox come out with me once. He is super tough. For the first six days, we didn't really hunt together; he killed a bull on his own, while I killed a buck on my own. After that, we happened to bump into each other at base camp, and he said he wanted to go out with me on day seven. He was there when I killed a nice bull. It was fun to have him accompany me to Eagle Cap, but other than that, I was always alone. Another time, I killed a 6x6 bull when I was hunting on my own. Since it was the opening day of the season, the llamas I had used to pack in were too tired to haul the bull out, but I did have friends on the other side of the mountain about 10 miles away. I had the bull broke down and the meat hanging in a tree before I hiked the 10 miles to ask if they could lend me a hand, and a few strong backs. This group—Tim Thompson, his cousin Joel, and Greg Miller—all helped me pack out the bull for 12 miles to the trailhead where my truck was parked. All the other times, it was just me hunting in isolation.

This rugged wild shaped me into the hunter I am today. Those years in the Eagle Cap showed me just how resilient I could be.

Hunting on my own felt like nothing else I had ever experienced. While hunting deep in the wilderness, I saw the world through a whole different lens. And through that altered perspective, I had a stark awakening.

I'm nothing deep in the mountain backcountry.
If I die for whatever reason back here, nothing changes. Absolutely nothing changes.
The wind will still blow the same.
The animals will still carry on the same way.
The mountains will remain unaffected.
Nothing will change if I die.

The wilderness puts life in perspective. In the outside world, in regular society, we can think we're so important, and we might have this misconception that the world revolves around us. Obviously, it doesn't, but that doesn't stop us from eliciting a response from people, weighing in on this and that, and feeling very self-important. But in the mountains, none of that matters. In the mountains, your life is similar to that of an ant. If you step on an ant, you just keep going. Nothing changes. The same thing applies in the wilderness for a human.

There is death every day in the mountains, and it has no bearing on anything. Coming to grips with this during those early hunting trips didn't adversely impact my confidence. In fact, it made me feel empowered. I thought to myself, *If I'm going to survive back here, I need to be at my very best.*

For some this might be too daunting, but for me it was exciting.

What types of challenges can I face?

I knew before I faced them that I had to prepare myself to overcome those challenges. That was the only way I was going to be able to consistently kill a bull elk with an arrow.

This wasn't overwhelming, it was incredible. I loved it. Even though I couldn't share this with anybody, I kept going back. Early on, I started with short scouting trips because I wasn't super comfortable being alone that far back. This was all before we had satellite phones or anything like a Garmin inReach satellite communicator. It didn't matter. I was addicted to whatever positives I got out of the wilderness. They outweighed any of the negatives, any of the fear or suffering that being out there might bring.

There were some intense moments in the wilderness in those early days. On the hunt when I killed my first wilderness black bear, I set up in this saddle that animals kept moving through. It was a low spot that connected a big basin with a water source—a swamp area—perfect for animals traveling the path of least resistance. The day prior to the bear kill, I screwed up on a nice bull, but the following day, a flash of movement caught my attention. I prepared for the opportunity but thought it might be a mountain lion or a coyote. A few seconds later, a cinnamon-colored bear, with blond highlights on its back, came through, and I shot him at 50 yards. I thought I made a good shot, but I was so nervous about trailing him. I circled around on high spots in the rocks to try to see him down there in the trees below. Even though the shot felt good, I just wasn't sure. A wounded bear deep in the wilderness when you're by yourself can be intense. Nowadays, after killing more than 50 bears, I would just follow the blood, slowly, and if it wasn't expired yet, I'd arrow it again, knowing that if wounded-bear-type shit goes down, that's just the way it is. But at that time, I didn't have the kind of confidence I have now. I was very tentative. While I was up high, I finally saw that he was down—dead after a quick death sprint.

Big, late-summer thunderstorms often come through the mountains and with them lightning. With it striking all around in the middle of the night, these moments always felt extreme. Lightning can get people off the mountain in a hurry, as most just don't want to deal with worrying about getting struck. But storms happen in the mountains. In that country, you have to choose very carefully where you're sleeping at night. You never want to camp or hunker down by a lone tree on a high ridge because that can draw lightning. It's in your best

"FIND SOMETHING THAT'S HARD—THAT SUCKS—BUT THAT MAKES YOU TOUGH. THAT'S THE WHOLE POINT OF WHY I DO WHAT I DO. IT'S JUST AS SIMPLE AS IT GETS. YOU WANT A GOOD WORKOUT? GRAB A ROCK, TAKE IT TO THE TOP OF A MOUNTAIN, THEN BRING IT BACK DOWN. BOX IS CHECKED."

—*Cam Hanes*

interest to pick places that are going to be safe for humans in the event of thunder and lightning.

Speaking of campsites, one time I made a mistake and bedded down right in the middle of a travel route that elk moved through to feed. In the middle of the night, while I was in my little bivy sack, a whole herd of elk started coming through. They became spooked because they smelled human (me), so they started to scatter, and as I heard the hooves pounding around me, I had a horrible thought.

Am I going to get trampled here?

These are some of the little things that I never thought about until I was back there, in deep. Storms. Pouring rain. Snow. Freezing temperatures. Getting soaking wet and not being able to start a fire. This was another way you could literally die. Hypothermia is a real risk out there when you're wet and that far away from any heat source or any way to get out of it. I had to learn tricks on how to dry out, where to camp, how to start a fire and where to find material to burn, kindling or anything dry that I could light and build a fire off of. It might be under a thick canopy of pine trees or maybe on the south side of a tree that might stay dry, whereas the north side was typically taking the weather, so it'd be wetter. I also learned where to find pitch you can use to start fire and what wood burned hottest. It's little things like this that were big challenges for somebody who has never done it before and who is on their own.

Every time something came up, I had the same mentality.

Okay, I gotta earn this confidence one more time.

Then I did it, and each time I did, I became more capable and more confident and more self-sufficient. It was a process that took a long time. A process where the first few times were very intimidating.

Those hunts in the Eagle Cap Wilderness definitely changed me. It changed who I was. It changed how I thought about myself. And it changed how I carried myself, the confidence I had. Everything changed with that newfound confidence.

During this time, as I was learning and growing as a bowhunter, Roy was doing the same thing up in Alaska with even bigger challenges, since Alaska is even more unforgiving. Although we were both on our own, we were kind of still together. Getting better. Getting more capable. We had always shared a mindset that if a man's ever done what we were trying to do, then we could do it as well. If a man has never done it—if it's never been done in the history of mankind—then who knows? Maybe our odds were 50-50. We both had earned so much confidence in our abilities by overcoming so many challenges and then sharing those stories in pictures and videos.

Eventually I started to travel to Alaska to visit Roy and go on epic hunts. I probably went up there 30 different times for bowhunting adventures in which we pursued whatever we could; from Dall sheep, to giant brown bears, to moose, to caribou, to deer. We always chased the biggest adventures and the biggest challenges. We lived through some of the most intense experiences. But we didn't just go from hunting in the backwoods of our homes to experiences like those in the wilderness and expect to succeed. It's night and day different from a normal hunt where you're coming home at night every night and getting up early in the morning just for the day. Hunting animals in Alaska that live amongst the wolves and the grizzlies. You can't just go from the typical Everyman hunt to extreme adventure hunts—it takes time to develop the skills. That's what we did. We put ourselves in those positions over and over and over again. Places of pain and pressure. Moments where we felt miserable. Hours of being on our own. All of that started to pay off. Every year, it paid off.

With that confidence and knowledge and experience, I wanted more.

Man, if I can do this, what else can I do?

I once signed up for a 10K and quit at mile five.

Yeah.

We all have to start somewhere.

This was during an unhealthy phase of my life, right after I turned 21. I was going down the path that I told Chris Williamson about where all I really expected out of my life was that little house and that truck. I was still hunting but had no real sense of purpose. I spent my free time drinking with my buddies and wasn't accountable for anything or to anybody.

During this time, I signed up for the annual Butte to Butte 10K race in Eugene, Oregon. Just as I got to Fifth Street at the five-mile mark, I felt awful. *This fucking sucks,* I thought. But nobody feels good living the sort of lifestyle I was living. With one mile to go, I quit.

I couldn't make it *one more mile.* What kind of father would I be if I couldn't finish a mile?

Becoming a father finally made me get my life back in order. After discovering a passion for bowhunting, I kept pouring it on in the backcountry. Chasing misery by trying to stay longer. Hunting harder. Hurting more. It seemed like I had the entire wilderness to myself back in those days. The hunting was good, and I killed regularly. Over time, however, I knew I could get better.

But by the early 2000s, I felt something was missing. After growing up with hardship, I now almost felt like life was too easy. I was married to a beautiful, supportive wife, Tracey, had healthy kids, and a good job. As a kid, I'd felt like I suffered every day, but now I only suffered for a few weeks the entire year. I convinced myself I was getting soft, and I knew soft would not excel in the mountains.

Bowhunting the backcountry was something I loved, a challenge that by now had defined me. If I lost my edge from easy living, what would I become? I didn't want to find out. I started to run. I worked my way up, from local 5K and 10K races that I managed to finish. Then a 7.3-mile race an hour away in Salem. Then a half-marathon. All to get into shape for bowhunting.

In 2003 I started to pile on the miles, running 20 a day before I entered my first marathon, the Columbia Gorge Marathon, and I came in third place overall. Eventually I somehow learned of something called an ultramarathon. They had 50-milers and 100Ks and 100-milers. They even had a 200-mile race. Those races sounded crazy. Or as Roy and I would say, "Crazy *awesome.*" An ultra was the perfect thing to help me not become soft, to help me take my hunting to the next level.

I wanted to run out of my comfort zone, not only to build my confidence but also to increase my ability to suffer. I wanted to hurt in training because I knew I would hurt during the hunt. Just like bowhunting was a test, an ultra would also be an incredible test.

Just like building up to a marathon, I continued to strive for long distances. Two years after my first marathon, I ran my first ultra. The McDonald Forest 50K was 31 miles in the mountains of the Willamette Valley. When I finished that, I was *wrecked.* It took me over five hours to complete and other than my ball-busting hunts, it was the toughest thing I'd ever done.

I'll never forget as I was nearing the end of my first ultra, I met four guys running back at me up the trail. I wondered what in the heck they were doing. After finishing and finally getting my wits about me, I asked someone if they knew what those guys were doing running back up the trail.

"They're doing a double," someone told me. "Getting ready for Western."

"A what?"

They had finished the 31-mile ultra and were now running the course *in reverse,* logging 62 miles for the day. I was in awe. I didn't think I could run even one more step and had a hard time fathoming how anyone could double what I'd just done. Then I found out that "getting ready for Western" meant they were preparing for the late-June running of the Western States 100-Mile Endurance Run.

Driving home that day, I felt dumbfounded. I was clueless to what the human body was capable of.

I thought I was tough . . . I'm not even close.

I wrote in detail about my first ultra in *Endure*. For me, running those 100 miles meant becoming best friends with pain and suffering. This was going to be the way I could become a bowhunting machine. I had gained confidence from hunting that big country on my own in an unforgiving setting, but now I was also able to run 100 miles through the mountains. Combining everything I gained from living and surviving and even thriving in both of those experiences, I had an undeniable confidence soaring in me.

There's nothing I can't do.

"Resilience is the ability to literally stand back or crawl back to your feet when you've been knocked down. And that is an experience that is common to all."

Former Green Beret Mike Glover said that during our conversation after his Lift Run Shoot. He knows something about resilience having spent 18 years in the US Army and being deployed multiple times. We were talking about having a survival mindset, and he summed up it as having the mindset of resilience.

"Most people think that going through trauma, going through difficult circumstances, overcoming adversity, that that is unique," Mike said. "It's not. It's common to all. When you understand the benefits of it, you intentionally put yourselves in those circumstances. So, when we do the Lift Run Shoot, what we're doing in a simplified format is overcoming adversity and building resilience."

Building resilience, Mike said, is so simple. It starts with action, with one step. It starts when you understand the benefits of taking action. When you stop and realize that overcoming a difficult workout or a climb up a mountain *will* make you better in your life.

"Foundationally, resilience is the key," Mike explained. "And we recommend that people expose themselves to weaknesses. It's one of the reasons why I'm here. If you dial ten of your close partners or friends and say, 'Hey, would you like to come on the podcast?'

Cam with Mike Glover atop Mount Pisgah

there is a ten out of ten likelihood that the people who come and do the Lift Run Shoot will find a deficiency in one of those three things. They're a good runner, but, man, they can't lift weights. They immediately identify their weakness. And if they're willing to volunteer and expose themselves to vulnerabilities, they become better."

The key is to be exposed to weaknesses. Mike discovered that he was suffering going up Mount Pisgah with weight. His cardio was not where he wanted it to be and therefore knew he needed to make a change. This is the sort of thing that builds resilience in all of us.

The truth is that not everybody wants to put themselves in that position. Nobody wants to hurt. Nobody wants to feel inferior in any way, so we kind of insulate ourselves from things like that. That doesn't help us in the long term. It doesn't prepare us for down the road when the shit hits the fan.

As Goggins and Williamson said, there is chosen and unchosen suffering. When you choose to suffer—even a choice to enter the military and then having to embrace the suck like Mike—this makes those challenges in life easier to face. That suffering and misery equip us to be ready. But a lot of people don't choose that, Mike explained.

"A lot of us, because we're so comfortable and complacent—more so than we've ever been in human history—don't want that discomfort."

Glover said that a lot of Americans aren't conditioned for stress, yet they have an expectation that they will rise to the occasion when the time is necessary. If they are unprepared, this, of course, won't happen. They will easily become overwhelmed by the circumstances. Mike compared this with his trek up Mount Pisgah with the weight of the ruck on his shoulders.

"It's small goals, small moments in time, even breath to breath. I mean, going up the hill: I know the tactics to not quit. But when you look uphill and you have eighty pounds on your back, and I see you're a hundred meters ahead of me, I'm like, *Man, this is suffering.* I know one step at a time, one breath at a time. Manage your heart rate. Continue to move, and you'll be fine. Just stop. Take a break. You get five breaths, a break, and then continue to move."

Mike had learned these strategies so that's how he navigated climbing up the mountain. For anybody else, they might look at the top of the hill and think it wasn't achievable. They would believe there was no way they could make it and then turn around and start walking downhill, defeated.

"A lot of people don't realize in life you're always fighting uphill, and that's the point," Mike continued. "Accept that reality. You're not special because you have suffered in

Mike Glover

trauma. Accept that reality. Harness that energy and then focus in on something beneficial, making you better."

Like so many of these outliers I have met—so many outliers in life out there—Glover has chosen to suffer in order to learn a lot about himself and become more resilient moving forward. This is how you become prepared in life.

"It's resilience. It's a mindset," Mike said. "It starts in your head. It starts in your body. It starts in your spirit. That's the first step in preparedness."

If my passion is bowhunting the mountains, then part of that journey will be marked with suffering. If not, then, by definition, it's not a true passion. Consider that the word *passion* finds its root in both the Latin word *passiō* and the Greek word *páthos*, which both mean "suffering."

If you're not willing to suffer for something, then I'd say you aren't truly passionate about it. You may have strong feelings for it, but it's not marked by passion.

I've read that suffering reveals the way to greatness. I have seen the way and now wonder: Does anyone ever really experience greatness? Or is the true reward in the journey attempting to attain it?

I know I'll never be satisfied or feel

"great," because I don't think I have that level of elite talent. But I can't imagine my life without suffering and appreciating real challenges. Yes, I'm addicted to suffering. The status quo is never something I'll be good with.

I've been lucky enough to share this same path of suffering with some true greats, which has been humbling for me. I've learned a lot during these experiences.

Every day is a new chance to learn. And to suffer.

STICK WITH THE FORMULA

I don't think about tomorrow. I just think about today.

My to-do list has three words: Run. Lift. Shoot.

Call my mindset one day at a time. Call it whatever you want.

But I don't think about the future at all. I focus on the next 24 hours.

My daily routine of lift, run, and shoot can be changed to any different order, but it has to remain a daily thing. The wins and the acknowledgment and the successes all happen through that daily work and dedication.

If you just keep doing the right thing every day, you're going to be more successful. I don't know what that's going to look like in five years or even a year, but my history tells me it's going to be better. I'm going to be better.

Hard work is always rewarded, and the results are never random.

I already know these things work because I've been doing them forever.

So, today I'm going to stick with the formula I know.

I can't do anything more about yesterday, and I don't want to spend time planning for tomorrow. The past has already been written, and the future is a tale yet to be told. Write your story today.

Live life in the present tense.

CHAPTER 2

FIND A WAY

DETERMINATION:

The strength that carries you through the path of success in the midst of obstacles

"WITHOUT QUESTION, PHYSICAL CONDITION PLAYED A FAR BIGGER PART IN MY SUCCESS THAN HUNTING SKILL OR KNOWLEDGE, AND I THINK THAT'S THE CASE IN MUCH WESTERN HUNTING. LONG MILES, LONG HOURS, STEEP GRADES, AND HIGH ELEVATION COMBINE TO MAKE WESTERN HUNTING TOUGH, AND IF YOU'RE NOT PREPARED FOR THE GRIND, YOU'LL FOLD."[2]

—*Dwight Schuh, author of* Bowhunter's Encyclopedia

There is no such thing as an "easy" bowhunt. I train for blood-and-gut epics.

In 2008 I had my first-ever sheep tag. The hunt was circled on my calendar for many months, and I felt like I had been training for it for years. I was putting a lot of pressure on myself to make the most of it. This meant going through lots of intense mental and physical preparations leading up to the hunt. I knew for this one to end like I'd envisioned, I needed to be at the very top of my game.

If my motivation to work hard ever waned, all I needed to do was look up the success rates for this hunt from seasons past. For comparison, success on elk is around 10 percent. This hunt allowed the harvest of any sheep, but I was focused solely on a mature ram. For the five-year span I researched on the Alaska Department of Fish and Game (ADF&G) website from 1997 to 2002, the most rams killed by bowhunters in one year was four. In 2000 there was one ram killed out of the 100 tag holders, for a mere 1 percent success rate. Not real high. Part of it is because the hunt takes place so late in the year that weather can make effective hunting nearly impossible; also, being that this is the last sheep hunt of the year, the sheep have seen humans. We learned firsthand that it doesn't take much pressure to push them into the cliffs, or "goat rocks" as Roy called them, which are completely inaccessible to man. So, out of the 100 tags issued, the best-case scenario finds only a handful of bowhunters holding sheep horns in their hands.

Before the hunt, Roy asked me a question.

Since Roy fell and died while sheep hunting in 2015, everything has changed for me, but especially my bowhunting journey. While I still find success, it doesn't seem as rewarding or sweet, being as I can't share it with the man that introduced me to the bow and arrow, Roy Roth. That said, regardless of the challenge or heartaches we face in life, we do not falter or fade. We must endure.

"What makes you so different from everyone else who drew this tag? Why are you going to be one of two or three guys who tags out?"

It was a good question.

"Because I pretty much suck at most things, but for whatever reason, I can get it done in the mountains with my bow. Maybe this is what I was born to do?"

I thought about what I had just said.

"That actually sounds pretty stupid," I said to Roy. "What do I know? On this hunt, success is my only option."

The only way to combat any doubt was through effort. I put in the hard work, and that keeps the doubt at bay because I know that I'm doing all I can. Because I've worked so hard, I know I'm going to capitalize. I am going to be successful.

Heading into the sheep hunt in 2008, I ramped up my training for what might very well be the most difficult bowhunting challenge I had ever faced. That found me running in three big races over a month period: the Boston Marathon, the McDonald Forest 50K, and the Forest Park Ultra. For the Forest Park Ultra in Portland, Oregon, I would be running a 50K consisting of 31 miles and an elevation gain of 3,185 feet. It turned out that I would end up running a lot longer than 31 miles.

For a good deal of the race, I ran with Ryne Melcher, who came down from Canada as part of the Montrail-Nathan trail Ultra Running Team. Right out of the gate, Ryne, Hal Koerner, and I were running together. Hal was an Ultra legend and the defending Western States 100 champion. About six or seven miles into the race, things went south for our group. We were running hard, following the flagging markers put out by race organizers on the muddy trails. We had been climbing steadily when the markers finally indicated that we needed to dive off the top of the ridge and head down. Running down hard and fast, we followed the trail all the way to the bottom of the drainage where we all stopped. The pink ribbon that was supposed to indicate which direction to go wasn't anywhere to be found. The course had been vandalized between the time the race organizers marked it the day before and the start of the race. Flagging ribbons had been moved.

What sort of dipshits would do something like that?

We had dropped off when we should have stayed up top. So, after dropping a ton of elevation for about one and a half miles, back up the trail we headed. A scenic three-mile detour. Right after we took the wrong trail, two local runners who apparently knew the course came through. Seeing that the ribbons had been moved, they fixed the markers before continuing on.

This was a good thing, but this didn't change the fact that Hal, Ryne, and I were way back. We had lost probably 25 minutes, which in a four-hour race is a lot. I tried to convince myself that there was a chance I could win the race, but honestly looking back now I can admit I didn't actually buy this self-talk. At the time, Hal was one of the best ultramarathoners in the world. I was a bowhunter. Had he completed the race, I would not have beaten him.

The truth is the worst part about losing the time and running extra miles isn't how it interfered with my goal of winning the race. It's the mental toll it takes. Ultras are similar to bowhunting because there are many mental hurdles to overcome. This is the case *without* screwballs messing with the course. Extra hurdles can be very difficult to overcome, even for the best. Hal dropped out, no doubt because of frustration. And if Hal Koerner dropped out, that couldn't be good.

I ran hard to pass all the runners I had previously been ahead of. On the muddy single track, in the pouring rain, this was no easy thing. I went down in the soupy muck once while trying to sneak past four runners single-filing it. I got to a few more trail junctions that had been screwed with. Ryne and I actually spent quite a bit of time frantically deciphering the course map (which, thankfully, he'd brought), looking for ribbons over the first 20K of the race. This felt more like an adventure race than an ultramarathon. As I reached the 20K aid station, I looked at my watch and thought that maybe I was 18 miles into the race. Nope: only 12.

"How many runners have come through already?" I asked.

"Around twenty."

Fuck.

I had already passed 20 or 30 runners, so the thought of still having to catch 20 more after having been in the lead pack disheartened me. For a short while, I thought about throwing in the towel, as Hal had done. But then I remembered why I was out here in the first place. This wasn't about earning a ribbon or a buckle or a victory or a personal record. This was about doing something difficult in order to be ready for that sheep hunt.

I kept running, determined to finish and hell-bent on reeling in as many runners as I could. By the next aid station (mile 18, finally), I had moved up to tenth place. Ryne and I were still fairly close. I got out of the aid station a little ahead of him and kept picking off runners. When I arrived at the last aid station at mile 24, I was in fourth place and felt pretty strong. The guys at the aid station said there was one runner just ahead of me and two guys a fair distance ahead of him. They were locals from Portland, so I assumed they never veered off course, as they'd no doubt run these trails before. After downing some quick-hitting carbs and refilling my water bottles, I took off, determined to hammer it hard for the last seven miles.

Things went well until I got to another vandalized junction. I paused, looking in the mud for tracks, unsure if the ribbons were right or if they'd been moved. The doubt sucked. I ran in what I felt was the right direction, but I was wrong.

I ended up out of the park down on the streets of Portland.

Back up the hill I went. I got back to the junction just as my good buddy from Canada was coming through. Knowing which way not to go, Ryne and I headed off for the home stretch. I ended up finishing in fourth place, Ryne in fifth.

Even though I didn't achieve my goal of winning, I felt like I did the absolute best I could.

Yes, I ran what I figure was five extra miles.

Yes, I did seriously contemplate quitting or dropping out.

Yes, my shoes were soaking wet for over four hours, and they were also full of rocks and mud.

Yes, I suffered and hurt, but, in the end, I pushed through the pain and the frustration to reel in more than runners.

I knew this would pay off in the coming bow season. In the end, I would need every bit of strength I could muster for that upcoming sheep hunt.

Undeniable people find a way. They are fine with doing more. They *want* to do more. They take pride in doing more than anybody else. And like Roy and I used to do, they always question whether somebody has ever done it before. Nedd Brockmann is one of those people.

When Nedd was 21 years old, the electrician from New South Wales in Australia discovered he loved running and challenging himself. After moving to Sydney and seeing the homeless situation there, he decided to raise money for people living in poverty by running 50 marathons in 50 days. And he managed to do this while working full-time. When he came to my hometown for a Lift Run Shoot, I asked Nedd what inspired the 50 marathons.

Nedd Brockmann has been an incredible inspiration to me and millions of others across the globe. Still in his twenties, he's proven to be an endurance warrior, running across Australia a few years back and just recently running 1,000 miles on a track in 12 and a half days.

"I think originally it was the desire to push myself, and I think that came from initially a weight loss journey. I wasn't morbidly obese. My body was symbolic for where my life was heading, and I just had to do something about this."

He knew how to train and how to eat healthily, so he asked himself why he wasn't taking the opportunity he had to do something with it. Nedd began to run and realized he could do it quite well. With each run, he added a little more distance, and in the space of around four months, he went from running a 3K to a 100K.

The morning after his first 100K, as he was lying in his bed in pain, he couldn't sleep. An overwhelming sense of pride and emotion came over him. Nedd was so hungry to do something else. A few weeks earlier, he had heard about ultra runners such as Dean Karnazes, who did 50 marathons in 50 states in 50 consecutive days in 2006, and James Lawrence, "the Iron Cowboy," who did 50 Ironmans in 50 days in 2015. So, Nedd asked himself a familiar question.

"Why can't *I* do that?"

In Nedd's mind, Karnazes and the Iron Cowboy were just other people. Where did they come from that made them so special?

"That was kind of this realization that, 'No, they're just people who've gone, "Fuck it, I'm going to do it,"'" Nedd told me. "So, I went back, and I did that and said, 'Fuck it, I'm doing it. But I'm going to work at my regular job too.' Who's done that?"

Being an electrician wasn't the easiest job in the world. He wasn't sitting on his ass all day and able to recover from running. Instead, he was cutting concrete walls and pulling cable. But he decided to do it, to find a way. Of course, there were people out there who decided to shit on his dreams and his goals.

"A doctor rang me up and said, 'What you're trying to do is physically impossible. I've spoken to four health professionals, and they said there's no way.' I went, 'Oh, good. I'll call you on day fifty.' And sure enough, on day fifty, I called him up."

During those 50 marathons in 50 days, Nedd realized that there were people in his life for the wrong reasons, so he had to move away from them. This was a powerful change.

"There are always people who say you can't do that because they put their own limits on it," Nedd said.

Nedd would work from seven in the morning until three in the afternoon, pack up his tools, and head home. Then he would head out his door around four in the afternoon, go run 26.2 miles, finishing anywhere between nine and eleven o'clock at night. Get in bed. Sleep. Then go again.

Fifty straight days of that. And after he was finished, he knew he could do *more*.

"I think that kind of instilled a bit of belief that I could run a whole lot more in a day if I wasn't working for nine hours," he said.

The following year, however, he ended up getting injured.

"I felt like I was Superman after running fifty marathons in fifty days," Nedd said. "You feel you can take on the world. And being quite young and quite new to the sport, you need to learn. You need to build that up. And I was quite stubborn with all that and just thought I could run ridiculous distances."

Like all of us, Nedd had to learn lessons the hard way, but he is thankful he learned them at a young age. He knew he needed to be smart about running and to do things better. But his desire to keep pushing himself only kept growing. He wanted to inspire more people and raise more awareness about the homeless, so in 2022 Nedd decided to run across Australia. For 46 consecutive days, he would run almost a 100K (62 miles) day in and day out. By the time he crossed the finish line, over 10,000 fans waited to greet him.

Nedd didn't just raise awareness; he created a movement.

Cam with Nedd Brockmann

I asked him how he trained for running across Australia.

"I was intentionally putting myself in uncomfortable situations every time I could so that when I was in the situation on the run after day one—when I was going to be in some fucked-up pain I knew I would be—my head would be okay with it," he explained. "Sure, my body might not, but that will follow when your head is right. I think when you let your head in, that idea of what's ahead of you creep in, it can be quite overwhelming."

Nedd is always wondering how to become uncomfortable before events such as running across Australia so that when he's doing it, he becomes more adaptive. But ultimately it comes down to one thing:

Determination.

"There's no real blueprint. It's just: find a way. And I think with making a decision on doing something, that's where I kind of thrive."

But there was hesitancy when he made the decision. He came up with the idea and then set the date for September 1. And he was sticking with the decision.

"When you say you're going to do something, you commit to it," Nedd told me. "And that's just how it has kind of always been for me. I didn't have the best lead-up for the run, but I just knew September first was it. Let's get to the start date, and you'll find a way because it means enough to you."

Retired National Football League defensive end Derek Wolfe is one of those guys who didn't grow up in comfort and peace and happiness when he was a kid. But he knew he wanted to play football when he was seven years old. Whenever teachers asked their students what they wanted to be when they grew up, Wolfe would always say the same thing:

"I'm going to play in the NFL."

The teachers would discount his desire and put down his dreams.

"You know how rare it is for a guy to make the NFL?" they would ask him.

Whatever, Wolfe thought. *I'm going to do it.*

That's exactly what he did. After playing football at the University of Cincinnati, he was selected as the thirty-sixth draft pick by the Denver Broncos. He played eight years with them, winning his first Super Bowl in 2016, and then two more seasons with the Baltimore Ravens.

Wolfe shared his journey with me when he came to visit Oregon to train and talk with me on the podcast. He said he was initially worried about the running, but I told him not to worry.

"You're carrying the rock," I said.

A guy like Derek Wolfe—6'5" and 285 pounds—is built for carrying anything and everything, and he killed it taking the rock up the mountain. He knew he had always been gifted with size, but he also knew that there were a lot of big guys walking around who didn't make it to the NFL. It was because they didn't have the ability and didn't have the mindset, Wolfe said. They weren't prepared the way he was prepared.

As it turned out for Wolfe, a rough childhood was the preparation he needed.

"I'm a super-blessed man for everything," Derek said. "Everything I went through, it's all for a reason, and it was all for a purpose: to prepare me for those ten years in the NFL."

All the pain and adversity he went through during a childhood marred by his parents divorcing, never knowing his father, and an abusive relationship with his stepfather only led to him being able to go through more pain and adversity in the NFL. But at least Wolfe was paid to do the latter.

"Everybody has a purpose," he said. "It's whether or not you're capable of finding that purpose. Are you capable of finding something that you love to do? Because when you find it, you know. You know it. You knew from the first time you stepped out in those woods and shot something with your bow that this is for you."

"Yeah, I did," I said.

His messed-up childhood prepared him to play professional football, Derek explained.

"To play defensive line in the NFL at a high level, you gotta be fucked up. You do. You have to be a savage."

When you've got two 350-pound guys trying to move you, then you had to be ready for that. You had to take yourself to a different place, and that's what he was able to do for a long time. When he became a father, this was more difficult to do, because it wasn't something he could simply turn off.

"It's like being a gladiator, fighting in the arena, then coming home and trying to be a loving father," I told him.

I asked Derek how he was able to do that—to be able to go home and turn it off—and he told me it was great coaching.

"You know, great coaches always used to tell me that you practice like you play. John

*Super Bowl champion Derek Wolfe is a mountain of a
man and has overcome so much to earn glory.*

Fox was one that told me this. He said, 'You get paid to practice. The game is for fun.' That resonates with me. It makes sense to me. When you tell me something that makes sense, I'm all in. Let's go. I'm going to grind in practice. That way when I get to the game, it's easy."

The players who didn't have that mentality, who didn't want to grind during practice, were not gamers. And those players didn't last long in the NFL. Very few do.

"It's only a matter of time in the NFL," Wolfe said. "As soon as they get you, they're trying to replace you with someone better. So, what are you doing to keep your job? What are you doing to stay there? Peyton Manning told me one time and I'll never forget it. He said, 'You either get better or you get worse. You never stay the same. And if you think you're staying the same, you're probably getting worse. Because guess what? The other guy's working hard. Whenever you're lying in bed at eight in the morning, there's somebody that's been up since five grinding.'"

Derek shares the same desire I have: to be around people who are trying to grow; people who are reaching for goals and always evolving.

"Like I said, you either get better or you get worse," he said. "My worst nightmare is working a nine-to-five job that I hate. Going in, clocking out. Clocking in, clocking out. And then living for the weekend. Going into the garage and drinking beers so my wife doesn't see. That's my worst nightmare."

I agreed. "That's a lot of people's lives."

"A lot of people are fucking miserable. And they're stuck. They're absolutely stuck. And I'm like, 'You allowed yourself to get to that. You allowed that to happen with complacency.'"

This was exactly why I had started the Lift Run Shoot experience, because I wanted to surround myself with people like Derek Wolfe. I've been lucky enough to bring people in here who are better than me at pretty much everything. I knew that if I can get a little shine from all these people, I'm going to grow. But we can do that anywhere—either as a little community or as a society. You can learn and evolve and have a whole different mindset from being around people who have done great things. And anybody can get better.

Wolfe said he loved that no matter what I do, I'm always going as hard as I can go.

"If you fail, you fail. But you're not afraid to fail, right? And you push and you push and you push. And what you've done is you've found something you love. You chased it as far as you could go, and it hasn't slowed down yet. It just keeps getting better. And that is inspirational. And anybody can learn. Anybody can do it. Anybody can go and find something they love to do and fucking chase it."

So many people—too many people—are afraid to chase those dreams. They're afraid of failure. Wolfe encouraged them to keep going.

"What if you do fail? Then try again, motherfucker. Go!"

In my mind, you need to figure something else out. If you pour yourself into whatever you're doing, there's really no such thing as failure. There's learning and readjusting and recalculating. But you have to just keep going.

Wolfe looks at it this way: "I played ten years," he reflected. "How many times do you think there was a pass play in ten years? How many pass plays were there?"

"Thousands," I said.

"Thousands."

Out of those thousands of plays, how many sacks did he have?

Thirty-six.

"I failed *a lot*. But that didn't deter me from keep trying. Next play."

Cam with Derek Wolfe

Sure, he would learn and adjust and change his tactics from play to play. When you go hard and play hard and work hard, Derek said, good things will happen.

"If I keep putting it out there that this is going to happen but I'm not doing anything about it, it's probably not gonna happen. But if I'm putting it out there, and I keep going and I keep going, I never waver from that. And there's going to be days where you're like, *Man, fuck this.* That's natural to feel that way, that you should just quit.

"That's the little voice in your head that you got to tell, '*Fuck off. Get out of here. No, I'm going to keep going.*' Wake up the next day before your feet hit the ground. Be like '*I'm going to win today. I'm going to win today. I'm going to win today.*' And you might not. But you're going to keep trying. Eventually it's going to work out for you."

It's going to happen today.

On my forty-first birthday, I'm standing on the edge of the amazingly beautiful, immense, and rugged Pioneer Peak, a 6,398-foot mountain in the Chugach Mountains of Alaska. It towers over the Knik River, just nine miles south of Palmer and about six miles outside the Municipality of Anchorage. Pioneer Peak is a prominent landmark in the Matanuska-Susitna Valley and the mountain I've come to in order to arrow a Dall sheep.

My guide stands beside me, pointing down the mountain and letting me know what he thinks. On my fifteenth hunting trip to wild Alaska over the years, this is my very first with a guide. All my other trips—Sitka blacktail deer, black bears, caribou, and moose— were do-it-yourself trips that Roy and I had set up together. When hunting sheep in Alaska as a nonresident, a guide is required. In pretty much a dream circumstance, my guide happens to be my high school friend and longtime hunting partner, Roy Roth. Roy has been working the last year as a state assistant guide under the supervision of an Alaska contracting registered guide-outfitter. That means he can personally guide me on my sheep hunt.

Being able to share my first-ever Dall hunt with Big Roy means the world to me. This is the sort of adventure we've always longed for—the kind we once dreamt of 20 years ago.

There is no one I respect more in the mountains than Roy Roth.

Sheep country and hardcore weather are a bad combination and make the use of crampons and an ice ax mandatory at times, so it helps to have a savvy, woods-wise, tough, and reliable partner. Roy is in rare company, having arrowed six big Dall rams himself. (He ended up with nine bow-killed rams before he suffered a fall and passed away in 2015.)

Our bowhunting passion has burned deep since we were young men. This passion has offered us so many life-enriching moments and experiences, so it's only right that Roy is on the mountain with me for this monumental occasion. Like I've heard him say, we are different in so many ways yet exactly the same: goal oriented to the max and able to keep our eyes on the prize when all hope seems lost.

Things looked good the day before the season opened. Roy and I had four hours of quad-burning, calf-thrashing, devil's-club-busting, slow-step-after-painful-step hiking to a bench, where we set up camp halfway up the mountain. While shrugging off my 50-pound pack, I spotted sheep. Scoping out the big group of ewes and lambs was exciting to see even though they were miles away. Then I noticed a couple other sheep closer to me, and one of them was a ram. He was only a half-curl—but I was pumped. I couldn't wait for daybreak and the opening of sheep season.

The following day, we hiked another four hours in some of the roughest country I have ever roamed to pack camp to the top of the mountain. It felt weird how seemingly we were on top of the world looking down on the valley below. So close to civilization, yet at the same time, we might as well have been a million miles away. It can almost give you a false sense

> "ANYTHING CAN HAPPEN IF YOU ARE WILLING TO PUT IN THE WORK AND REMAIN OPEN TO THE POSSIBILITY. DREAMS ARE REALIZED BY EFFORT, DETERMINATION, PASSION, AND STAYING CONNECTED TO THAT SENSE OF WHO YOU ARE."[3]
>
> —*Michael Jordan*

of security when you see the lights of the city and headlights moving along the highway. But make no mistake, if you got into trouble on the mountain, there is nothing anyone in the valley could do for you. Alaska sheep country is as unforgiving place as there is, regardless of the view.

Perched on top of one mountain while surrounded by snowcapped peaks, I see him. The Dall sheep in the distance sits like a king, wearing his massive, curled-horn crown. Right away, I begin to approach, mindful of where I step. These mountain ledges can be treacherous; one slip, and you can die. I move down an incline, then up another peak. My legs ache, but I'm not tired. All those miles from the past year—the past decade—are paying off. I ease to within bow range.

At a chip-shot range of 23 yards, I try to sneak my arrow over a rock into the ram's vitals. I hear an almost inaudible *tick* as my arrow arches toward the ram but catches stone, causing the arrow to hit low, cutting the ram's leg. I have confidence I can make the thread-the-needle shot.

Maybe too much confidence.

My dream animal is so close, and I make a bad hit on him.

My goal in the discipline of bowhunting is perfection, and I work toward it every day of the year. Every day I'm working to hone my craft and my abilities, and then I just fucking fail miserably like this.

I feel sick.

After watching a puff of long, white winter-coat sheep hair float off in the wind after being cut loose by my razor-sharp broadhead on impact, I sit on that lonely ridge and reflect on my failure. I walk over and pick up the hair to inspect it.

Is this the closest I'll ever get to my ram?

My heart aches as I watch him intently through my binos as he slowly navigates his way among the rocks. Doubts and questions race through my mind.

Could I have sacrificed more?

Was I ill-prepared for crunch time?

Did my focus wane because I felt the shot was a gimme?

My goal is to be on autopilot, but I didn't remember "picking a spot," which is, of course, a key step of the aiming process I obsess over. I think of all the effort it took to get 23 yards from my ram. The hours of shooting, miles of running, logistics, travel, the time away from my wife and kids, the money, humping it up the mountain, trudging through the snow, living in a Spartan camp in extreme conditions, and so on.

This photo was taken near the top of Pioneer Peak on my 41st birthday in 2008. I had just killed a Dall ram and success felt sweet and we seemed to be on top of the world. As fate would have it, this was near the spot Roy Roth fell in 2015.

I will never ever have a better chance at a Dall.

It simply doesn't get any easier than a 23-yard, broadside, looking-down-the-hill-as-I-was-on-the-up-hill-side, all-the-time-in-the-world shot.

How could I screw that up?

This is the *exact* situation where I expect myself to be infallible.

The despondency doesn't get rid of my resolve. One thing I have learned over the years is that successful bowhunting is more about overcoming obstacles than anything else. Yes, my lip has been bloodied, so to speak. I let myself down big-time, but I have no other choice than to bone up and get to work on what is sure to be a tough blood-trailing job.

Roy doesn't say a word; he doesn't have to. We are both on the exact same page, prepared to give all we have to make it right. More than anything, I owe it to the animal. Respecting the life of the animals we hunt is *the* most important part of the hunter's creed.

We get on blood just like we have so many times over the past two decades of bowhunting. "Blood, blood, got blood, good blood here . . ." You know, every once in a while, a guy catches a break, and I catch one this time. I let out a thankful sigh when I spot an ample amount of crimson-colored blood staining the powdery snow and splashed over rocks, marking the ram's path.

In the steep, rugged country, we keep working, unraveling the blood trail until I am eventually able to sneak in and finish off my trophy of a lifetime. He dies at the edge of a sheer drop-off we estimated to be 400 to 500 feet high. I make the final shot at 25 yards and hustle down to him over snow-covered ice.

When I reach the Dall sheep and grab onto his horns, I suddenly realize he has more life left in him. I hold him as he bucks and kicks violently in his final death throes. He begins to slump and slide as I struggle to hold him.

He's going over the edge.

Maybe I'll join him in a freefall to the snow-covered rocks below.

I keep holding him, one false move from certain death.

This is *my* sheep. I've waited a lifetime for this moment.

How many get to this point where they're holding a longtime dream, literally, in their hands?

I'm not letting it go for anything.

I picture all those who are important to me—those I love—and I wonder if this will be the last thing I ever think. Here I am holding a 250-pound wild beast, and with one false move—one weakening of my mind and spirit—he will pull me over the cliff.

The struggle seems long, but it lasts only about a minute before the sheep dies. I didn't know if I could hold on to him that long. But I remained steadfast, and I kept going.

As a cold breeze sweeps over the mountain, I wedge his ground-side horn into a crack in the rock, using my body weight to anchor him while I fight to get my pack off. After slipping it off, with one hand I unzip a pocket and fish out a length of nylon cord. Throwing it with my left hand while holding my trophy with everything I have, my crampons digging in, I pseudo-lasso one of his back legs and pull it toward me. Letting go of the cord, I quickly snatch his leg, and by using every ounce of strength I have left, I am able to somehow yard his body up on the small rock ledge. I don't know how I do it, but I do it.

It's all determination.

After Roy methodically makes his way down to me, he asks me how I feel.

"I feel awesome. It was—how shall we say?—not textbook, but he's lying here. He's dead, and I killed him with my bow."

A part of me can't believe I killed a Dall sheep. I never thought that sheep were ever in my future. I'm a blue-collar guy, and sheep hunts are usually for upper-crust type of people, so I never really thought sheep were ever in my cards.

Of course, by having Big Roy at my side, anything is possible. I have to thank him because without him, it never would have happened.

"You could have found a little bit easier spot though, Cam," Roy says as we both laugh. "We're on a rock that's going to fall off here any second."

I look around. "This is brutal. How far is it? I mean, right here there's about a five-hundred-foot vertical. At least."

"Maybe more."

"I probably wasn't the smartest person trying to hold a bucking and kicking ram like this from going over the edge, but, man, he was mine, and I wanted him. So, I did what I had to do and held him up on here on this ledge."

Surveying the scene, I have to chuckle again. "I don't even know how we're getting out of this mess. We will somehow. We have to be real careful."

"This really makes me nervous," Roy says as he gives what can truly be called a nervous laugh.

"I know. It could go."

"It's not held on by much."

"I think we'll be all right. I mean, if this goes, it was our time to go." We both chuckle. "I mean, we're here with the sheep. What do you do?"

"I don't want to go right now, though," Roy says.

"I know. I want to be back at a camp."

"I want to go to Chili's."

That good-natured and gentle laughter drifts into the wind off the edge of Pioneer Peak. There is a lot of work ahead of us, but for now, I cherish this special moment.

I turned 41 years old today, and I've never felt more alive.

When I think back to that hunt in 2008, in many ways it resembles a Lift Run Shoot. I was with an outlier named Roy Roth. He was my guide for that hunt. He was also a friend and a mentor and a brother. Just before we were going to haul the sheep out of the mountains, I asked Roy how he managed to constantly find success with his bow. His words at the end of that hunt still resonate with me. They weren't just lessons for surviving in the mountains. They were lessons for life.

"I wish there was one thing that I could come up with and say. Do this, this, and this, and you'll find success. But just like with any of our other hunting, I'm trying to find pockets where other people are not going to be."

Roy explained how since this was the last season of the year, the rams had been pushed to pretty inaccessible areas. So, he was always trying to find those pockets to try and figure out how they were going to work.

"You just go the extra mile," Roy said.

It doesn't matter what the daily forecast looks like; things can turn very ugly out there in just a matter of hours. You have to be prepared for bad weather. You have to be ready for a long, tough climb in and an even tougher climb out.

"You have to find that lone ram, and you got to exploit those opportunities and just make it work," Roy said. "It's a tough hunt. Every time I'm up here, I'm going, *This is impossible. There's no way I'm going to get a ram with this bow and arrow.* And then you just kind of keep working at it."

Like anything great in life, you remain determined and you keep going. You keep searching and keep moving, and then when the opportunity comes, you move fast and make it work.

Roy and I knew that when you were in sheep country, good things could happen. But you had to be there to make them happen. Even hunters with tags can become intimidated; they say that 40 percent of the people with tags don't even show up. These mountains are so dangerous and daunting. It's easy for people to think the same thing as Roy: *What'd I get myself into? There's no way I can do this.*

The key is to never stop.

"I'm proud of you," Roy told me. "It's a tough one—not a lot of people do it."

I will always be grateful that Roy gave me this opportunity. I couldn't be more proud of my first bow ram and the mountain lessons I learned on this tough hunt. From less than zero to one of my hunting life's sweetest rewards. This was an achievement I thought I'd never, ever realize. Not me, with my modest life. But as they say, dreams can come true, and one did that special day on Pioneer Peak: October 2, my Birthday Ram!!!

Always keep working hard. The greater the sacrifice, the greater the reward.

"A GREAT BOOK BEGINS WITH AN IDEA; A GREAT LIFE, WITH A DETERMINATION. MY LIFE MAY NOT BE GREAT TO OTHERS, BUT TO ME IT HAS BEEN ONE OF STEADY PROGRESSION, NEVER DULL, OFTEN EXCITING, OFTEN HUNGRY, TIRED, AND LONELY, BUT ALWAYS LEARNING. SOMEWHERE BACK DOWN THE YEARS I DECIDED, OR MY NATURE DECIDED FOR ME, THAT I WOULD BE A TELLER OF STORIES."

—*Louis L'Amour,* Education of a Wandering Man

BE BETTER ON THE TENTH DAY

There is a reason you are here, all alone, putting in the work with seemingly no reward and nobody watching.

Determination isn't a desire. It's a destination.

A place you plan to reach.

An invitation you can't refuse.

A journey you have to take.
You start with a goal in mind. Maybe it's an aspiration. But maybe, like that Dall sheep, it's a dream too good to become true.

So why can't you grab onto it?

I am proof that no dream is too big.
Sometimes after all that hard work and long preparation, you can appear to fail right at the moment you seem to have found success.

Sometimes you can be kneeling on the edge of failure.

And then sometimes you literally grab the bull by its fucking horns.

What is holding you back?
My dreams were deliberately difficult. The success rate was incredibly low. The odds were not in my favor, but as Roy said, you have to keep working at it.

I don't like accepting failure; it doesn't feel good. That's why I want to do everything possible to put the odds as much in my favor as I can.

So, I run. A simple 10K turns into a marathon turns into an ultra.

It's that easy, but easy doesn't get the job done.

I was prepared and had an easy shot on my dream Dall, and I fucked it up.

Preparation is the assortment of tools you carry, but determination is the attitude you bring with those tools.

Preparation gets you to the excitement of day one of a hunt, but determination keeps you there on the tenth day, when you're so beat down and mentally fatigued and pretty much ready to go home.

The goal is to actually be better on the tenth day. You are acclimated and know your surroundings better, and you are more hungry than ever.

Always keep the legendary pro football coach Vince Lombardi's words in your head: "The price of success is hard work, dedication to the job at hand, and the determination that whether we win or lose, we have applied the best of ourselves to the task at hand."

You begin with hard work.

You continue with that dedication to the task.

And you finish with determination.

Determination allows you to know that whether you win or lose, you've done the best you can possibly do.

FOCUS:

Careful attention that is given to something such as a task, or the ability to give your full attention to something

"I NEVER HIT A SHOT, NOT EVEN IN PRACTICE, WITHOUT HAVING A VERY SHARP IN-FOCUS PICTURE OF IT IN MY HEAD."

—Hall of Fame golfer Jack Nicklaus, winner of 73 PGA tours, in Golf Digest

Crunch time. This is when everything comes down to one heart-racing moment. The bowhunter shooting at his target. The game-winning basketball shot. The putt for the victory. The sprint toward the finish line. This is the high-pressure moment when all the work you've put in and all the time you've spent and all the resources you've used come down to one single point.

The key to my archery success over the past 35 years and the way I've been able to master those crunch-time moments has been consistent practice. I want to make shooting a bow as natural as taking a breath, and the only way I have found to do that is through daily dedication. Shooting every day. Weight vest, no weight vest. Pack or no pack. Sun or rain or snow. Coat on, no shirt, shorts, pants, in bathrobe, one sock only and nothing else. It doesn't matter. I just shoot. I focus on the process and perfect it. Yes, you can be the best hunter in the world and in better shape than anyone, but if you can't make the shot at crunch time, you simply won't find consistent success.

There's no way to ever simulate the true intensity of those crunch-time moments that come in sports. For me, I find ways to put pressure on myself to make a perfect shot in high-intensity moments; those moments in practice help me on my hunts. That's why I do things like shooting through my truck window. It comes down to simple focus. Eliminating distractions and being able to put the arrow where it needs to go in the heat of the moment.

One of those moments happened in 2011, when a new Cabela's store opened in my hometown of Springfield, Oregon. I lobbied for the chance to cut the Grand Opening ribbon with an arrow; it had never been done before, so I had to come up with a way to do it. Talk about pressure. There was a crowd of 2,000 people, along with television crews attending the opening. My plan was to shoot at the ribbon and break it, then afterward conduct a seminar in the store. Yes, this was simply a chip shot, but with a bow, I've seen people blow slam dunks plenty of times.

Adrenaline can do crazy things to a human.

Every sport demands serious focus from athletes, especially at crunch time. For example, making a putt in golf can test the nerves of even the best professional golfers. Some say that, in terms of focus, making a putt in crunch time is as hard as it gets. All golf fans know what Tiger's Eyes are. Tiger's Eyes originated when TV cameras zoomed in on golfing legend Tiger Woods as he squatted down and put his hands up on the sides of his eyes like horse blinders, essentially blocking out everything but the ball and the hole in an attempt to read a putt. I am sure in such a situation a pro golfer is likely feeling tons of pressure, but let's be honest: that ball is lifeless, and the cup is just a hole in the ground.

In other sports, guys must constantly react to things all around them. In football, the players are reacting to the guys in front of them. In baseball, the batter is reacting to the pitcher, and vice versa. Fairly straightforward, reaction-mode stuff. Granted, it might not always be easy, but, in relation to focus, it's not as tough as bowhunting.

Here's a good example of the difference between reacting and being faced with a challenge that requires extraordinary focus. Ask any basketball player what he would rather do: attempt a game-winning shot within the flow of the offense as the clock winds down, or to be standing at the free throw line for two shots with one second left and his team down by one. Almost every player will take the "make the shot within the offense" option, because making two clutch free throws—when it is just you, the ball, and the rim—is as tough as it gets for most.

Yes, these sports scenarios are hard, especially in the pros. But in my opinion, they are nothing compared to making a shot on a bull elk full of rage that comes crashing in. A live wire of blood, muscle, and raw energy, blowing snot from his nose. There is nothing tougher than drawing your bow, staying focused enough to pick a spot, and sending one arrow on its way toward 800 pounds of wildness with only one goal: of stopping his heart.

That's no game like golf or basketball. That's life and death.

There are plenty of mainstream sports stars people love to worship, but the real

For the Cabela's Grand Opening in my hometown in 2011, they asked if I'd cut the Grand Opening ribbon. I said no, but I would shoot it with an arrow. And that's what I did. The moment is captured here.

Photo courtesy of The Register Guard

admiration should go to the guy down at the local pro shop who has killed a handful of bulls with his bow.

Learning to bowhunt takes lots of time combined with supreme focus. It can be overwhelming at times, and when you're by yourself in the wilderness and a bull is flashing through the timber, headed your way, it's hard not to crumble. You've been thinking about this moment all year, practicing and preparing and planning, and suddenly it's here. Some people pull back and don't even aim but shoot anyway, then the arrow misses, and they're wondering to themselves, *What just happened?* They don't even know. This is what you call "buck fever." It happens even in rifle hunting. Guys will lock up, or inexplicably jack all their shells out of the gun without even shooting. People who are with them will wonder what just happened. "What'd you do?" they will ask. "You didn't even shoot!" There's just so much adrenaline pumping through your body, and there's this giant bull standing so close to you, and there's all the pressures of costs and expectations and a whole lifetime of dreaming waiting for this moment.

The high intensity of hunting is a lot to handle.

My focus always remains on making a perfect shot and being the best I can be. I am able to block out everything. That's how I can continue to shoot 10 arrows and kill 10 animals in a season. My heart rate doesn't change, because I've been doing this for over 30 years. I've had a black bear popping his jaws at me, I've been lion hunting in Africa, and I have killed Cape buffalo. I've had so many high-pressure reps. Including that ribbon-cutting pressure.

I loved the pressure and excitement of that Cabela's grand-opening event. For weeks before, I practiced in my house. And to be honest, I think I had more pressure shooting in my house than in the ribbon-cutting ceremony. I put a target a few rooms away. To make a shot here, I had doors and walls and lights surrounding me. My wife's computer was nearby, and there was a nice family picture above the target. I didn't want to send an arrow into any of those things, so that meant I really had to focus and block out everything else.

When the moment came at Cabela's, I was ready. Sure, there were people talking to me, some joking and telling me, "Don't screw up." Cameras filming me. I knew that if I did, in fact, screw up, I would be "that guy who missed" at the ribbon-cutting ceremony. And that was something I did not want to be known for.

When my crunch-time moment came at Cabela's, I made the shot. I succeeded dealing with the pressure around me; the sort of pressure every bowhunter knows.

This is the type of training that has helped me with focus. Is it mandatory for a bowhunter? No. But it is necessary if you are going to succeed when crunch time comes.

Not everybody has a goal of being undeniable, but if you want to be undeniable, you have to put in the work and the time. You have to force yourself to focus under extreme pressure. That's how the best maintain their mastery.

"I just was this redneck from the Carolinas that wanted to shoot a bow and had this dream that still to this day burns and has never been put out. I just love to shoot."

If you took out the part about the Carolinas, this statement could have come from me. World champion archer Levi Morgan is the self-proclaimed redneck who loves to shoot. He has the most amazing ability to focus on each and every shot when he's in a tournament, better than anybody I have ever come across, known, or shot with. He is the best to ever do it in archery. So, when he came out for a Lift Run Shoot, I was thrilled and honored. I was also a little nervous.

So far, I had hosted a lot of great people for the Lift Run Shoot experience. Incredible runners and amazing athletes. Fighters and hunters. So many strong individuals. But shooting some arrows with Levi, knowing that he was doing it better than anyone has ever done it in the history of archery—that was a little intimidating.

Levi Morgan grew up in Rosman, North Carolina, a small town in the mountains where he says there wasn't a lot to do except for hunting, fishing, and playing sports. His father was a bowhunter who shot in local archery tournaments, most of the time for practice. When Levi was around five years old, he started going to those local shoots with his father and quickly began to pick up on archery. Soon Levi started winning everything, so his dad quit shooting tournaments and instead started to take him around and coach him.

After winning locally and nationally and even on the world level at a young age, Levi knew that archery was something he wanted to pursue. It was a dream and a goal he chased all the way through his teenage years. But as he told me, there was no template for how to become a professional archer.

"We didn't have a lot of means to do it," Levi said. "But my mom and dad sacrificed everything for me to go to these tournaments when I was younger and went through the amateur ranks."

Levi Morgan

At the end of high school, he found himself at a crossroads. He had experienced success over the years as an amateur in archery, but during high school he quit to focus on other sports and girls. After graduating, he realized how much he missed archery.

"I'm hungry, and I still have this thing burning inside of me that I want to go do, but I didn't know how to do it," Levi recalled.

He turned down college scholarships and decided to focus all of his efforts on establishing an archery career. Levi wanted to be the best that ever lived. Since his dad was a rock mason, Levi was working 60 hours a week as a mason to pay his way. His rookie year in 2006 as a professional archer was rough.

"No sponsors. No free gear. No nothing. I never even made a top five and struggled big-time," he told me.

While working full-time and starting a new relationship with the woman who became his wife, Samantha, he battled through that first season. Even though Levi won rookie of the year, he never won a major event or even came close his first year.

"I'd be the first guy out of the finals," Levi recounted. "It was always one little thing. I was like, *I know this is what I want to do. I can feel it burning. I know I got what it takes, but I can't figure it out.* Right when I'd get there to win, it was like something would happen, and I just missed the final."

When the offseason came, Levi remained determined. *I'm gonna figure this out,* he told himself.

"I'm like, *Where am I weak? Where do I suck at this game? Where am I missing it?* So, I went through that entire offseason—every spare second, I was working at this craft with this burning desire."

Levi explained that he took a lot of notes back then, so he logged everything.

"I would shoot certain targets, certain lighting, certain lanes, sunny, rainy, shady, varying terrain, different targets, and track it all. After I was logging this for months and months, I went back and looked, and I started to see tendencies that I had and weaknesses in certain scenarios and weaknesses with certain targets. And so, I slowly started to fix those because I'm like, *I'm just missing it by* this *much.* I started to fix all my weaknesses and still stay strong where I was strong."

The first event for his next season, in 2007, Levi missed the top five cut. He was at an all-time low. He had spent every dime he had to chase this dream that seemed to be slipping away from him. Discouraged and convinced he needed to walk away from the sport, Levi decided to go to one last event after talking with some of the people that mattered the most to him. He set an all-time high score of 462. For the next 15 years, Levi would become exactly what he'd set out to be: the GOAT of archery. The greatest of all time. He would go on to win 16 Shooter of the Year awards, 16 world championships, and over 60 national titles.

As someone who grew up loving to shoot a bow, I was thrilled to shoot arrows with Levi. It was such a great day. I compared myself to Happy Gilmore in the Adam Sandler golf movie, while Levi was Shooter McGavin. It was incredible to watch somebody who's the best in the world at what they do.

In the archery tournaments that Levi specializes in, a range finder is not allowed, so archers have to judge the distance to the target basically to the yard in order to be perfect. Levi is perfect. He can just look at the target and know the yardage.

Being able to shoot with Levi and walk around the range with him was incredible. It was interesting for me to get into his mind and hear how he gauges all these shots in the different conditions. To learn how the weather impacts arrows, how the sunlight coming into his sight window impacts where he holds his pin, how the terrain can impact that. How everything around him comes into play. He's the best to ever do it. And his ability to focus is what sets him apart. He is able to focus on every single arrow every time, and most people can't do that at the same level he can.

What is Levi's secret? Was it just that he was born with this amazing gift to shoot the bow?

"There's a kind of art to what we do," Levi told me. "We have to be great shots, but we also have to judge great and make good decisions. But growing up, all I had was a bedded buck target and a bag target in my front yard, where I didn't have a range.

"Everybody thought I was just blessed with this forty-target, pristine range, but I just had a bag target that I shot up. My dad would get old rags from a clothing place and stuff it in chicken mash. It sat at thirty yards in my yard. I would shoot that all day as a kid. And so still, to this day, I can find thirty yards. I think I call it my absolute. No matter the situation, I can find thirty, all because that's what I practiced over and over as a kid."

During our discussion, I asked Levi to compare his archery tournaments to hunting.

"I guess in that final moment, they're very similar in how you handle the pressure. The difference for me is that, in a tournament, it's a controlled environment. I know the time I have on the clock. The target's not going anywhere—it's not looking at me. So, inside, I'm not rushing. I know what I have time to do. Pick my spot, fix my footing, make a good shot, and mentally prepare for that. Hunting is so much more unpredictable. A buck can stand up out of his bed and look at you, and you've got eight seconds to make it happen. And in those moments, when everything inside of you is screaming for you to hurry, I think this is where a lot of people screw up. With hunting, you're just faced with so many different scenarios—frantic things that make your chances of success go way down in those moments."

You have to be able to adapt to all the different situations in bowhunting, Levi said, whereas in the tournament world he knows the situations he's dealing with. That's why hunting teaches him a lot. It prepares him for those tournaments.

"You can't replicate that feeling when your heart rate's up and you're nervous and you know if you don't make a good shot what's riding on that. It could be an animal of a lifetime. It could be a world championship. That feeling you can't replicate. There's no way to practice it."

For Levi, the only time he could learn and grow as an archer was during the moments when he was failing; when he knew he couldn't win. If he couldn't win, at least he could learn. What could he do differently to make this moment easier, or to make sure that the next time this moment comes, he will come out on top?

"In the tournament world, I've learned what I do wrong in those moments when I start to feel that panic inside—like my pin's not sitting still. When you're nervous and your heart rate's up, you have to learn to execute through that and make a good shot. And so that's where it's very similar to hunting. When I pull back on a giant bull that just screamed in my face, and I know I've got five seconds to make a perfect shot or else it's all over and I won't get another opportunity, it's very similar in how you execute in that moment, whether it's hunting or a tournament."

Levi's unbelievable ability to focus earned him a nickname in his early 20s: the "Manimal." A fellow archer gave him a custom quiver with this term on it.

"I never really thought much about it, but he called me that because of the way I attacked those tournaments, when I had tunnel vision and all I thought about was attacking that opportunity. I never got crushed by those heavy moments because I expected to be there. I prepared for it. I wasn't trying to guard second or third place. I was never nervous in second or third place. I had one thing on my mind: winning."

Levi credits this mental toughness to his dad being an unbelievable coach when he was young. All the things he went through early in his career prepared him to be strong mentally.

"I've seen so many talented people get crushed because they have no mental strength," he observed. "You have the key to that, and you can't let anybody else in there. You own that."

Focus often breaks down for one reason:

Fear.

It can be fear of failure or fear of falling behind. It can also be fear of being mauled by a giant bear! There are many ways fear can wreck and ruin the focus you must have for the task at hand. Being able to conquer your fears is just part of the journey that takes you from a humble beginner to a seasoned veteran in whatever field you might be in.

Years ago, I sat in a crowd at a bowhunting seminar at the Bow Rack in Eugene, the same place we bring people for their Run Lift Shoot. The speaker that day was Oregon bowhunter Jim Hodson. As he shared hundreds of slides with an eager audience, I sat awestruck at what I was seeing and hearing. That one night made a huge impact on my life. Listening to Jim's experiences from Oregon to Kodiak Island, I craved to do the kinds of things that he had done. At the time, I didn't know or appreciate how tough the road would be. How could I?

During my first year in the woods with a bow in hand, I figured it out real quick. I remember thinking it was going to be completely impossible to get within bow range of a bull elk and get him on the ground with one of my arrows. No one told me I would feel utterly harmless in the woods with my stick and string. I kept plugging away, though, and each day I learned. Finally, after nearly three weeks of hunting every day, I was starting to get it, and the effort paid off when I arrowed a spike bull elk.

The key to that success? Time. It took me 18 straight days of elk hunting, every day a supreme effort, to take that bull. But with something as difficult as bowhunting, you have to walk before you can run. And one of the things you have to learn quickly is to control your fears. As I wrote in my book *Backcountry Bowhunting: A Guide to the Wild Side,* "Learn to control your fear or your fear will control *you.*"

It's interesting that one of the book's most popular chapters was the one I wrote about facing fear. No guy ever wants to talk about being afraid of the dark or scared of being attacked by an animal, but that's exactly what I talked about. I admitted that when I first went into the mountains by myself, I was afraid. I wanted people to read this and realize that these were normal feelings. Here's an excerpt:

Fear is a defense mechanism, which kicks in naturally because above all else the human body wants to survive. When fear hits as a big fat dose of adrenaline rushing through your veins, it leaves those who aren't mentally strong enough shaking, panicky, and not in position to make the best decisions. Outside of the backcountry, our normal life seems secure and comfortable, but in deep, that will change. We will definitely be separated from all the other conditions that make us feel safe: our home, our family, our circle of friends, the money in our bank account, our physical health. Uncomfortable thoughts racing through the minds of new wilderness hunters can be debilitating.

How do you use fear or anxiety as an advantage? As we know, fear is normal, so the big question is, How will you react?

The key is being able to answer that question. When you can anticipate and understand your fears, then you can do something about them. Like Levi Morgan, you can figure out how to adequately adjust to those fears. Once you do that, you will be that much more deadly and lethal as a hunter.

The other day, I was in the gym, and a guy told me that he had one of my old bows from years ago. He used it on a hunt.

"I almost got a bull," he told me.

> **"FOCUSED ATTENTION IS INFINITELY MORE VALUABLE THAN AN IDLE MIND."**
>
> —*Cam Hanes*

"What happened?"

The man explained that the bull was 35 yards away and came in bugling.

"I had your bow, and I'm standing there watching him. He's thirty-five yards, and he's right there. And I was shaking so bad, I don't even know how I could have shot it."

"That's normal," I explained. "That's how everybody is at the start."

That's the moment you practice over and over for. That moment when you realize, *Okay, I need to be in control, and I need to do everything that I practiced and make that shot.* A lot of people are overcome by fear and are never able to make precise shots. That's because they're difficult to make.

The pressure is *always* there. Even after you've hunted hundreds of times.

In 2005 I went on my first expensive hunt in Colorado while I was working with *Eastmans' Bowhunting Journal.* The cost for the hunt probably ended up being more like $12,000 because it was a pretty good bull. The bigger the bull, the more you have to pay. Being that Gordon Eastman was one of the pioneers of outdoor film, and since the Eastman family was paying for the hunt, I felt a considerable amount of pressure from that. The following year, Gordon's son, Mike Eastman, accompanied me on another expensive hunt in order to film me, and once again I felt the pressure to make a good shot and kill while he was filming. I had a great amount of respect for Mike, who was a legend of Western big-game hunting and film, so I didn't want to let him down.

Over the years, when I'm hunting, I'm always thinking about the numbers. My odds of success.

Okay: This animal is seventy yards away and unaware. I can make that shot perfectly eighty percent of the time. But if I get to sixty-nine yards, then my odds of making it go up to eighty-two percent. And if I go to sixty-eight yards . . .

I factor in the weather and the wind and everything else. All the different variables. Everything is a calculation to me. Some things are out of my control. But for the things I can control, I am prepared. The better shape I'm in, the better decisions I'm going to make at crunch time. When it's time to focus, I'm going to be thinking clearly instead of huffing and puffing. When you're tired, you lose focus and take shortcuts. Therefore, if I'm never tired, I'm never losing focus. If I'm physically ready, then mentally I will be focused on what I need to do to kill that animal. To not be affected by everything around you is a huge advantage.

In order to squelch any fears you might have, you have to spend the time to prepare yourself. This can take years of work. That's why now I'm not affected by anything outside during a hunt. I'm the one in control. The animal is the prey; I'm the predator. I'm the one calling the shots.

That's the mindset it takes to conquer your fears. It's taken lots of years and hard work to acquire. But when you do all the little things that need to be done, that's how you are able to overcome your fears with focus.

"Nothing clears a troubled mind like shooting a bow."

This is one of the most well-known quotes from the legendary Fred Bear (1902–88). Virtually every passionate hunter about my age has heard of him, and so far as I know, Fred was the first world-famous bowhunter. Even though bowhunting has been around for thousands of years, Fred was one of the first to become a household name in the sport. My dad bought me one of my favorite books, *Hunting with the Bow and Arrow* by Saxton Pope, published in 1923, that had a special introduction by Fred Bear. I still have some of his films.

There is such truth in his statement about shooting a bow. In our busy and boisterous world, there is something wonderful about the experience. That's one of the things I love about Lift Run Shoot. I get to see people shoot a bow, sometimes for the first time. For those unfamiliar with the feeling, it's incredible.

When Andrew Huberman—podcaster, neuroscientist, and associate professor of neurobiology and ophthalmology at Stanford University School of Medicine—took part in a Lift Run Shoot, he summed up his experience of the moment his arrow hit the target.

"It's just something so satisfying. There's a lot of steps for somebody who's never done it before. I knew which direction the arrow goes out. That's about it. Learning how to use the right musculature to actually be able to draw back. I always thought that on a compound bow that when you draw back that it just sits there—like you could take your hand off. I didn't realize you have to provide some additional, ongoing tension. Sighting up on it. Bringing the mind's focus to such a little narrow cone of attention. And then there's the contrast between that stillness, a decision, and then ballistic movement."

He made a sound of the arrow flying.

"And then the arrow leaves the bow. That's it. You've set it all up, and it just feels

Andrew Huberman

amazing. It's very hard to describe because (a) I am brand new to it and (b) it's all kinesthetic. I'm not sure there's a word to describe all of that and how good it feels, but it feels so good."

Huberman explained that even though he had shot rifles and pistols before and enjoyed that, it didn't resonate with him in the same way. He didn't feel as connected to the mechanics of shooting a gun versus a bow. With archery, he realized he loved every step of the process. Taking the right position with your feet and forearm and back. Breathing. Making adjustments. There was something about the contract between the stillness and so much motion that moved him.

"You have to be relaxed," I explained. "You have to be calm, relaxed, and precise at full draw. And then, as you said, it's just like a beautiful explosion."

With enough distance, we could watch the arrow arc and then hit home. That's why so many times when we put up a balloon for people to hit from a long distance, they can see that arrow arc, and then there's that immediate indication that the arrow has hit when the balloon pops. Seeing people's reactions is a joy for me.

"I'm completely taken by the experience," Huberman said. "One of the things that I'm absolutely obsessed with is

Cam with Andrew Huberman

time perception and how elastic our perception of time is. And when we get our eyes into a narrow area . . . getting into that narrow cone of attention, it's almost like things are in slow motion right before you release the arrow."

This reminded me of why I love bowhunting. There are many things like this in today's day and age when we're so distracted all the time. We have our phone sitting there with the universe at hand. There is so much information out there, so many topics to talk about. It's difficult to focus. Everybody walks around thinking they have attention deficit disorder.

Shooting a bow requires tunnel-vision focus.

That's one reason why I feel taking ice-cold baths are good. Because when you get in the water, you can't think about anything else but that fucking cold tub and how miserable it feels. It takes your brain and does something to it.

For me, archery does that. Running, too. I do think about other things, but I'm pretty much focusing solely on performing.

Ask yourself this: Do you have something in your life that requires tunnel-vision focus? If you do, how often do you get a chance to experience it? If you've never found something like that, what sort of thing might it be?

As humans we're so easily distracted. We are such a complicated species where we have doubts and fears and emotions that can overwhelm us. You have to have things—maybe just one thing—that requires you to shut out all of that other shit.

Having something good to focus on in your life is one of the healthiest things you can do.

Being able to have that tunnel-vision focus, or as Huberman called it, being able to bring your mind to focus on such a "little narrow cone of attention" is something that is necessary in life, and something that those who are undeniable are able to do. But we need big-picture focus as well. That view of the world that I began this book talking about. Seeing the world as only 20 miles big.

As I've said so many times, like a lot of kids growing up, I lacked direction in my life. After high school, I had nothing even remotely resembling focus or purpose. I longed to define myself. The problem was, I didn't know what I wanted to be and had no goal to shoot for. Bowhunting put everything in perspective. Just as I began to discover a much bigger world, I was also able to begin narrowing my focus in order to find my purpose.

When we find something positive to focus our energy on, we can get going in a positive way. That's what happened with me. Bowhunting gave me something to focus my energy on. When I was younger, working during the week and drinking away the weekends, I was very average, but when I became laser focused on bowhunting, it changed me.

Bowhunting has defined me. For me, bowhunting is the key to everything.

When professional trail runner Sally McRae came to do a Lift Run Shoot, she spoke about being laser focused in life. Sally is one of my favorite people in the world, and her story, which I'll share in detail later, is incredible. As she was talking about the experience of shooting the bow, she spoke about the theme of having focus in your life.

"I have so much respect for what you do. You trying to get me to focus on that little balloon today and just all the little things that I had to do before I even lift the bow. It's so technical. And I had told you a couple times, 'Cam, this is so peaceful for me because I literally cannot give way or give attention to anything else.' I was off my phone this entire trip because I was so focused on the need to learn the technique on this bow—where my elbow is and, like, the string needs to touch the tip of my toes and just everything. And I think that your ability to be laser focused on one thing is also why you're the best hunter in the world. But it's such a simple thing.

"We don't talk very much about focus. We don't talk about wisdom and patience. I mean, those things aren't sexy, right? Wisdom, patience, and focus. But come on. I want *strong* and *perseverance!* But oh my gosh—the only way I was able to get that balloon today was that I had to be all in focus on this little, teeny, tiny dot."

Sally said that too many times our focus is on the wrong things.

"There's that phrase 'comparison is the thief of joy.' And we say it so much that we actually forget about what it genuinely means."

"It's a cliché," I told her.

"But it is pretty incredible," she replied. "If you are in a point of struggle in your life where you're really down on yourself, you're just so overwhelmed. It's like, get off your phone. Close the social media apps and actually think about the steps that you have planned for yourself. What steps are you planning to change the life that you're in? Because if you keep looking to your right and your left, you know what we call that? It's distraction. And distraction is one of the greatest thieves of you achieving your goal. It is the best way

MAKE A GOOD SHOT

to get you off track, and it's the best way to frustrate you and to make you bitter and to turn inward and just be upset all the time."

Instead of being overwhelmed, anxious, and frustrated, Sally observed, you have to be laser focused on the path before you.

"If you are at a point of frustration, pause, turn off your distractions, and ask yourself, What am I focusing on? Am I focusing on the pain and everything that's not going right? Am I focusing on what *she has* and what *he has* and how I don't have it all? That I'm just in this darkness, in this dismal spot? Or am I actually focusing on where I want to go?"

"The goal," I said.

"On the goal."

"The goal is a balloon," I said. "But you can't get to break that balloon without all the other stuff. Those distractions are not going to make it happen. And the distance you shot the balloon at was hard. Very hard. You had to do everything perfect. And as you said, it required intense focus. And you did it. It was amazing."

Finding the right thing in life to focus on isn't always easy. Keeping yourself laser focused can be pretty damn hard. But that's the only way to reach those amazing milestones in your life.

Focus over the long haul has made up for my lack of talent and ability. The only reason for any success I've had is because I've stayed focused and not given up on my dreams.

So, what are you focused on? Because *that* will become your reality.

The dream is to find a goal you can be laser focused on. And then never, ever waver.

Dr. Andrew Huberman has become a dear friend, and his podcast episode in which we discuss his faith in God blew up. I'm eternally grateful for his friendship and willingness to write the foreword to this book.

BUILD ON TODAY

All you need is a shitty bow.

That's all.

An old pair of sneakers.

The dusty set of weights in storage.

A no-name brand T-shirt.

A faded and stained cap.

It's not about the equipment.

It's about the exercise and the effort.

It's about starting.

Then starting again.

Day after day after fucking day.

All you need is an hour.

A half hour.

A lunch break.

A break from text messages.

A break from Instagram.

A break from Netflix.

30 minutes before dawn.

Or 30 minutes after dusk.

1/24th of your day.

5 hours of your week.

All you need is a spark.

A yearning for change.

A goal to get you outside.

A desire to do something different than yesterday.

A chance to build on today.

A target to aim for tomorrow.

A mission to simply start.

A determination that you will finish.

And a belief that you can ultimately find some success.

As for me?

All I need is a mountain and a rock.

A high summit and a heavy stone.

All I need is one word.

"Poser," written on that rock.

A reminder that some people aren't that impressed with me.

That's good because I'm not that impressed with me.

All I need is a story.

The joy of hearing when others find the fuel for their dreams.

The power of seeing people overcoming difficult odds in life.

They are all I need to push through when I am at my lowest on a hunt.

They are reminders that every single one of us has the chance to overcome anything.

CHAPTER 4

GET UP AND GO

CONSISTENCY:

The quality or fact of being consistent: such as the quality or fact of staying the same at different times

"INFINITE PATIENCE AND PRACTICE ARE NEEDED TO MAKE A HUNTER. HE MUST EARN HIS RIGHT TO TAKE LIFE BY THE PAINFUL EFFORT OF CONSTANT SHOOTING."[4]

—*Saxton Pope,* Hunting with the Bow and Arrow

The first time I met Joe Rogan, as a guest on his podcast, *The Joe Rogan Experience*, I introduced him to my daily routine.

"People always ask, 'What do you do?'" I said. "It's real simple. I got it on my shirt."

"Lift Run Shoot," Rogan quoted.

"I lift, run, shoot every day."

Rogan looked surprised. "You don't take Sundays off? Nothing?"

"Every day."

"You don't take a day off a week for anything?"

"Every day," I repeated.

"Wow. I take days off, son," Rogan said with a laugh. "I like days off."

"Hey, I would like days off too, but I can't do it."

If there is one constant theme about undeniable people, it is that they are consistent with how hard they work and the effort they give when performing. This doesn't apply just to a sport; it can apply to your business, or your ability to lead, or your relationships, or anything else in life. Through the highs and lows of life, one thing must remain constant: work. Make no mistake, without consistent effort, the whole ship sinks.

Every outlier I've met and run alongside and shot bows with works hard. Every single one is a testimony to the value of toiling away every single day. Each of these individuals has a trait I could share in this chapter. They all have a common thread inside of their DNA. It's not their rare genetics that they were born with—although some of these outliers were indeed blessed with those. It's an idea that anybody can latch onto:

Consistency will set you apart.

Growing up, I didn't have a lot of confidence. I didn't have lots of direction, either, nor did I have a lot of support from my peers. Discovering bowhunting and the feeling that came from success with a bow changed everything. I wanted more and more of that. I discovered that the harder I worked, the more success I had, and that just evolved into where I am right now.

I'm not some amazing athlete, and I'm not the best shot in the world. There were lots of better hunters out there when I first began, but I refused to stop. I knew I had to give everything, so that's what I've done. It's a daily grind; a life of never being satisfied with where you're at.

One person who has reached that summit and continues to climb higher is Nick Bare. I was super pumped to host Nick in my hometown for a couple memorable days. This US Army veteran is a beast known for being strong and fast and full of endurance. Not only that but also he's a good guy at his core. He's also the founder and CEO of Bare Performance Nutrition (BPN), a multimillion-dollar company.

As a kid growing up in a small town in central Pennsylvania, Nick said he was pretty average. "Average athlete. I was an average student. Socially I was average, from my perspective." He loved baseball and dreamt of playing in the pros, but he eventually realized that wasn't going to happen. After a severe eating disorder during his childhood nearly killed him, Nick was able to build a healthy relationship with food. This sparked his eventual love of fitness, training, and nutritional supplementation. He went to college to study nutrition before entering the army, and before graduating, he created BPN. During his time in the military, he began to document his journey as a business owner and an athlete on social media. A decade later, he remains on a journey to build a community that helps people find their full potential.

For our Lift Run Shoot, it was no surprise to see Nick excel at our 20-mile run. He has shared his journey in running from the very beginning. After transitioning out of the military, he publicly declared, "I will never run a day in my life again." But after he stopped, Nick discovered that he missed running. Starting back has ultimately led to marathons, triathlons, and 100-mile races. But early on, Nick had a moment like my 10K experience when I gave up and quit the race.

Nick Bare

Halfway into an 18-mile training run for Nick's first marathon in 2018, he was running in downtown Austin, Texas, on a cold and wet day. He felt tired, and voices in his head were asking him what the hell he was doing out there. Why should he keep going? He stopped and began to walk back home. But something inside of him told him that he was quitting. And if he was quitting on this, what else would he quit on in his life? Nick forced himself to keep running. When he made it to the 18-mile mark, he didn't stop and consider the run a success. Instead, he kept going, running one more mile. When he got back home, Nick wrote two words on the bill of his hat: "One More."

Nick Bare's "Go One More" mantra has given a generation focus and drive to push harder and chase their dreams.

This would eventually become Nick's slogan and saying: "Go One More." Like "Keep Hammering," the "Go One More" saying has become a meaningful mantra to so many athletes out there. As Nick talked with me about his journey into becoming a successful hybrid athlete and also a successful entrepreneur, he spoke about the theme of consistency. With Bare Performance Nutrition, there wasn't some overnight success story but rather that long, steady grind toward success.

"It was just this compounding consistency of building a true, authentic, and real brand, and connecting with people and building this community with great products," Nick told me. "That kind of has gotten us to where we're at almost eleven years now. I'm a big fan of compounding consistency over time. Just show up and be consistent. One of the things my running coach, Jeff Cunningham, says is that it's better to be consistently good than occasionally great. Think of the runner who wakes up every single day, goes and logs their miles day in and day out. It's hot, it's cold, it's rainy, it's sunny—they're still going to log their miles. Then you have the other person who wakes up, then they snooze. They don't go to run their miles. They don't log their easy runs. But occasionally they go out and they run the fastest mile they can. Or they sign up for a marathon and blow up. And they're occasionally great. But to be consistently good—that compounds and is going to get you so much further than the person who is chasing quick greatness."

Like all outliers in today's online community, Nick has had his own share of haters. The first time he put out on the Internet that he was going to run a sub-three-hour marathon, there were articles and forums and YouTube videos and posts from people saying he would never be able to do it. The first time he went out, he ran a 3:24 marathon, missing his goal by 24 minutes.

"I trained for another year, and I fucking did it," Nick said. "I ran a 2:48. And people still talked shit. People still criticized. But if I would have let those people bring me down the moment I didn't do it and just give up, I would never have accomplished some of those goals after that."

Nick has been one of those outliers doing amazing things over the years—things that have inspired me. I had to admit to him that even I was skeptical when he announced that he was going to run a sub-2:50 marathon.

"I know you could run, but I'm like, 'That big fucker? Is he going to run a sub-2:50? I don't think so. I mean, come on!' And sure as shit, you did. I've been proven wrong in a good way with you."

I shared that seeing Nick do something like that inspired me to want to know more about his training plans and to ask myself what I could be doing better. Could I be doing a little more of what Nick was doing?

"I'm a fan," I told Nick. "I have looked at some of your goals and been like, 'Is he going to be able to do that? I don't know'—and then been pleasantly surprised that you did it. I love to see people win, and you're a fucking winner."

Nick's mindset reflects his winning attitude. "I think I've learned over the last just couple of years that there's nothing that's unbelievable or unachievable if you truly—it sounds clichéd—like, if you put your mind to it, you make a plan, you follow that plan, you can do it. But it's pretty fucking true."

The key is to make a plan and stick to it, Nick said. To not deviate from it. And if you miss the goal, you have to go back and revise and refine that plan.

"You hop back on that track and you keep working toward it," Nick said. "Once you realize you can pretty much do almost anything you want, you're unstoppable."

Like myself and so many others out there, Nick was just this average guy with no big aspirations.

Courtney Dauwalter has redefined mountain endurance running for women. She is generally regarded as the Greatest of All Time, and I can't even put into words how much joy I get seeing her succeed. I train as hard as I do many days, just to hope to halfway keep up with her on the mountain training runs we share.

"So many people, they have such limited beliefs in what they can achieve," he reflected. "You know: 'I came from this family. I grew up here. I don't have this money. I don't have these opportunities.' *Create* them. Create the opportunities. If you create the opportunities, it's going to get you to exactly where you want to be one day."

If anybody's life is an example of true compounding consistency, it has to be Courtney Dauwalter's. She is the legendary ultra-girl who is considered the GOAT of trail runners. But this didn't happen overnight. For Courtney, it was starting young and seeing her ability grow with each passing year. Her love for running began in fifth and sixth grades, when she had to run a mile for gym class and discovered she liked how it felt.

"I'd always been a soccer player before that," Courtney said. "And my favorite part of the game was that I could run the length of the field the whole time. And that was like my one thing I could contribute."

In seventh grade, she joined the cross-country team and discovered a deeper love for running. Instead of playing a team sport, where your success hinges on other athletes' performances, and there's action going on all over the field, or the court, or the diamond, running allowed her to exert full control over what happened, and she enjoyed that. Even as a young teenager, she was discovering her true passion in life.

"It felt like I could push as hard as I wanted until the finish line," Courtney recalled. "And that was satisfying. I enjoyed going as hard as I could. I loved the feeling. I loved how afterward I always felt like every system was working. It felt like recharging for my brain and the rest of my body. And then when I joined the cross-country team, I learned that it can be this huge social activity, too. It suddenly was a space where I was sharing miles with my best friends and going on adventures."

Racing on cross-country and track teams established her love of running. She had great coaches who taught her the value of working really hard. But it was her teammates that had the biggest impact on her passion for the sport.

"Cross-country teams are special because often you get really close with them," she explained. "And running has a way to make people *real* right away, so those were my best friends growing up. They're still some of my best friends—my cross-country team from when we were thirteen years old together."

Running provided Courtney with not only social opportunities but also a meditative space.

"I remember in high school going on runs by myself and composing my whole English paper in my head, getting home, and scribbling it down on paper so I could turn it in. It was when my brain seemed to work the best."

Her journey into ultramarathons wasn't something that happened immediately. It was a process that she built up over many years of running. Some people in the sport learned about ultras when they were kids and dreamt of running them one day, but not Courtney. She had never even heard of an ultra. In fact, when she was growing up in Minnesota, the concept of just a regular marathon sounded insane to her. She couldn't believe people ran them, so it wasn't a path she pursued early in her life. But that consistent routine of running began to change her. In her mid-20s, Courtney ran her first marathon: the Twin Cities Marathon, which starts in Minneapolis and ends at the state capitol building in Saint Paul. After that, she began to yearn for bigger challenges.

"I think I was just, like, looking for a thing outside of normal workday life," Courtney told me. "What could I sign up for just to see, because who knows what will happen?"

She signed up for a Tough Mudder, an obstacle race with events held in a variety of cities. Participants have to go through mud pits, climb walls, and avoid electrical shocks. She loved the experience and laughed as she shared some of the details.

"We did jump from this really high platform into this freezing cold lake and swim across it," she said. "Electric wires were dangling, and they were zapping me, and I was flopping through like a dead fish and just started giggling. I was like, *This is so absurd. I can't believe that I'm willingly doing this.*"

When Courtney finished the Tough Mudder, she thought to herself, *Okay, what else is there that I can try?* A buddy of hers was going to enter a 50K right in her neighborhood of San Antonio, Texas, where she'd moved to take a teaching job. Since she had already run a marathon, a 50K sounded like the perfect amount for her.

"I was running every day," she remembered. "I would consistently get maybe an hour before work and maybe on the weekends, up to two hours. But I wasn't following any plan or anything. I was just doing normal, basic maintenance because I loved it. It felt good. That's what I wanted to do with some of my time, but I wasn't putting in a ton of effort to it."

The 50K that Courtney ran in 2011, at the age of 26, was on dirt trails, something she hadn't really run since her cross-country days in high school. Those trails through the

Courtney Dauwalter

woods felt a lot different from doing a road marathon, where watches would be beeping all over the place and everyone was checking their pace the whole time.

"To get to the peacefulness and weaving through that single-track dirt in the woods and people just chatting and joking and filling my pockets with jelly beans, I was like, *This is cool.* And that then opened up the whole ultra-running world to me."

Her first 50K went better than expected, and Courtney wondered immediately which distance she should try next. She decided on a 50-mile race.

"The 50K that I did in Texas exposed me to the sport, but the fifty-mile race I did was in Steamboat Springs, Colorado, in the mountains. That's what hooked me on the sport, for sure. It was incredible scenery. It was so hard. Like, fifty miles was insane. A huge day. And then just the people and their attitudes got me fully hooked on it. It was terrible weather: sleeting, windy, awful. All signs pointed to *We should hate this,* but the people around me were having so much fun. I was like, *That's cool. I want to be surrounded by those kinds of attitudes.*"

Courtney entered her first 100-mile race a year later, in 2012, and as has been talked about and reported so many times, she quit 60 miles into the race because the pain was too much. She had not yet found her famous "pain cave" that she always talks about.

"Now when I think of it [the pain], I'm like, that was normal," Courtney told me. "I just didn't know that I had the mental tools to push past that."

One of the things I love about Courtney is how she bounced back from her initial "failure" of not completing that 100-miler to become one of today's ultra-running greats. Imagine if she would have let her running dreams get derailed after that first 100-mile attempt?

Courtney's conquering those ultramarathons and her going deeper into her pain cave didn't just happen. As I've said, it was a long journey that continues to this day. I asked her what advice she would give somebody who wants to become a runner.

"That it's hard at first, but it's tiny, consistent blocks that you're adding, or grains of sand on the pile. Like you're just putting one more grain on there, one more tiny block each day, but that consistency is the huge thing. So, if you want to run five miles eventually, you shouldn't start by running five miles. You should start by running around the block and then around a couple blocks. Go tiny, but be consistent."

"I think that's it," I said. "I've never heard that analogy about a grain of sand at a time. Because people do want these big gains. If you think of it in perspective as a grain of sand building on that block, that's a small increment, but that is what it takes."

"Yeah. And then you look back, and suddenly you've got a pile there. They add up for sure. It's just you don't see the gain every day."

It's easy for people—especially those who are just starting to run and exercise—to feel discouraged when they see all those people running marathons and smiling and having a great time. They go out and they're thinking, *Oh my God, this fucking sucks! How do these people smile?* Everybody needs to realize that it's hard sometimes, even for people like Courtney, but it's okay if it's hard. Because once you get done with a run, you know you're moving in the right direction. It's a positive. The key is to move in a positive direction. But it doesn't happen overnight.

"Sometimes it's putting in that huge burst of energy to *just put your shoes on* at the door that can be the hardest part," Courtney said. "Put in a bunch of energy, get the shoes on, walk out the door, and start walking away from your house. Then it gets a little bit easier."

When I think of consistency—of working hard day in and day out; of having that sort of undeniable work ethic—I think of Rich Froning Jr. I'm not a big CrossFit guy, but I'm

It was such an honor to share a few days running, training, and shooting arrows with CrossFit legend Rich Froning.

a big icon guy. So, it was a thrill to talk to Rich, once called the Fittest Man in History after winning four back-to-back individual CrossFit Games championships from 2011 through 2014. In the same way that I loved watching Lance Armstrong, even though I never biked, I loved watching Rich compete and win, even though I didn't do CrossFit. After retiring from individual competition after the 2014 season at the age of 27, he has been the captain of six CrossFit teams to win the Affiliate Cup championships.

When I asked Rich what it took to rise to the top in CrossFit and remain the best in the world for multiple years, he couldn't pinpoint one factor. Rather, it was a bunch of things, he said. "I think it's just the perfect storm of things coming together. Obviously, genetics play handily into that. You can outrun genetics a little bit, but not completely. I had really good parents growing up. My faith is a huge part of who I am. And then, also, playing sports growing up and having really good mentors and coaches and learning a ton through that."

So how in a sport where every guy there looks shredded and every guy is coming there to compete totally in shape, how did Rich manage to beat every single other guy? If essentially they are all genetic freaks? What makes him stand out?

"Most guys there, and then the girls on the women's side, *are* genetic freaks," he agreed. "They are outliers, for sure. But I think the missing piece is the mental side of it that came from the fact that I was one of the first ones to really play or do CrossFit kind of as a sport. A lot of guys in my era when I first started were, 'Oh, I'm just going to stay in my lane and just do what I can.' But I was always watching and trying to either play games with them while we were competing or watching and pushing them more than they wanted to be pushed."

According to Rich, when he played high school baseball, his team ran more than the track and cross-country teams. His coach was big on mental toughness, and he was also always doing CrossFit before CrossFit became cool.

"We would just run, and it was more of a mental conditioning than it was even physical. I think that laid the foundation."

That, along with Rich's inner drive to always want to win and hating to lose, made him into the competitor that he became. When he first started out competing in CrossFit, everybody would do the same workouts, and the athletes could gauge where they were at with one another. Rich figured out how to not take significant losses in events that weren't in his wheelhouse, while also throttling down on events when he could shine. He was one of the first ones to figure out that you're playing a big game one event at a time. As he discovered ways to make his body stronger and more efficient, people began to notice.

"People were trying to figure out what I was doing," Rich said. "One of our buddies, Jason, would write on his wall, 'What's Rich doing?' He would always go out to the garage and try to do more than what he thought I was doing."

"To work harder," I added. "To sacrifice more."

I understand this desire to do more, as I explained to Rich. "Sometimes I go running and probably shouldn't run, but it's like, *No, I gotta sacrifice more.* I want to run by these houses with everybody inside all warm and watching TV, and looking at each house as I pass, I'm like, 'Pussy'; 'Pussy'; 'Pussy.'"

"'Got you,' 'got you,' 'got you,'" Rich agreed.

Being consumed by his sport was eventually one of the reasons Rich decided to step away from individual competitions once he had kids.

"There'd be times where I'd be in the house at ten o'clock at night, and I'd be like, *I didn't do enough today. I'm gonna go get another 5K on the road or go out in the garage.* And I can't do that when I have my kids. They need to be front and center. That was why I stepped away at individuals—because I was obsessive. I was all consumed by winning and grinding, and it started to affect relationships."

To be at the top of his career, he was constantly wanting to do more. It was fun to win, Rich said, but it was also a mental and physical grind.

"It got to the point where it was like this: Remember when you were a kid at Christmas, and you got pretty much everything you wanted? And then the next day, you're like, 'Christmas is three hundred sixty-five days away!' That's how it was. The day after I won the games, I'm training again. We're taking a family vacation in September after the games in August, and I'm training two or three times a day just because that's what I did."

"Isn't that the price of greatness?" I asked.

"It really is."

"People say, well, you should be balanced. Balanced in your family, balanced in this and that."

"There's no balance," Rich said. "Not to be the best."

I agreed. "You can be average and be balanced."

How did Rich do it? It's not some secret formula, and it doesn't come down to his unique set of genes. It comes down to that consistency.

"Man, every day there's a grind," Rich said. "You wake up. 'Ah. Today I just don't feel like it.' But you just get up and go. Once I get going, I'm good to go."

Growing up in a small logging town, I was accustomed to seeing people putting their heads down and going to work day after day without much change. Tomorrow was going to be same as today, and that meant more hard work. I realized early on that I couldn't be a guy who just goes to work and comes home. I couldn't do that. Then I discovered hunting.

I can't claim to know the sort of greatness that defines someone like Kobe Bryant or other undeniable icons, but I do understand the mentality of outworking others. I know that if you work hard at something every single day, you're going to get good. For me, it's been over 30 years of working hard at this every single day. Basically, the only reason why I'm where I'm at is because I'm grinding away. Because of hard work. It's not about talent; it's about grinding everything.

For so many years, that grind came along with working a full-time job at the Springfield Utility Board. After I got to know Joe Rogan, he was constantly encouraging me to quit my job to focus on hunting. Most people work at something all day that they don't want to do, Joe said, but I experienced all this sort of adventure in my life on top of my daily job.

"But a lot of people don't," Joe said. "Their existence is this dull drone of doing things they don't want to do all the time. And then when they get home, they just watch TV and eat. And when they see people that are daring, that take risks, they attack them. They hate on them. And that's through the comfort of their own phone and through computer keyboards. They like to shit on people that make them feel uncomfortable, and they'll talk shit about your ambitions. 'What the fuck is wrong with him? Why is he running every day? Why is he working out so much?'"

Cam with Joe Rogan

Joe joked that even though he never reads negative comments about himself, he will read ones about me.

"They do it because they feel inadequate, because they have not lived. They're not living a maximized life. But they *could*. That's the thing. They could. It's not easy. And the longer you get into that life, the harder it is. If you're fifty-five years old, and you've been living a dull and boring life your whole life, and you've never taken any chances, and your body looks like shit. It's fat, doughy, and you're tired all the time. And you decide, *I want to be a beast today*. Like, *Boy, you've got a long road, son*."

"I've seen people do it," I told Joe (though I'm not sure that they turned into "beasts").

"If a guy loses pounds, he's a beast," Joe said. "That's a true Herculean effort."

I've said it before many times, but I've been hearing people tell me for years that if I kept up running, I wouldn't be able to do this and that. That I would need knee replacements by the time I was 40. That my body would break down. But I believe your body does adapt to the load you put on it. Running strengthens your body. Runners actually have stronger joints and stronger knees and stronger hips because their bodies have adapted. Everybody can see a change that happens with consecutive running and working out, but it's only after consistent work—*years* of work—that you see your body adapt.

"Everybody gets all fired up, energized to do something," I said to Joe. "Then that drops off. They might do it for a week."

"Like folks who lose weight and then gain it back," he said.

"Yeah, but if you can just continue to put in the work, punch that time clock, your life can change dramatically. Your body will change. Everything will change. How you look at things changes. But it takes that consistent effort."

Consistent running and lifting make sense. But why consistent shooting?

Do I *really* need to be consistent with that?

I'll let the great Fred Bear answer that hypothetical question:

"It is important to practice during a hunt. Not when you're sneaking around expecting to see a deer, elk, or bear, but at times when you're having lunch or when you have a group talking together . . . You should practice, because the first shot that you get in hunting is an important shot. And if you haven't shot for three or four days, that first one might be the worst arrow you ever released. So, you should keep yourself in shape and sharp. You should get that potentially first bad shots out of your system by practicing."

Early on, when I first started to appear on podcasts as a guest, I grew tired of hearing myself in the long form because I felt like I was always telling them the same thing. I always felt like I didn't really have much to say that I haven't said a million times already.

"My secret? Work hard. That's it. End of interview."

Even though I love my own podcast and love all the incredible outliers I've been able to talk with, my own core message remains the same. It ain't rocket surgery. It's putting forth consistent effort. Period. Work, sweat, hurt, win. To do this every day, no exceptions, no excuses, regardless of how I'm feeling or what challenges I have. For me, this means lifting weights, running the mountain, and shooting my bow to prepare me for the challenge of bowhunting.

I know personally that good is the enemy of great. I know that because I have been lucky to have spent time with people who are truly *great* at their craft, be it hunting, running, endurance racing, lifting, training, writing, and so much more. These people fascinate me; I can't get enough of true greatness.

I feel as if I am not great at anything. On my best day, I'm good at one or two endeavors. I can't be satisfied with "good," because I've learned that the greats are never satisfied. They are always working, learning, growing, and giving more. They are disciplined in their drive to keep pushing, getting to the next level. In following their lead, I find myself doing the one thing that in my mind means discipline: I run. When I run, I feel like I've put in work, and working in one aspect makes me want to work in all aspects.

If I'm being honest, I know that, in all likelihood, I'll never reach the level I dream of. In anything. Most of us don't. That said, I'll never stop trying.

Maybe you're in the same boat. Maybe your mantra is that you'll never stop trying. But how do you keep growing and becoming better? I asked Courtney Dauwalter that very question. How does someone like her improve? She said she focuses on the things she needs to keep working on, places where she can still improve greatly on. Courtney calls it "sharpening the dull blades" on those areas she can improve.

"You're building a little bit at a time," she explained. "It just takes that consistency of adding another little bit to it. So, if I can keep on growing the endurance so that maybe it's more possible to push even harder."

"How do you look at growing endurance?" I asked the world's greatest endurance runner.

"Just consistently adding to it, adding to the fire a little bit at a time. For sure, you don't want to just keep training more. That's how you go over the edge of that and start breaking down instead. I guess adding little bits to the fire every day through just consistent work. And then signing up for the stuff that's hard and just seeing and learning from it."

Adding little bits to the fire. I love that.

LOVE THE GRIND

VERB

Grind is an action.
  To crush and pulverize by friction.
    To shape and sharpen by attraction.
      To rub and reduce by repetition.
        To wear down your wants and your will.
        To grate and to gnash.
      To get going day after day and night after night.
    To get going and keep going.
  To go far, and to go farther than that.
To stop guessing how far you will go.

ADJECTIVE

Grind is an attribute.
  Describing the difficulty
    Summarizing the struggle
      Naming the never-ending toil
    Labeling the long-standing routine
  Distinguishing the drudgery
Epitomizing the effort

NOUN

Grind is an attitude.
  One word for the countless steps up the mountain.
    One way to picture the pain and the persistence.
    A daily goal.
      A weekly routine.
    A yearly regime.
  The ache and the sweat.
  The hard work and the exhaustion.
The lifestyle of longing for more.

If you want to be undeniable, you have to grind it out.
You have to put in the work.
You have to love the grind. Period.

CHAPTER 5

JUST WATCH WHAT HAPPENS

DISCIPLINE:

*(a) control gained by enforcing
obedience or order
(b) orderly or prescribed conduct or
pattern of behavior
(c) self-control*

"AS YOU GO THROUGH LIFE, THERE ARE THOUSANDS OF LITTLE FORKS IN THE ROAD, AND THERE ARE A FEW REALLY BIG FORKS— THOSE MOMENTS OF RECKONING, MOMENTS OF TRUTH."[5]

—*Lee Iacocca (1924–2019), American auto executive*

Bowhunting is a discipline that will humble you. You have to be prepared to hike up any mountain and weather any storm. You hunt animals that are used to being hunted every single day, so they're dialed in. Getting into bow range, in the red zone, is difficult. You have to be patient and quiet. You have to battle being alone. You basically have a sharp stick, and you have one chance to make a perfect shot. And then you see these majestic, mythical creatures, and you have to keep calm and steady.

Don't start bowhunting unless you can deal with failure. It will humble you no matter how good you think you are. That is why you need practice and to prepare for it. There are many things you need to do. But there is also a trait that you have to embrace in order to be successful. Not just as a bowhunter, but in life.

That's discipline.

In this chapter, I want to talk about one aspect of discipline. I don't want to focus on the aspects covered so far, such as being consistent and having determination. I want to look at the ability to have self-control in your life.

I've heard people say it's the little things or that the devil is in the details, but I think that's wrong. It's the *big things* that matter if you want to be the best. And one of those big things is not sabotaging yourself with choices such as overeating or overindulging in alcohol. You can't sabotage yourself with going to McDonald's and boozing and then also think you're going to be great at something. It just doesn't work.

So many of the outliers I've spoken with share similar

experiences of having to overcome their battle with alcohol and other addictions. My own story is similar, and so many of you know it. I don't drink alcohol and haven't in decades. Since I ask a lot of my body every day, I know that alcohol isn't going to help me with any of my goals and plans. Like everybody, I had to face the choice all of us have to face at some point in our lives. It's like the opening line of the classic Robert Frost poem "The Road Not Taken":

"Two roads diverged in a yellow wood."

At some point in our lives, we all arrive at that fork in the road, where we face having to choose which path to take. In my early 20s, I came to that point.

The mantra of my life back then consisted of four words: same shit, different day.

Things in my life changed when I was 17 years old. That's when my mom, stepdad, two brothers, and sister moved away to Arizona. I stayed in Oregon and bounced around, living and sleeping wherever I could. They eventually came back, but I never moved home. Instead, I stayed at my girlfriends', a couch, a couple trailer parks, a year of living in the dorm while trying to play college football at Southern Oregon University, and rented an apartment with three other guys. At each stop, I flirted with disaster, all alcohol related. I was just like everybody else. Low self-esteem. Low ambitions. Low expectations. I'd go out because I thought I'd be missing something if I didn't, but then I'd go out and nothing would happen. I would do the same thing as always: drink, get a little buzz on, and pass away the time. When it was all over, it was like nothing had ever happened. Sometimes I'd show up somewhere and realize that the last time these guys saw me, I had blacked out and didn't even remember what I did or what I said. It was a good guess, though, that I'd probably made the biggest idiot of myself. So, I'd think, *Well, I better get a little buzzed, so I won't even worry about it.*

I'd wake up the next day feeling bad from having drank too much and knowing my life was going nowhere. So, after work, I'd drink to mask *that* pain. Deep down, I knew I was letting everybody down, but I didn't want to deal with any of it. I didn't want to face reality.

In *Endure*, I shared one of those lowest moments I experienced, when I crashed my truck, totaling it, and they had to tow it away. I was suddenly faced with two paths I could take in my life. One path led to that small trailer on the side of the road I called home, and the other path led to the mountains.

Author John C. Maxwell wrote in his book *Failing Forward: Turning Mistakes into Stepping Stones for Success* that "every major difficulty you face in life is a fork in the road. You choose which track you will head down, toward breakdown or breakthrough.[6]"

Every single outlier I've met came to that fork in the road, and every single one had a breakthrough. Some have had similar battles like I had.

Sometimes to be undeniable, you have to choose to *deny yourself* of something.

Natalie Eva Marie might seem to be living in a whole other universe than I'm in. She's an actress, fashion designer, and a model, but she's known best for being a professional wrestler in the WWE (World Wrestling Entertainment). As of late, she's become an ultramarathoner and hunter. The beauty of social media is that, many years ago, Natalie began to follow me, and now she credits me for getting her into running and racing in her first ultra. I took her on a run up to the top of Mount Pisgah.

"I have to say, I'm not surprised that you're a savage, but this shit is no fucking joke," Natalie told me.

Our childhoods have some similarities. She could relate to my story because sports played a huge role in her life. She grew up in Concord, California, wanting to be with her brothers, so she'd play every sport that they played. In high school, Natalie played every sport, but soccer was the one she began to home in on. Then, she told me, "I tore the ligaments in my ankle my senior year. I made the choice that after my senior year to be done. Even though I came back and played through the remaining season, I made the choice to hang up my cleats."

At junior college, though, Natalie got the bug to play again. Not only did she make the team but also she earned All-American honors. After transferring to Arizona State University, she wanted to try out for the team there. But self-doubt led her to abandon her dream. From ASU, she transferred to California State University at Fullerton. This time she decided to try out for the soccer team—and made it—but ultimately wasn't permitted to suit up. The reason? Her NCAA (National Collegiate Athletic Association) eligibility had expired because she had exceeded the "five-year clock" rule.

"It's a perfect example of self-belief," Natalie reflected. "You're your own worst enemy. So, it's like you have to face yourself every single day, and the belief is imperative with anything that we do in our life. It can take you there, or it can take you out. You have to be honest and ask yourself, *Am I good enough?* I battled with that, because I was like, *I don't know.* I think that I am, but I never really felt like I was."

One of a kind in so many ways, Natalie Eva Marie makes an impact wherever she goes and I love it.

Being disqualified from soccer at Fullerton left her feeling deflated and purposeless. She beat herself up and decided to head in another direction. A self-destructive direction.

"Oh my God, that's when shit was on and poppin'," she recalled honestly. "And then the beast came out, and that beast was not pretty and not good. And that's where things went downhill real quick."

Just like I did at her age, Natalie found relief in drinking. And just like I did, she totaled her car while driving drunk. The difference there was that I walked away without injuries, while Natalie broke her nose and developed a hematoma. This was the last straw. With the help of her brother, she became sober at the age of 23. Once she began to attend Alcoholics Anonymous and started hearing other people's stories, she was warned how easy it was to relapse. In Natalie's mind, however, there was no way that was going to happen to her.

During the next three years, Natalie began to get her life back in order and regain the things that she had lost. Things that normal citizens in society already had, like a driver's license and a stable job. Her confidence began to come back, but with it came an accompanying voice.

"That little voice," Natalie described it. "That bitch is trying to take me out every day."

One day she called her AA sponsor to tell her thanks but she was okay to be on her own. Nine months later, Natalie was back to her old ways. Once again, her life

Cam with Natalie Eva Marie

began to crumble. Thankfully, she had parents who loved and supported her; who had laid down a foundation of discipline and hard work for her. It was these qualities that would be required for her to get her life back in order.

At the time of her relapse, she was dating professional fitness coach Jonathan Coyle, now her husband. He had seen her strengths: her discipline and her work ethic and her drive. Jonathan knew what she wanted in life. When he realized that his girlfriend had a serious drinking problem, he gave her an ultimatum.

"We had a serious talk," Natalie recalled, "and he basically said, 'If you want anything to work right here, then you not only have to be sober, you have to work the sobriety program.' And that was that pivotal moment where I'm like, *What do I want?* The old me would have been like, *Fuck this, I'm out.*"

"What was different?" I asked her.

"He's the calm to my storm. I'm the tornado. He's able to reel me in and go in the right direction. But what I also appreciate is he doesn't put up with my shit. I will run the show, and I have no problem running the show, but I need someone to put me in my place as well. And so, him being that anchor was super important."

This was a pivotal moment in Natalie's life. A game changer.

"You always hear people talk about forks in the road," she said.

She was dating the man of her dreams and had just gotten her third callback from the WWE to try out for the WWE diva search.

"I ended up in rehab," Natalie said. "I put myself through it, because if you're not ready to get sober, it's not going to work. You have to make the choice yourself. No one else can." As the old adage goes, she added, "You can lead a horse to water, but you can't force it to drink it."

Natalie called back her sponsor with her tail between her legs and asked to be taken back, and her sponsor did. That's when her life got amazing, Natalie told me. She signed a contract with the WWE and began training for a sport she had never done. She also starred in the long-running reality TV show *Total Divas*. It was all by the discipline of working a 12-step program and keeping her priorities in the right place.

For her, it comes down to living day by day, making meetings, working out, and eating as clean as she can.

"Once you actually make that choice and get sober and do the deal, you got to put the work in," Natalie explained. "It's actionable steps on a daily basis. You can have a life beyond your wildest dreams. Sitting here with Cameron Hanes—a life beyond my wildest dreams. That's what it's all about. And it's a testament to doing the program. In March of this year, I'll have, God willing, ten years of sobriety. It's been a journey, man."

I asked Natalie why so many people get sober and then fall back into their bad habits.

"Because it's hard. You have to battle your demons every single day. You gotta show up.

Natalie Eva Marie

That's why I love guys like yourself and David Goggins. Seeing you guys actually together and seeing how you guys get after it every single day is inspiring. Because it's a daily choice. It's a daily thing that you have. It's a daily reprieve that you have to kind of face."

I fully understood where she was coming from.

"It's hard to just focus on what's in front of you," I said. "That is a talent or an art. You stay the course day after day, month after month, year after year, and then who knows where the hell you can go? Because just like you, I shouldn't be here, either. I should have died in a drunk-driving accident. We beat the odds, and now we're here sharing an amazing experience and influencing others with being able to share this content like what we did yesterday. And it's going to impact others. We shouldn't be here, but we are, and we're going to make the most of it."

My younger brother Taylor is somebody who is making the most out of his life. He could easily have landed in a very different place—a very dark place—and it would be easy to understand why. He is someone who has chosen to take the hardships and heartaches in his life and do something with them.

Taylor is technically my half brother. When my parents divorced, it was just Pete and me. My mom remarried, to my stepdad, Greg, and they had Taylor and Megan, my sister. My dad remarried Kandi, and they had Justin. So, I have a wide variety of brothers and sisters, who I never categorize as a "half."

There is a 10-year age difference between Taylor and me, so it was hard to form a great connection with someone so much younger. He said I had a positive influence in his life, which I'm glad to hear, since I feel like I was probably the worst big brother when I went away to Southern Oregon University. There were several memorable times when I took him hunting with me. Like the time I pulled him out of school in his first year of hunting, when he was 12, so he could shoot this big buck I found that was bedded. Or after his second deer kill, when I told him it was time that he gut a buck himself, and he damn near sliced his thumb off. (I had to finish for him). I wasn't the best teacher for such a young kid, but Taylor learned a lot, regardless of my impatience.

By the time Taylor reached his 30s, he found himself going nowhere. Back surgeries and being overweight had him relying on beer and prescription drugs just to cope. Finally, at 34 years old, Taylor took an inventory of himself and started choosing complete and honest sobriety. But even tracking in the direction we want to go does not guarantee a destination.

"Life always catches up with us," Taylor says.

For a long time, he believed he was coasting through, unnoticed and unaccountable. Then in 2016 Taylor got a phone call in the morning that no parent wants.

"I remember it, plain as day," Taylor told me. "I had a dentist appointment at seven o'clock, which is crazy early, and I saw a car accident on the news. Saw the pickup and thought, *Dumb kids, driving too fast, drinking and driving.* As I was driving to the dentist appointment, my phone rang. It was Pamela, my wife, sobbing."

Pamela told Taylor that their son had died in that accident.

"I had come into Donovan's life when he was about ten. That's a tough age for a stepdad to come into a situation. We had our bumps in the road, and he'd straightened himself out and then was killed in a car accident. He was twenty-one. Young kid. Whole life ahead of him."

The entire family was heartbroken and lost. Rather than caving into old habits, Taylor launched himself into encouraging recovery in others and leading by example. For starters, he began running.

"Life experiences make us better, not worse," Taylor will tell you honestly. "Life gives us all roadblocks."

For him, running is a different way to cope with discomfort. Running provides him a different way to process the pain instead of escape it. Those obstacles are no longer excuses. Life is gritty, raw, and real.

Taylor's running journey began when he was trying to get back into shape. He had signed up for an 8K race without having any idea how far it was. At the time, I had entered the Western States 100, and Taylor was intrigued, knowing that it had become a big goal of mine. So, I asked him to come out and pace for me, but he ended up having surgery so he couldn't pace me. He tried a 25K next, then ended up doing the Frozen Trail 50K on Mount Pisgah.

"I did that 50K in a rain slick, wool socks, carrying a Gatorade, and almost died," Taylor said. "It was raining and rough."

It's fun to look back at how far Taylor has come. Everybody knows him now as this very talented ultra runner who just crushes miles in the mountains, but we all have to start somewhere.

"Those first ones are way worse than anything I've done now," Taylor said. "The first two miles I ran with Donovan one afternoon brought me closer to dying than any two-hundred- or one-hundred-mile ultra I've ever done. Those moments when you first start trying to run? God, it's miserable."

I hear people say all the time that they have a hard time completing just a mile and can't fathom doing a half-marathon, something that Taylor and I might do in a day. But as I always say, your body gets used to what you ask of it. If you haven't asked your body to run before, of course it's going to be hard. But once your body realizes, *Oh, okay, this is what we do,* then that's what you do.

Taylor recalled one of the first times he and I ran a race together.

"You're just crushing me, and I'm just flip-flopping across there, thinking, *I'll never be able to do this.* But then I started thinking, *You know what? He's a man. I'm a man. If he can do this, I can do this. I just need to toughen up and stick with it.* And that just kind of progressed: getting past that 8K and setting new goals."

It took him 10 years before Taylor truly felt like a runner. He never focused on the races; he just loved being out in the mountains. It was when he ran the Tahoe 200 that he ultimately decided to focus on having a successful race. The first two years he ran the Tahoe 200, he placed third. One of the runners in front of him was Courtney Dauwalter.

Taylor is like me: he can't just sit around and be bored. He used to sit at home drinking and watching television. Now when he sits at home, he says he feels like the laziest person in the world. When he finds extra time, he will get outside and run some miles.

Taylor Spike

I can't imagine what it feels like for Taylor and Pam to have lost Donovan, but I have seen what an amazing job my brother has done trying to honor him. A few times on the races and trips we've done together, Taylor has spread his stepson's ashes at meaningful moments.

"Watching your family suffer is hard," he reflected.

Going through that pain included watching his wife holding the urn of Donovan's ashes at night and falling asleep on the couch.

"Seeing how that impacts your family, you don't have any choice but to do better," Taylor said. "And to be the best version of yourself. During that same time, we were forced to move. I lost my job after twenty years. All those are really good reasons that probably everybody else would use to drink or do something they really shouldn't. But I had running. People were encouraging me to do it. It's like I was going to engulf myself in that and go bigger and go farther and go faster. And that's what started to drive that."

"You can't really blame anybody for wanting to numb that pain," I told Taylor. "And that's where people turn to drugs and alcohol, because it hurts so bad. You just don't want to hurt. You're tired of hurting. But that doesn't change the pain."

Running was a far healthier way to deal with his heartbreak because he was forced to deal with it rather than numb it. The discipline of running in the mountains gave him more time to think about his emotions.

I asked Taylor what life has looked like since he's been sober.

"What I try to tell people is that, in the moment, you don't realize what you're doing," he said. "You think it's okay if everybody else is doing it. But you have way more purpose than that in life."

Taylor's mission in life now is to inspire people, even if it's just to make them smile and encourage them to live their lives a little bit more.

"I've made a lot of bad choices, but I've made a couple good choices that have positively impacted my family and my life and then others. I just want to keep doing that."

"Somebody save me, me from myself."

If there's ever a song lyric that everybody should sing, it's that one. It barely needs any introduction since it blew up in 2020. I remember listening to and watching the video for Jelly Roll's "Save Me" a million times. I loved the song because it seemed so real and authentic. What struck me was that the Tennessean singer-songwriter-rapper conveyed so much soul and emotion with just his voice, and that was before knowing his life's story.

After years of toiling away at his music, he became a household name in 2023. When he visited Joe Rogan's show, he shared his incredible journey from a turbulent, troubled childhood to his rise to stardom.

"I spent my fifteenth, sixteenth, seventeenth, eighteenth, nineteenth, and twentieth birthdays incarcerated," said Jelly Roll. "They didn't even give me an extra piece of cake for dinner. I didn't have a guard tell me happy fifteenth or sixteenth birthday. I missed high school completely; I think I was in high school for, like, six weeks. I knew I got a woman pregnant. I'm back in jail. She's pregnant. She hates me. We're not talking. I'm a bad human. She's right: I was a horrible human. And I'm sitting in there, and that guard knocks on my door on May 22, 2008. He goes, 'You had a kid today,' and he walked away.

Jelly Roll has overcome so much in his life, from being locked up in jail for years to becoming a Grammy-nominated country music artist and more importantly, a man filled with the most love and graciousness I've ever met.

I immediately thought to myself, *I've got to quit this shit.* Now, I'm in the violent offender gang unit of this jail. And immediately, I went and signed up for that education and got my GED. I didn't know what I was going to do, but I knew that I was dead set on not selling drugs ever again."

From that moment on, he decided to change. Jelly Roll enjoyed rapping, but didn't realize he had a voice to sing. He had assumed a guy like him would die in prison, but that changed when he kept working on his music and his life. At the start of 2023, he was stunned to win three Country Music Television (CMT) Music Awards, including Breakthrough Male Video of the Year for his hit song "Son of a Sinner." I loved what he said at the beginning of his acceptance speech:

"They let a loser win tonight, baby! They let a loser win tonight."

I was talking to Joe Rogan not long after Jelly Roll's visit to his podcast, and I expressed just how much I loved the musician:

"There's no denying that talent, that storytelling, the voice itself. And then how he delivers it, and then on top of it is the lyrics. You put that all together, and you get something magic like Jelly Roll. I think a lot of people can identify. Like, nobody's praying when things are going great. Most people don't. They're like, *God, please just give me another chance* when something fucks up."

The song "Son of a Sinner" was so powerful to me because that *is* me!

"It's everybody," Joe said. "It's every human being. It's human nature. You got to cherish those kinds of people. It's a rare diamond that it's created by that kind of pressure."

After talking with Joe about Jelly Roll, I connected with the musician, and we messaged each other for a while. He asked if I could come to one of his shows, and I eventually was able to see him at the Grand Ole Opry in Nashville. I took my son and his fianceé to the show. Before the performance, we met Jelly Roll for dinner with his family. They were all so nice. He is the most gracious and humble and giving person ever, with the biggest heart of anybody I've ever met. At the show we met the iconic rapper, Nelly, who was there to perform as well. Jelly put on a hell of a show, and he sang with an open soul.

The next day, I met Jelly Roll and some others for lunch. He brought a copy of *Endure* for me to sign and said he planned to put my book alongside his gold and platinum record awards.

"I used to think I wanted records on the wall, but now I want things like an autographed book by you," Jelly Roll told me.

Seeing this bighearted guy who's turned his life around makes me want to be a better person. I realized that when I got back home. I saw firsthand how he treats people. And I witnessed how his singing and his music not only positively impacts people but also emotionally *moves* them.

"That's a guy where life gave him a fucking terrible hand, and he got through it, and he came out on the other end, and now he's amazing," Joe Rogan commented. "Now it's like this amazing journey that he can, like, really, truly appreciate every aspect of it. And he's so good at expressing that. He's so good at spreading that love, spreading that positivity. And it really does make you want to be a better person. It makes me want to be a better person."

In his acceptance speech for his surprising Country Music Award, Jelly Roll sounded more like a preacher than a musician as he inspired anybody listening.

"There is something poetic about a thirty-nine-year-old man winning New Artist of the Year. I don't know where you are in your life or what you're going through, but I want to tell you to keep going, baby. I want to tell you success is on the other side of it. I want to tell you everything's gonna be okay! That the windshield is bigger than the rearview mirror for a reason! And what's in front of you is much more important than what's behind you!"

Hallelujah and amen, brother!

When the man dubbed as the "World's Best Marathoner over 50" by *The New York Times* visited Springfield for a Lift Run Shoot, I knew he would come ready.

"You're dealing with a pro," Ken Rideout told me moments after I picked him up. "When you do this every day, you always come prepared. It's refreshing listening to your book and your podcast because trying to explain what you're talking about to someone who doesn't do that every day is a hard concept for people when you start telling them. 'You run every day?' 'Every day.' 'What about if there's a hurricane?' 'Every day means every day.'"

Ken knows the drill. He's a man cut from the same cloth as me and all the other outliers who have visited. Someone who doesn't think he's super special, but who's willing to suffer in order to get better. He's a beast: his marathon personal record is 2 hours and 28 minutes, which is elite.

With Mount Pisgah being closed, I took Ken for a five-mile run up 2,058 feet of rugged terrain to the summit of steep Spencer Butte, near Eugene. His verdict? "Hard. Not that

I'm the litmus test, but I can't imagine many people making it up there as fast as we did. That was a workout."

"Felt it?" I asked.

"Everywhere."

Ken grew up in Somerville, Massachusetts, a city northwest of Boston. Living in a lower-income and dysfunctional household, he was able to pay for an education at Framingham State University only by working as a prison guard at the same penitentiary where his brother and stepfather had served time. In college, he boxed and played hockey. A successful career in finance transformed this poor kid into a rich man living in both London and New York, flying back and forth on the Concorde supersonic airliner.

"Money won't make you happy," Ken told me. "I say that to people, and they look at me like I'm crazy. Well, I was poor, then I was rich, and I became a drug addict. So, did the money make me happier? No. It exposed weaknesses that were always there."

An ankle injury led to Ken being prescribed the potent opioid pain reliever: Percocet. His dosage quickly tripled from 7 tablets per week to 20; a mom-and-pop pharmacy in New York City would refill his prescriptions with no questions.

"From there," he told me, "I was off to the races. And I was very resourceful. I was making money, so I could buy them on the street. And I was a very good drug addict. I could keep myself in supply. And I was very good at hiding the addiction."

Ken said he wasn't a complete lunatic when he was high, but he was just . . . different. Very high and low, with a lot of energy. He could function, but it was a vicious cycle and a horrible experience. According to Ken, not only did he still have to contend with the same unresolved painful feelings from childhood, but also now he had to battle his addiction.

"I think that once you go through that, you come to the realization that everyone's struggling with something in one way or another. And, you know, talking about it is great. But the only real way out is to deal with it."

After defeating his addiction and becoming sober, Ken discovered endurance sports.

"I was doing the Ironman triathlon when I got sober," he recalled. "I started riding my bike, running again. I didn't know what I was doing. I knew how to swim if I fell off a boat."

I asked Ken if the training was a replacement for the prescription drugs he had been abusing.

"Yeah, it probably still is. I don't profess to have all the answers. Matter of fact, I always tell people, don't take my advice, don't do what I do. I'm not saying it's the healthiest thing, but this is the only alternative I have found to doing the wrong things. The balance works for me."

From addict to one of the greatest master's marathoners of all time, Ken Rideout has a true "You'll have to die to beat me" mindset.

When he finally qualified for an Ironman tournament in Hawaii, Ken was on a high. He was euphoric to be there, but the experience was one of the most brutal of his life. The pain he felt wasn't just physical; it was the toll it took on his pride that really hurt.

"When I got onto the run, I just shit the bed and quit. I was just like, *I'm not going to have a good race. I'm going to shut it down three miles into the run. I'm so ashamed of myself.* Even when I think about it now, I get choked up because I'm like, *What a fucking quitter!* It was the most painful lesson. My friend Teddy Atlas talks about this all the time. It's always harder to quit because it lasts forever."

"Because you have to live with it," I said.

"I'm telling you—I'm getting choked up. I could get emotional thinking about how I fucking quit like a dirty dog loser. There was no reason."

"Did you finish your race?"

"No. I thought, *That is just too hard.* I walked back to the start line. And literally as soon as I started walking back, I was like, *Oh my God, what have I done?* And my wife was there, and I was basically in tears. I was like, 'I can't believe I did that. What the F? I can't believe I just didn't walk.' And she was like, 'Oh well, go back next year and fix it.' And I did. The next year, I did 9:39, which for me was really good."

In 2016 Ken began to focus all his efforts on running. He would run in the morning before work; soon he would be running 10 miles a day. He progressed steadily to become one of the best marathon runners in the world, clocking 2:30 or better seven times. I asked Ken how I too could run a 2:30 marathon, chuckling because I knew the answer.

"You just got to run a lot. Run a lot with purpose."

Ken's entire life now has a bigger purpose.

"I want to give people an example with my own actions of what's possible—like you would say—when an average guy doesn't want to settle for mediocrity. When you decide that you're not going to settle for being average, it's amazing what you can do. And it's all a very simple formula. The person who works the most typically is the best. The guy who has the biggest muscles in the gym? He probably lifts weights a lot more than you do. The guy who's winning the running race? He's training more. And as soon as I came to grips with that concept and just started training, it became both my therapy and my advantage."

Ken likes the life he has now more than the life he had as an addict. He no longer has to lie to himself and his wife and his friends about when he is going to become sober. Maybe his daily regimen of running and enduring pain is his penance, Ken said. He doesn't get

Cam with Ken Rideout

any days off anymore because he feels he's used up all his free passes. But he wants to demonstrate the hope that comes with his daily discipline.

"I'm hoping that I can inspire and provide some motivation to a small handful of people that are going through addiction. When you're in it, it doesn't seem like there's a light at the end of the tunnel. The reason athletes and runners become good is because you know the commitment, the sacrifice, and the delayed gratification that they had to deal with to get there. That doesn't happen overnight.

"When you're going through recovery, that first week of detoxing and withdrawing from the drugs is hell on earth. Imagine being the sickest you've ever been, and it won't go away. And you know it's not going to go away for ten days. You can end it any minute by being like, 'Oh, let me just take a couple pills.' This is the big lie all addicts tell ourselves. 'I just got to wean myself off. I'll just take a couple.' Two days later, you're back to full-blown taking pills every single day three or four times a day. I'd take them in the morning, I'd take them at lunch, and I'd take them after dinner to chill. And I'd justify every single one of them. What I'm hoping that some people realize is this: I promise you, you go into that dark tunnel of recovery, there is a light at the end of the tunnel. But it's like training. You might not see it for a little while, but you have to fucking blindly believe that it's at the end of the tunnel. You just have to keep going."

Ken Rideout's life is about turning his weaknesses into strengths. It's about realizing

"WANNA GO HAVE AN EARLY DINNER, TALK, AND DRINK WINE? I'D RATHER BE DEAD. BUT I'D LOVE TO SKIN A BUCK IN THE DRIVEWAY WHILE DRINKING COFFEE AND LISTENING TO GOOD COUNTRY MUSIC ON A CHILLY NOVEMBER DAY. HOW'S THAT SOUND FOR A COMPROMISE?"

—*Cam Hanes*

we can't control what happens to us, but knowing that we can control our reactions. He has shown that you can take the weakest and most humiliating part about yourself and use it as a building block in your life to see what is truly possible when you finally bring discipline back into your life.

"I'm not the same person I was. And I used to like myself more than I do at times now, but I can't ever go back there. So, there's no sense in fretting over it. Like Jelly Roll said when he won the CMA, 'The windshield is bigger than the rearview mirror for a reason.' It's important that you recognize what happened and why it happened. But it's much more important to focus on what's in front of you. You can't change anything, but you can change what happens tomorrow. The reason that these corny old cliché sayings stick around is because they're true. Tomorrow can be just one day, or it can be day one of the new journey."

There's nothing to stop you, Ken says. There are lots of people out there who are watching what he's doing and what I'm doing. And neither of us have superpowers. Everything we do are skills that have been earned. We are simply two people out there who are demonstrating what is possible.

"To use your own words, we're two very average guys that just decided we don't like being average," Ken told me. "I don't. It sucked. I felt like I wanted to be recognized as being successful. I wanted to have traits that people admired. There was only one way to get them, and that's to go through the fire. And it's available to anyone. The gates are open. Come on in."

There is a common theme to the people that I follow on social media. Maybe it's just the algorithm controlling my life, but every person I see who is influential right now—Goggins, Jocko, and Rogan just to mention a few—are all fit and disciplined. This prompted me to ask Chris Williamson, another person I put in this category, are there are influential people who are not disciplined?

"Well, think about it this way," Chris answered. "Do you think that the most successful people in the world became successful and then got disciplined? Or do you think that they became disciplined and then got successful?"

I agreed with him that obviously it's the latter. Chris said he can't say that there aren't undisciplined people who manage to become super successful, because there are flukes out there. He puts himself in that category.

"I came from this reality-TV, obligation-free status, plucked out of obscurity, and six weeks later, two million followers and a million-dollar fast-fashion deal. That's the world that I came from, and that is the most transactional, low-investment way that somebody can become super famous and successful from nothing. However, I don't think that's scalable. The only way that that happens is you beat the odds. It's like a lottery. It's like being plucked out of obscurity and hoping that you're going to be given this opportunity. That's not how most people are going to win. Most people are going to win fame through discipline."

Growing up in the United Kingdom, which Chris calls a big "lager-lout culture," he was used to everybody getting smashed most nights of the week. The drinking culture was his life. He not only did that recreationally, but he also spent a lot of time working with monetizing this alcohol culture as a club promoter and contributing to it as well. When he reached 23, 24, training became important to him, so Chris dialed back his partying. By the time he turned 27 and 28, he had an epiphany.

"I thought, fuck, I need more time," Chris told me. "I need more consistency. I felt like I would make good progress, and then I got the Friday-afternoon itch, which is this compulsion to just be a degenerate and get on it with the boys, which is fun. But I knew that I needed more time, more money, more energy, and more consistency if I wanted to make the changes that I needed to. Fundamental changes to the way that you see the world are really, really hard to do. If I was resetting my progress every two weeks because I was spending a day hungover in bed, I wasn't going to get anywhere."

Chris became sick of being stuck in a *Groundhog Day*–version of taking two steps forward, then two steps back, then two steps forward, then two steps back again and again. His life resembled an Etch A Sketch that he erased every couple of weeks, so he decided to see what would happen if he went sober for six months. Would it improve his performance?

"I loved it," Chris said. "I found I had basically an extra day every two weeks free to myself because I wasn't getting drunk. I had better consistency that started to compound over time. I went back to drinking for a little while—didn't really enjoy it. Did another six months. Went back to drinking after that for, like, two or three months. Didn't really enjoy it. Then was like, 'Right. Fuck it. I'm just going to do a thousand days.' And that was incredibly impactful to me because it gave me focused consistency."

Chris believes that going sober is the most effective competitive advantage young people can do because it gives you so much more mental clarity to be consistent. He didn't have a problem with alcohol; he wasn't dependent on it at all. He just wanted more from his life.

"A lot of young guys feel that it's a rite of passage when they're away on holiday or going to Vegas, or whatever. Like, that's what you bonded with your friends over. That's cool. But you also used to play with Power Rangers when you were eleven, right? You don't play with them anymore. The tools and the experiences that formed you when you were younger aren't necessarily the ones that will serve you when you're older."

This chapter isn't about me standing on my soapbox or preaching from a pulpit. Look: I've been there. I understand what it's like to self-sabotage. As I've said, for me, alcohol was not helping any of the things I cared about. I wanted to be more fit. I wanted to be more disciplined. I wanted to be the best bowhunter and the best athlete I could be, yet alcohol was always a step backward on all those things. I wouldn't be who I am if I kept drinking. That's how powerful it is. That's how powerful of a drug it is. Yet it's a societally *acceptable* drug. Most people don't truly understand the poison that it is.

The great thing about life is that beauty can emerge from the ashes. For proof, look at the individuals covered in the previous pages. Good things can come out of bad choices in your life. My father is an example of that. I shared this during a conversation with Joe Rogan.

My dad was an amazing athlete and track star who had a lot of potential that he never got to take advantage of because of drinking. He eventually became sober and didn't drink for 30 years. He died at the age of 62, which is pretty young for someone to die of cancer. He hadn't smoked or drank in many years, so who knows why he got cancer. But in the prime of his life as an athlete, he sabotaged his talents and abilities a bit.

Maybe this was a blessing in disguise.

Who knows what would have happened if he had received the individual glory he was capable of receiving? I wonder what might have happened if he had made the Olympics and won gold and set a new record. Would my father's life have been different? Would the road he traveled down have been different?

My father's life was about making an impact on so many kids as a high school coach. I still get messages from kids that he coached telling me about the positive impact he made on their lives. My dad knew how hard it could be growing up and navigating life in general, so he would take kids that needed support under his wing. Over 30-something years of coaching, he impacted thousands of kids. So, I don't think he would regret anything. That's life. That's how it plays out.

That's also the reason why I am the way I am.

My father was a legend to me as I was growing up. I didn't get to be around him as much when I was a kid because of the divorce, but we grew close before he died. I saw the impact he had on people. He's always who I wanted to make proud.

The ones we love the most in our lives are the ones who often force us to be more disciplined. But discipline hurts. Discipline can feel devastating.

There is always hope on the other side.

I see this hope in the first 200-mile ultramarathon I ran, in 2016. The Bigfoot 200, in the Cascade mountains in Washington State, is actually 205 miles and includes 42,000 feet of elevation gain and 86,000 feet of elevation change. I had competed in some 100-mile ultras, and I never thought they were easy, so I'm not sure why I thought a 200-miler would be a good idea. But that's where my brain goes. You have to find new tests and new limits to see what you're capable of, so I signed up for the Bigfoot 200. My brother Taylor agreed to pace me during the night.

It was close to 90 degrees in Washington State at the start of the race. I took off way too fast, but I was feeling good, like most people do at the beginning of an ultra. You've trained really hard, and you're excited, so you want to start getting some miles under your feet. Around mile 40, maybe seven hours in, I was way ahead of everybody, by hours. But I was also dehydrated. I had not planned well enough. We were running on the side of Mount Saint Helens, exposing me to the hot sun for hours, with no shade. I didn't have enough water. The other runners were being conservative, knowing that this race posed a long test of endurance.

Naturally, I hit the wall. As they say, when you get dehydrated and run out of food, fuel, and calories, and your salt level drops too low, it's like a *bonk*. It took me quite awhile to get out of that "bonk." People started to pass me, and it took me almost a full day to recover because I was still in motion. It wasn't as if I were resting, getting caught up on calories and hydration. I was still running, and hiking when the terrain turned steep, still burning calories, so it took about a day to catch back up.

After 30 hours, I reached the 100-mile mark—not even halfway!—and was *smoked* already. It was the farthest I had ever run, and the thought of having to do it all again felt daunting. At least I had Taylor running with me in the pitch-black night.

When I reached mile 130 at about midnight, I was able to somehow grasp this incredible moment. It was raining and dark, yet I had my brother by my side.

"Man, this is what it's all about right here," I told Taylor. "These moments."

You can't get 130 miles into a race and have 75 miles left until you've gone through the fire. But when you go through the fire and reach this point, you suddenly realize it's a place that very few people will ever get to. I couldn't contain my excitement.

"How lucky are we to be here right now, a hundred thirty miles into a race?" I exulted. "It's awesome."

Yes, it hurt, but we hadn't given up. We were still going.

Bigfoot 200 contained the usual ups and downs of running an ultra, but I was loving every minute of it. I kept pushing. Taylor ran mostly at night with me and ended up running 100 miles of 205, sticking with me in the dark and recovering a little bit during the day. There wasn't a lot of recovery, however, because jockeying around vehicles in the mountains to different checkpoints takes time. So, I'm not sure how much rest he actually got. Watching him run—seeing him soldiering on after everything he'd gone through in life—was an inspiration. Taylor is tough as hell. He actually

"TWO ROADS DIVERGED IN A WOOD, AND I— I TOOK THE ONE LESS TRAVELED BY, AND THAT HAS MADE ALL THE DIFFERENCE."

—*Robert Frost,*
"The Road Not Taken"

had a hard job himself. Simply running a race and just thinking about covering miles is sort of the easy part in some way, as opposed to having to deal with logistics of getting a vehicle with supplies to certain points of the race.

Near the end of the race, I had emotionally been in the valley, then back at a peak, then went back in a valley feeling fatigued. During the last 13 miles, I was back in a groove. Maybe I could "smell the barn," which is horsespeak for when a horse will walk real slow until you turn around. Once he realizes that he's heading back to the barn, all of a sudden he'll often have more energy. Pep in his step. Even double-timing it. So where you used to have to try to coax them to walk, now they're double-timing it because they're headed home. I don't know if that was the case for me, but with just 13 miles left, I was feeling better, for whatever reason, and was picking up to pace. After 190 to 195 miles, I was running in the sixes (under seven minutes) per mile. I finished eighth overall in my first 200.

After the race, Dwayne "The Rock" Johnson put up a post basically saying how impressed he was by my performance. I was wearing one of his shirts from Under Armour that bore the words "Blood, Sweat & Respect." To get a shout-out from him definitely had a huge impact on my social media and helped to raise the awareness of this type of race, one that not a lot of people knew about.

The Bigfoot 200 was one of the toughest races I ever ran. But I know that there are different kinds of pain we have in life. The pain in a race is going to ease and go away. But when I think of Donovan and the pain that Taylor carries with him, or I think of my father or of Roy, I know there is life-changing pain that's never going to go away. Death is so permanent, and those left behind will always feel it.

Sometimes when I'm running—even running up Pisgah—and I'm feeling the aches and pains, and in my mind I'm being kind of a pussy, I stop and ask myself what I'm doing. I'm going to be home later today. Even if it's a 200-mile race, that's only a few days out of my life. But it's my *life,* and I'm still alive and still breathing and still able to do something with that life. So, I try to enjoy the moment.

The pain that comes with discipline can pay off. If you stick to your goals and your plans, then you will see the positive results. Yes, it will take sacrifice, and you might find yourself aching in the deathly dark of night, but, as Ken Rideout said, there is light at the end of the tunnel.

START CHIPPING AWAY

Beat the odds.
    Break the cycle.
        Be different; be better.

Everybody has a mountain they need to climb in life. What's yours?
What summit do you want to reach? And what will you see when you get to the top?

What self-inflicted habits will prevent you from getting to the peak?
What sort of self-sabotage will keep you in the middle of pack?

Imagine this: What would your life look like if you changed
from being passive to passionate?

Do you have an elite-level talent? No? Well, neither do I. Those with a ton of talent
generally aren't running at midnight after a big couple of days of hammering miles
and long plane rides.

To everybody out there with talent, congratulations. I'm just a scrub compared to you.
I know that, and I accept that. But all I know is that you won't outwork me.
Whatever talent you have—and we all have some untapped talent inside of us—if you
don't sacrifice, then you won't reach your full potential. That's what they call wasted
potential. Don't ever live with that.

When you live a disciplined life, you deserve to get to those mountaintops.
Are you standing at the bottom looking up? That's okay. We've all been there.

The beginning can be overwhelming, but you just gotta start chipping away. Day after day.
There is one thing anybody can do in life, and that's work hard. What I do to be
undeniable is to work every day. I don't know what's going to happen next month or
even this coming weekend, but I do know what's going to happen tomorrow. I'm going
to run that fucking mountain. I guarantee you that.

It's never too late to begin. To be someone new. To stop the bad habits. To start new ones.

Yesterday is over, and tomorrow isn't guaranteed. Today matters. Make the most of it.

CHAPTER 6

BET ON YOURSELF

WE MUST ENDURE

CONFIDENCE:

A feeling of self-assurance arising from one's appreciation of one's own abilities or qualities

"A MAN NEEDS TO PROVE HE IS BETTER THAN ME, RATHER THAN SHOW ME HIS BIRTH CERTIFICATE."

—*Tommy Shelby*

There is a difference between believing that you will find success and believing that you deserve it.

In September 2023 I find myself deep in the heart of the untapped country of the San Carlos Apache Indian Reservation in southeastern Arizona. This is the sixth year I've been here. If life were fair, I wouldn't be here. I don't deserve the opportunity to hunt the best elk country in the world. Life is not just, and not fair.

As I look over one of the most incredible elk-hunting drainages in the world, I recall watching a film twenty years ago called *San Carlos Apache Tribe Elk Hunting* with the Stevens brothers. I dreamt of hunting this legendary country. Back then, the Stevenses—Homer, Mark, and Tim—were larger than life and elk-hunting legends in my eyes. I was convinced they knew giant bulls better than anyone. That hasn't changed. The Stevens brothers call the San Carlos Apache Indian Reservation home.

I have become familiar with a place that has elk the size I didn't know even existed when I was growing up in my small town of Oregon. As I soak in the setting, I wonder why I've been afforded opportunities like this. Did God's blessings bring me here, or is it some form of retribution for the pain I've endured?

No, others deserve God's favor, not me. Others have endured far worse pain for longer than me.

Yet here I am, thinking of how blessed I am to be standing here, to be alive in this moment.

That's when I hear a deep bugle rising from the depths of this canyon.

When I finally got to the point where I stopped moving through life with my head down and my ambitions buried, when I started to look upward and outward, I began to be filled with dreams. Ever since, I've always had big dreams, probably bigger dreams than I deserved to realize. Fact is, I didn't really have any redeeming qualities or any special talent, but I had big, unrealistic dreams. Hunting in a place like San Carlos was one of them.

Of course, I had many other dreams as well. One of those was to be sponsored by a major sports brand just like other prominent athletes were in other sports. I always believed I could make it happen. Even though I hated the business part of hunting, I also knew that was part of the deal. Bowhunting was my passion, not my job, but I still wanted to win, and I knew that I offered value. By the 2000s, I thought I deserved more opportunity because I was working harder and was better at bowhunting than most others. I was mad and had a chip on my shoulder that the industry couldn't see that.

In 2004 I was walking on the carpeted floor of the Shooting, Hunting, and Outdoor Trade Show, otherwise known as SHOT. Over 2,200 exhibitors from 64 different countries gathered in Las Vegas to talk about the business of shooting, hunting, and outdoor recreation. One booth I was surprised to see at the show was Under Armour. To me, the sportswear company was synonymous with major sports like the NFL and Major League Baseball. I pictured their performance apparel being worn under football shoulder pads or baseball jerseys. But hunting? I asked one of their salesmen what they were doing at the show, and he informed me that Under Armour was launching a hunting division.

The company booth featured a huge photo of legendary NFL defensive tackle Randy White, who spent 14 seasons wearing the uniform of the Dallas Cowboys. He looked intense wearing Under Armour and holding a bow. Though he'd retired a decade and a half before, Randy was all jacked, veins bulging in his arms, his Super Bowl ring shining on his finger. As I studied the photo, I noticed something wrong, so I asked the man in the booth, Eric Crawford. He was my first contact at the company.

"You know, that picture would be a lot more realistic if that bow had a rest on it," I told him.

I wasn't trying to be a smartass; I was simply being honest. I assumed that the bow had been bought from a store and then handed to Randy for the photo shoot, so it hadn't been set up properly. Any bowhunter could see that you could never hunt with it as it was, so the advertisement didn't feel authentic. And when it comes to advertising, authenticity is key. People know when something is real and when something is simply a marketing ploy.

I exchanged contact information with Eric, and then stayed in touch with him. Under Armour ended up bringing me on. At first, the company didn't pay me, but rather just asked if I would represent Under Armour. They told me they would get me set up and do a photo shoot with me. That's how my journey with the company started. I ended up being one of its longest-tenured athletes, staying with the brand for almost 17 years.

Years ago, the very idea of making *any* money in hunting would have been ridiculous. When I grew up, I could barely afford to even hunt elk. For years, I hunted only deer, since elk tags were $25 each. For me, that was a lot of money. A deer tag set me back only $10 or $11.

It was great to have a big sports brand recognize hunting as something legitimate. Nike wasn't going to do that, and neither was Adidas. Under Armour had ambitions of being one of the top performance brands in the country that accepted hunters. It got behind people like me and created an outdoor line. I eventually became the face of that. This was when I first met Kip Fulks, one of the original founders of Under Armour and the guy who took over its outdoor division.

There's a part of me that has always hated the business aspect of what I do with hunting, like contracts and royalties. I'm good with numbers, and I understand that side of the hunting industry, but I've never enjoyed talking about money. The truth is that I've never really cared about any of that. I wanted to get paid just because I knew this was a natural step in my journey as a hunter. I'd be getting paid now as if I were a professional hunter, a sponsored hunter.

Being paid meant you were one of the best.

As far as how much that was worth—how much *I* was worth—that was a good question. A year later, 2005, I signed a deal with the bow company Hoyt Archery, which I am still with currently. When it came to discussing the terms of the deal, I was up front and honest with them.

"I don't want to negotiate," I said. "I don't want to go through all of this. I hate contracts and all that shit. I just want to do a lifetime contract."

Hoyt told me they couldn't do a lifetime contract, but they *could* do something they called an evergreen contract. It was one where every year as a term dropped off they would add a year onto the contract, essentially making it a lifetime deal.

Becoming sponsored by Under Armour and Hoyt wasn't the grand plan I had when I started hunting. There was no plan at all except to keep hunting year after year. Our family had no money. For a long time, we owned only one car, until my wife's sister gave us another. The only state I could afford to hunt elk in was Oregon, so that's what I did from 1989 to 2003, killing a bull virtually every year on public land. It was only in 2004 that I went on my first out-of-state elk hunt in Wyoming and killed a 6x7 on public land.

The only place I wanted my obsession with bowhunting to lead me to was bigger and better hunts. I never thought about the money aspect of it. But over time, the business end of bowhunting became a natural part of my life, and with it has come many blessings.

However, my focus has never changed.

Someone who understands the business of hunting as well as I do is Michael Waddell. He grew up in the backwoods of Booger Bottom, Georgia. As a good ol' Southern boy born to hunt, Waddell has said that "if it gobbles, quacks, bugles, or grunts, chances are I've chased it more than a time or two."[7] After winning a turkey-calling contest in his late teens, he began to start guiding and filming hunts for Realtree, a camouflage company. He suddenly found himself filming legends like Chuck Adams and Jim Shockey on their hunting adventures all over the country. A few years after this, he came up with the idea for *Realtree Road Trips,* a successful show I loved to watch on the Outdoor Channel on Sunday nights. Waddell's presence and personality on that show changed the hunting industry.

In a lot of ways, both Waddell and I began to get opportunities in hunting around the same time. His personality is one of a kind. A lot of hunters aren't made for television, but Michael was born for entertaining *and* hunting. *Road Trips* was much-watch television back in the day. This was when you didn't have a digital video recorder to record it, so you had to watch it when it came on. Everybody in the hunting world began to watch Waddell. It happens in every industry that once somebody has success, people see a blueprint to copy. While Michael was just being his quick-witted self, he had the "it" factor. Very few people have that "it" factor.

When I spoke with Waddell for the podcast, it was fun to reminisce about those days. I found a photo of the two of us from an Under Armour photo shoot in 2004 that I had sent to Waddell for him to sign. Almost two decades later, the one thing that hasn't changed is that we still love to hunt and love what we are doing.

"I remember that particular photo shoot," Waddell said. "I remember me and you were both looking at each other, saying, 'What are we here for? I bet they're gonna let

Michael Waddell came from Booger Bottom, Georgia, and turned into a hunting rock star as his fun personality changed the way hunting TV impacted viewers.

us have these shirts for free! I think they're gonna give us this whole box of camo!' We couldn't believe it."

In 2008 Waddell became a cohost on one of the Outdoor Channel's highest-rated shows, *Bone Collector*. He also started a company with the same name that was dedicated to standing up for the hunting culture. Since then, he's become one of the most recognized and beloved ambassadors for the hunting industry.

In discussing our journeys, Waddell knows that we have both been very blessed with opportunities. It started with a belief in ourselves and where we could take our hunting dreams. But before it all happened for Michael, his belief seemed crazy at the time. Coming from a blue-collar family, Waddell had gone to school to earn a degree in HVAC. He had his own service van working for this HVAC company in Georgia, so he encountered a lot of resistance when, in his 20s, he decided to give it all up to pursue a career in hunting. Waddell said his family didn't understand when he told them he was going to be a cameraman for a hunting show. He had a good job in HVAC with good benefits and a company Christmas party and vacation days, but he wondered if there was more.

"I've always looked at life almost in percentages," Waddell said to me. "Let's say you've got a fifteen or twenty percent chance of making it in something, whether it's as a country singer, an influencer, a YouTube star, on the Outdoor Channel, an actor, a comedian— whatever it may be. You always have that percentage that you can make it, but you understand the odds are going to be against you, because that's twenty percent of people or maybe less."

Waddell looked at his chances of succeeding in the hunting industry and decided to go for it. Even if he only had a 10 percent chance to make it, he knew that if he failed, he could always go back to his former job. After a while, he began to realize he was pretty good at what he was doing. He just kept working hard and chipping away.

"I went from a ten percent chance, to now I'm in the door, to now I might have a forty percent chance, to, all of a sudden, here we are."

Seeing that photo of the two of us, Waddell said it showed two guys that didn't have a pot to piss in; two hunters happy to be there as they looked at the journey ahead of them.

"But nobody can say we didn't work hard," he added. "We're in our fifties. I don't want to say we found peace, because I don't want to think we're satisfied. We're still striving forward. But there is a different dynamic that feels good."

Waddell said that he has enjoyed seeing my success in hunting and running and with the people I've been able to meet.

"If I were to somewhat brag on you and me, it's cool because I feel like we really truly have become ambassadors," Waddell said. "We're getting a chance to influence our life and our culture."

As we spoke about Waddell's decision to take a chance and leave his stable job to go into an uncertain profession—one of those crossroads moments in his life—I noted that I thought a lot of online hate toward people like us came from guys who *didn't* make that tough decision.

"'Should I take the van with my name on it, or should I chase this dream?'" I said. "And then they get down the road, and it's too late. And then they're bitter, and they're jealous of where you're at now. Not the journey you did, because nobody wants to talk about the challenges, the failed marriage, the missing your kid. Nobody wants to talk about that. They just see where you're at right now."

"There are so many roads," Waddell added. "But it is crazy about the timing and how we had our opportunity to work in this space and everything that has transpired. It's been pretty wild. But I will say that that's what makes America great. And it has caused me to kind of have less empathy for complainers because I realize how hard I have worked. I realize that they're spending so much energy being mad at the people that succeeded, when I see something in them that they don't see in themselves. It's not that I'm mad that they're being negative. I'm mad because, like, did you not look in the mirror? Are you just looking at social media and seeing this person? Did you not look at your *own* ability and talents? And if you did, and you can admit that you were talented, why did you not take the gamble? You'll sit here in Vegas and put a hundred dollars on a blackjack hand, but you wouldn't put down ten bucks on yourself. Why are you mad at me? If you can't bet on yourself, who the hell are you gonna bet on?"

Waddell said that some of his buddies never would bet on themselves, but guys like us are used to betting on ourselves. I agreed with him.

"I'll say again—and I know you've probably said this also—but if *I've* made it, anybody can," I told Michael. "Where I grew up, there were no big dreams out there. Twenty-four kids in my high school class; a hundred in the whole school. People just worked in the woods or at the mill. There was nobody with his big dreams. So, if I can come from here, and you can come from Booger Bottom and be the most famous hunting TV celebrity there's ever been, anybody can."

"Anybody can!" Waddell repeated. "You have to believe in yourself. You gotta believe."

"Not only that," I said, "but you have to be tunnel-vision focused and work. Because you've worked your ass off. You say you're not good with numbers, or whatever. You're a definite visionary because you had a vision for this brand. And this brand—your brand—is iconic. God dang, you had a vision."

Waddell thanked me for those compliments.

"It's crazy because as crazy and visionary as it might seem, inevitably it becomes this simple conception to just stay focused and work," he said. "Life is such an amazing thing. Even your mistakes and regrets are almost blessings, too. I'm thankful for them, because all of that makes you better."

"If you can't bet on yourself, who the hell are you gonna bet on?"

I love that quote from Waddell.

Every single outlier I've met has bet on himself time and time again in his life. It comes back to what I said at the start of this chapter: just because you believe you will find success doesn't mean you deserve it.

You have to believe in yourself. For me, that meant I needed to believe in my abilities in the wilderness. But I also needed to believe in my value in the business. That's why I would sometimes be a pain in the ass to the people that sponsored me. One of my closest friends and biggest supporters in the world, Kip Fulks, knows this all too well. He was one of the original founders of Under Armour, who, as I mentioned, ended up leading the company into hunting.

"It's funny because I kind of quit to get that job at Under Armour," Kip explained. "Kevin Plank and I started the company together and spent many, many years traveling all over the world to make stuff. And I was like, 'I can't do this anymore. I want a division I can believe in.' You know, football, basketball, lacrosse, some of the core sports, I love them, but I wasn't passionate about them anymore. And so, I actually quit to start that division. I said, 'I want that or I'm out.'"

When Under Armour really got into hunting, the company truly made a mark on the industry, providing hunters with kickass boots and badass performance clothing. That was all because of Kip. And since I was the face of the outdoor brand, I ended up benefiting from all of that. I owe a lot to Kip, but he was initially hesitant to bring me on board he later told me.

I've used the term "bowhunting brother" many times throughout my life, but it's never more accurate than when I talk about Kip Fulks.

"I have to give a lot of credit to some people at Under Armour that brought you to the table," Kip said. "They're like, 'We want to sponsor this runner from Oregon.' And I'm like, 'You don't understand; we're doing a hunting division.' And they're like, 'No, no, he's a badass bowhunter, too.'"

I will never forget seeing an Under Armour billboard at the Shooting, Hunting, and Outdoor Trade Show years ago that featured me decked out in hunting gear with the tagline "Athletes Hunt" on it. I prided myself on training like a professional athlete would and exhibiting the same type of dedication that they did in attempting to perfect their craft and compete at the highest level. Seeing those words, "Athletes Hunt," only made me want to hammer harder and to keep improving. It also made me want to work harder for a company like Under Armour. I never hesitated to speak my mind to UA, either.

"You guys need to pay me more money," I once told Kip. "I should be your number one athlete."

For me, this was about the belief I had in myself and in my value to them. Kip admits that he was hard on me as a sponsor. He refers to himself back then as my "oppressor." He explained once on someone else's podcast, "I was the corporate douchebag that sometimes Cam had to wage war against. I didn't give in to all Cam's demands.

"I'm like, 'Nope,'" Kip continued. "And yet you just keep grinding it out. One of the things I got to give you a ton of credit for, Cam, and I don't think people know this: for a long time, you did some writing, you did some shows, and you just kept hammering the hunting and bowhunting, but you were also one of the early adopters of social media and figured it out. You started doing it yourself. You didn't have a company behind you. There wasn't a bunch of investors. And if you look at what your social media has done over the last ten years versus other people in the hunting industry, it's not even close. I remember thinking, *Wow, Cam's kind of an innovator.* And it wasn't necessarily about Lift Run Shoot. It was more like, *Wow, he's kind of attaching himself to this social media.* Back before people understood what Instagram and Facebook could be. So, I got to give you a lot of credit over those years for stepping in where other people weren't going."

I remember those early days very well. I had worked so hard for so many years just to get to a place where I had a platform, because, before social media, you had to have a magazine or a TV show like Michael Waddell had. You had to have somebody putting your work out there, so I didn't want to screw up those relationships.

"I was already just a pain in the ass to work with as a hunter because I grew up hunting on my own," I said to Kip. "And you know as well as anybody that I don't like anybody telling me what to do. I don't like anybody slowing me down. And that's kind of what I was starting to feel like back then."

Working in the hunting industry has always been a love-hate relationship for me. I have loved the people I worked with, but I have hated the strings attached to working for a company, writing for a magazine and doing television. Social media was a godsend because it finally gave me control. I could say what I wanted to say and write what I wanted to write and do what I wanted to do. Kip understands that.

"Whatever the impetus or whatever the reason or motivation was behind it, it ended up playing in your favor, in a huge way, over time," he said. "And I think that's the definition of innovation: seeing things that other people don't see and being willing to stick with it. Because a lot of times people go, 'It didn't work. I tried Instagram, and it didn't work.' No, you got to actually do it for, like, ten years, and *then* come back and tell me it didn't work."

Sometimes I used to feel as if some of these companies signed me just so they could control me. As if they would be saying, "He's not working for the competition because we got him locked up," and then they didn't really have to use me. I began to feel that Under Armour would sometimes do that because I saw other athletes being promoted, and I wanted the same thing. I wanted the same sort of exposure, the same platform.

"I'm working my ass off," I told Kip. "I've been working my ass off for decades, and I want it. As a business, the Western market was tiny—maybe five percent compared to ninety-five percent for the East and the southeast whitetail hunters. So, I had the small market, and I wanted all this love, I guess, or essentially support. It was frustrating for me because I'm busting my ass over here."

Kip smiled when recalling those days. "Yeah, I was the douchebag executive going, 'Nah, nah, we're not doing that with him. No, he's fucking crazy. Nope. Not going to do that.' But over time, I think you did a good job of explaining and continuing the partnership, I will say, because you're loyal, you stick through with companies, and because you're authentic. You're not really pulling any punches. You have had a lot of great sponsors that have stuck with you for a long time. Because you're loyal, I think once companies figure that out, then it starts to open them up."

The progress was slow and sometimes hard-fought and consisted of many ups and downs. For a while, I was ecstatic to even be sponsored. I was like, "I can hunt for free, and you're going to pay me ten grand a year? What? I'd do this for nothing!" But then it got to a point where that began to change. "Wait a second—I have value to you now."

Before, I wanted to be used for this, and then it becomes how they're now using me. Then it becomes, "Wait, *you're* the one benefiting from all this." I'm getting a little from this, but the company is making bank off me. "Wait a second: How many units sold? How much did you sell of those shoes with my name on it? This many units times this much? And I got this small percentage?" Before, I was just happy to get scraps, but all of a sudden I knew I should be getting more. I looked at this as a business and knew I couldn't be stupid. I had a family that relied on me to make good decisions.

"It's really hard for certain people to self-promote because it feels like you're letting your ego talk," Kip said. "But in this world, you have to self-promote. You have to be okay talking about your skills, what you're good at, what you're great at, and what value that brings people obviously from a sponsorship standpoint."

Self-promotion is not comfortable for a lot of people, Kip said. If you have a small business, if you're starting one or if you've taken over your family business, or even if you're working at a big corporation and trying to make that next big move up the ladder, you have to self-promote yourself in a way that's humble and authentic so that you don't come off like that jerk. In this space, you *really* have to self-promote.

> "LEARNING AND INNOVATION GO HAND IN HAND. THE ARROGANCE OF SUCCESS IS TO THINK THAT WHAT YOU DID YESTERDAY WILL BE SUFFICIENT FOR TOMORROW."
>
> —*William Pollard, nineteenth-century English clergyman*

"Who's going to toot your horn if you don't?" Kip stated.

Those antagonistic days between Kip and me are long gone. He retired from working at Under Armour to do other things. We've gone on many hunts together, and he is someone I trust. He was with me on a hunt when I got the news that Roy had died. He went from being that "corporate douchebag," as he said, to becoming my friend and bowhunting blood brother.

It might be easy for some people to look at Kip and think those three words that lots of people think: *Must be nice.* As one of the original founders of Under Armour, when it went from a private company to a public company, Kip's net worth essentially became around $50 million. He was only 32 years old.

I like to sometimes poke fun at him and say, "Yeah, you're fucking soft and rich." But the truth is that Kip is one of the hardest-working people I know, if not the hardest.

"I didn't grow up with any money," he said. "I put myself through college and graduated. I got a scholarship to University of Maryland, finally, after playing at community college and being a walk-on at UMD. I paid my dues. And then I worked at Under Armour for twenty-one years. I didn't work there two years. I didn't work there five years. It wasn't a tech stock we ran up and sold. There wasn't a bunch of rich daddies behind the scenes. We just grinded it out, and we got lucky. But we also worked really hard. And you got to give a lot of credit to a lot of other people at Under Armour. I'm never going to say it was all me or all this or all that. It was a group of people that just wanted to crush it. Over time, it adds up."

When people ask Kip how he did it, his answer is simple:

"I worked my fucking ass off. I had four jobs. I slept an hour and a half. I kept an in-out log at my front door because I was deciding whether I wanted to buy my house. I said, 'Why would I buy a house if I'm never here?' It turned out that I spent something like just two and a half hours a day—including sleep—at the house. So, I was like, 'We're not buying this house.' If you want more in life, you need to do more. If you want something, you're going to have to give up something."

Kip has been doing lots of things lately, from starting new companies such as Big Truck Farm Brewery, to partnering with companies like Origin apparel and Jocko Fuel. He's also sharing his expertise and knowledge in a 12-week intensive online class call Method & Mindset. He has a lot of wisdom to share, but he also admits that he's had to learn a lot over the years.

"I've made a lot of bad mistakes," Kip said. "I also think that being in Under Armour for a long time wasn't good for me. I think my ego got big. You're a corporate executive; you start believing your own shit. I don't think that's healthy. I think you need to wake up every day and *fucking earn it*. Like, what have you done for me lately?"

Kip doesn't want to be known only for cofounding Under Armour years ago. That's in the past. He's keen to do something new today. That's one reason he loved coming to do the Lift Run Shoot.

"I love the mindset and the method that you preach and these outliers that you're bringing in," Kip said. "I mean, the people you're bringing into this—it's just freaking cool people. You shine a spotlight on these interesting people. Very successful in their own ways, all of them different. But they all have like a lot of commonalities, too, when you start peeling back some of their work ethic."

They're all people like Kip and me who have worked their asses off.

They're all innovators. Risk takers.

Most importantly, every one of them believed in themselves.

In 2018 I decided I wanted something new.

"I don't want to do just another bowhunting film."

Once again I was certain that my sponsors couldn't stand working with me, but I knew it was time for something different. I gave Under Armour an ultimatum:

"I've done the films. We've done it. Everybody knows I'm hunting in September, so I don't want the film to come out six months after the fact, like always."

Why do the same damned thing every fucking time?

Why can't I share what happened during the hunt as soon as possible?

"I want to hunt, and every single day I want to edit up a one-minute clip and post that daily teaser on Instagram and Facebook," I told Under Armour. "One minute every day capturing the highlights of that day. The next day, a one-minute clip, and then at the end of the week on Friday, I want to release a film."

Naturally, the people I spoke with had doubts and questions and all that other shit.

"Well, we'd have to have editors there . . ."

"They'll have to be up all night . . ."

That didn't matter to me.

"I don't care. I don't want to do the same thing. I want to do this."

Was I being a pain in the ass? Maybe. I can accept that. But did I have a vision and a belief that it would work? Definitely.

Under Armour agreed. The company hired the best film editors, from a media production firm called Sub7, known for its quality outdoor TV shows and commercials, and they had to film during the day and edit during the night. It was quite an expense; I think around $50,000 for that week. It was also a lot of company on a trip. Two camera guys, an editor, and a still photographer with you on a hunt? Man! That's a lot when you're trying get within range of an old bull, say, around 10 years old, who has seen a lot and been hunted a lot.

It was a tough hunt and a long week. I'd get mad if someone made noise. So many things were going through my head. At the end of the day, everything worked out. The film turned out amazing, and Sub7 did an incredible job editing the clips and getting everything done by Friday. I owe a lot to Marc Womack, Sub7's founder, for knocking the film out of the park.

To date, this film, titled *Cam's Bull of a Lifetime*, is the second most popular video on my YouTube page, with over four million views as of this writing. The bull was truly one of the biggest and most beautiful I had ever shot. It was what every bowhunter dreams of. It was unreal. And I didn't have to wait six months to share the adventure with the world.

What does it take for an undersized high school kid to become one of the best NFL quarterbacks of all time? Aaron Rodgers says it's believing in yourself.

"The best players, the most successful people, are self-motivated," he told me.

The former Green Bay Packers and current New York Jets quarterback understands self-motivation. When he came to Oregon for an incredible Lift Run Shoot experience, he shared his own unlikely journey from being overlooked in high school to becoming a superstar in the NFL. It was enlightening to hear the things that have mattered the most in his career.

"As I look back over the last twenty-two years of my life playing, the greatest moments of growth and learning experiences were associated with an ego death in some way or another," Aaron reflected. "That's kind of an interesting term, and it's thrown around from time to time. It just means that the idea of who you think you are gets destroyed."

NFL legend, Super Bowl champion, iconic QB, and sure-to-be Hall of Famer Aaron Rodgers came to Springfield, Oregon, and took on my Lift Run Shoot challenge, which was surreal to me.

Growing up in Chico, a small town in Northern California, Aaron loved watching college football on Saturdays and then NFL football on Sundays. During his senior year in high school, he set a single-season total-yardage record, but no four-year colleges showed interest in him. "I just always thought I was going to be playing on Saturdays," Aaron said. "The best opportunity for me was to go down to Butte Community College, just down the road. There, Coach Craig Rigsbee, still a dear friend to this day, came over to the house, and we had a great conversation. I told him, 'Listen, I'd like to play on Saturdays in Division 1 after a year if I have a good year.' And unlike some junior college coaches, who'd want you to play for them for a couple years, he said, 'Of course.' Now, he was probably thinking, *Hey, take it easy! Let's just see if you can be a starter here first!*

"The ego death of going from high school to a D1 school and starting on Saturdays allowed me to deal with adversity that made me a better player and a better person. It broke me down, and I had to rebuild myself. And it happened again as a backup at the University of California. And it happened as a backup in Green Bay for three years. It happened a couple other times during my time in the NFL. And every time I've kind of gone through one of those ego deaths, it's been a period of really intense growth. And I think it happens for all of us."

In his freshman season, Rodgers led Butte College to a 10–1 record and a number two national ranking. The following year, exactly as he'd planned, he enrolled at the University of California at Berkeley and became the Golden Bears' starting quarterback. After breaking school records and placing in ninth in the voting for the coveted Heisman Trophy, Rodgers decided to skip his senior year to enter the 2005 NFL draft. Considered a top 10 pick, possibly even top 5, he would be one of a half dozen guys who came to the draft in person. San Francisco had the first pick, so it made perfect sense that it would select a California native. Aaron had a great interview with the 49ers and an excellent workout. In the end, however, the 49ers decided otherwise and picked QB Alex Smith of the University of Utah. A disappointed Aaron Rodgers famously had to suffer in the green room as pick after pick was chosen while the cameras captured his every moment.

Rodgers was finally selected in the first round by the Green Bay Packers, as the twenty-fourth pick overall.

Looking back, he said, "Anytime you face adversity that questions who you are as a person and what you want to be about and your identity, it allows you to return back to yourself. Or return back to your center and take some time thinking about the kind of person you want to be. So, I'm thankful for those moments in adversity. Some people struggle with that. I've always gone inward and been reflective and try to come out the other side a better person. And it's in turn made me a better player."

"That seems like a very healthy way to look at it," I told Aaron. "Me, I would have a chip on my shoulder."

"I have plenty," he said with a big grin. "'Oh, you fuckers don't think . . . ? Okay, let's see.'

"Just because you have an ego death doesn't mean you don't stack up some chips on the shoulder," Rodgers added.

In hindsight, Aaron said he understood why colleges had overlooked him when he was, as he put it, "this skinny kid wearing a knee brace from Pleasant Valley High School in Chico." He didn't blame them. And he was thankful for the motivation it gave him.

"Whatever it takes to motivate," he said. "I was passed on by twenty-three teams in the draft. You know, I didn't forget that. I've given that up. That's long since passed. But you always got to find ways to stack some chips on your shoulder and just get a little extra motivation."

Aaron Rodgers

That little extra motivation helped him to become the Most Valuable Player of Super Bowl XLV, when the Green Bay Packers edged the Pittsburgh Steelers, 31–25, on February 6, 2011. As for the other guys in that infamous 2005 draft?

"Nobody from my draft class is still playing and hasn't been for a few years," said Rodgers, who turned 41 during the 2024 NFL season, his twentieth. "Obviously, I outlasted all those guys."

Rodgers detailed his long journey of joining a team with a beloved legend playing quarterback. It couldn't have been easy playing backup to veteran Brett Favre. At one point, it looked like Favre was going to retire, but then he decided to stay on. Then it happened again. Even after Favre officially announced it, there was discussion that he was thinking of coming back. Rodgers wouldn't start his first NFL game until 2008, his fourth season.

"Everybody's like, 'Oh, you're the guy,'" he said. "And I'm like, 'Okay, I'm the guy.' And then it goes crazy the next few months. I'm actually the guy, then Brett's going to come back, and then there's a bunch of crazy stuff. So, there was a lot of opportunity for motivation that I drew from comments from a number of people, including our fans. There were some really bizarre statements: death threats, bodily harm, threats to my face while walking back from training camp practices. I actually had some chips built up against some of my own fans during that offseason. I think anytime you take the field, it's never a bad thing to feel like you've got something to prove."

Rodgers understands that he is in the entertainment business, since sports is about entertaining fans. Anytime he walks onto the field, he knows there are people who have never seen him play in person. That's when he has a chance to entertain them.

"I've always found ways to motivate myself," he said. "And then also just the responsibility to your teammates has always been a good motivator for me, too, because I know how they look at me, the expectations that they have of me, and I love that. For some people, that pressure is hard, and you can maybe shrink in those moments. But I've always enjoyed that pressure to perform for your brothers. And I think there's a lot of honor in having pride in your performance. I've always really felt like I want to go out and prove the kind of player I am not just to myself but also to my guys, and the fans, and somebody who's never watched me play before. So, there's always been fun ways to motivate myself. And then there's been plenty of detractors and critics over the years who just made motivation a little bit easier."

I told Rodgers I couldn't imagine that sort of pressure. "You're in the business for being criticized. I mean, everybody's got an opinion. Every fat fuck sitting on the couch watching you as a professional athlete compete 'knows' what you 'should' have done."

Not only are there a lot of armchair quarterbacks out there, but now you have fantasy football "owners" and people betting on the game who are wanting you to win. "But I would guess that all that external pressure couldn't compare to the pressure you put on yourself," I said.

"For sure. I think every great athlete has that quality. It goes back to the pride in performance. Your hating to lose more than your loving to win can be a big motivator. And it is for me. You just hate that feeling of disappointing yourself, teammates, and the fan base more than you even love the win. Winning is fucking awesome. I mean, it's incredible. It's embracing that. There's so much that goes into playing quarterback outside of just the throwing and the plays and checks and everything. The most

important thing is: Who are you in those big moments? Who are you when the lights are brightest and the game's on the line, and you either shrink in the moment or you rise to the occasion?"

Do I wake up believing in myself? Do I carry self-confidence around on a daily basis?

Most of the time.

But there are still times—*lots* of times—when I feel I don't deserve all the opportunities and benefits that have come my way. I've earned them and suffered for them, but do I *deserve* them?

It comes back down to feeling like an imposter. I wrote some about this in *Endure,* and I've had a chance to talk with other outliers about this. It turns out I'm not alone in feeling this way.

Chris Williamson addressed this when talking about his own success.

"Sometimes I feel like success is a fluke, and nobody knows I'm not supposed to be here. It almost feels like one day someone's going to come out of the woodwork and go, 'This actually isn't your life. You actually don't deserve that.'"

I totally could relate to that. It's a feeling I sometimes still get in my head: *You're the lonely kid all by yourself.*

Chris said it's easy to think that you're undeserving of success, and he knows too well the demons of self-doubt that come from his crappy childhood, as he explained.

"For anybody that has suffered with bullying as a kid, that felt lonely, that felt isolated, and that feels like they need to prove something to the world—I feel for you, because that's me."

One way that Chris is able to battle these doubts is by having an "undeniable stack of proof that I am who I say I am." He said that Joe Rogan calls it building a mountain with layers of paint.

"It's just one iteration after the next," Chris said. "Better. Meaner. Better, better. Each single time to do something, you can get yourself to a stage where you've disproven your imposter syndrome so many times in the real world that it's crushed under this ridiculous weight of evidence. There's no way that you could continue to exist. And the other side is to find people that just want you for you. You know, this is friends, this is family. This is partners."

I couldn't agree with Chris more. The only worry—the only problem—is when you sometimes still feel like that kid. When you still believe he's never gone away.

This subject has come up when I've gone on Rogan's podcasts. He likes to encourage me by giving me a hard time about these feelings. At one point, I was talking about the opportunity to train with David Goggins and how much it had changed my life.

"I feel like it's another blessing I don't really deserve," I told Joe.

"You always talk like that, and it drives me crazy," he replied. "All this 'I don't deserve shit.'"

"I don't," I said.

"It's the one thing I hate about you," Joe said, laughing. "Drives me nuts."

I tried to explain my thoughts. "I always say what I think somebody eventually is going to say: 'What the fuck? What is this guy doing here?' And I'll be like, *Well, they figured it out. It was a good run.*"

"That's called imposter syndrome," Joe said.

I replied, "I see you guys—you, Goggins, Jocko—you can change people's lives. And I feel like pretty soon they're going to go, 'Why is *this* guy, this bowhunter, here being mentioned?'"

"That's how I feel, too," Joe said. "I just don't express it."

I asked Joe if he hated himself for that.

"No, I don't hate myself for that," he said.

"But you hate that about me?" I countered.

"Well, you say it too much. Drives me nuts

"IF PEOPLE DON'T BELIEVE IN YOU, THERE ARE TWO CHOICES: SHRINK AND GO AWAY OR BECOME UNDENIABLE."

—*Cam Hanes*

because I admire what you do. It drives me crazy because you've taught me so much. For one thing. I feel the same. I used to feel the same about everything. Like, it's called imposter syndrome. It's when people have very high standards, when people work hard and they have very high standards, and then they become successful, they feel like an imposter. It's, like, there's no way because you're always wanting better and more."

Joe talked about meeting other people who are even more famous than him and feeling like an imposter. Feeling crazy having dinner with celebrities or going onstage to speak before a sold-out arena of people. He gets it.

"It's just because I have a very high standard, and I work really hard, and I'm never satisfied."

Success, confidence, self-belief—it's a mindset. You have to find it in the morning and carry it up the daily mountain.

I have to believe in myself for those daily wins, but at the end of the day, I leave them behind.

When I do something, it doesn't matter if it's monumental or epic, I do it, and it's gone. I don't even think about it. Some people rest on their laurels, but I refuse to.

When I wake up, I think to myself, *That was yesterday. What's today?*

It's easier to think about times I failed and didn't reach that goal rather than replaying my successes. That's what drives me forward. What's next? What's tomorrow? What can I learn and how can I grow?

This is what keeps me going.

This is my destiny.

Destiny brings me to those moments I don't deserve. Moments like the one I started this chapter with at San Carlos Apache Reservation.

That bugle I heard came from the bull I would ultimately kill on film perhaps an hour after I heard it. This massive bull worked his way up the creek drainage, right up to me. I didn't even have to make a call. After my shot, the bull takes off, mortally hit. I find him right before dusk and begin butchering him to haul off the mountain.

It really feels like destiny. All of this. Being at this place that has such a rich tradition. Seeing dreams I had as a kid become reality once again.

This is my place and my purpose. Do I believe in my abilities? Fuck, yes.

Do I remain honored and humbled? Definitely.

This is what success and winning look like to me. Worldly riches mean little when we look around and see all that God has blessed us with. On this mountain hunt, He gave me handfuls of gold. I'm so grateful for another day in which I was able to look over a wild, elk-filled valley at sunset. Thank you, God, for one more day.

PUT IN THE WORK

You have every right to be delusional with yourself.

To tell yourself you're awesome and incredible and you're the fucking shit.

Don't tell anybody else this unless their name is Roy Roth, because they're gonna probably doubt you or think you're delirious.

Yes, I'm being honest when I talk about the imposter syndrome and feeling humbled, but don't get these words wrong.

Feeling like an imposter doesn't mean I'm ignorant of my abilities.
Feeling humbled is not a sign of humility.

When I was young, I looked up to the greats, like Fred Bear in Michigan, the godfather of modern archery, who shared his experiences in print and videos. Times change. Sports evolve. Fred passed away in 1988 at the age of 86.

The fact is that Fred Bear couldn't shoot like I shoot. He couldn't run like I run.

That is truth.

The standard back then was different than today. Years ago, I decided something. I'm going to redefine the standard.

I've always thought I could do it.

Yes, it sounds delusional to say it, but I believed it back then, and I still believe it today.

Did I share it? Hell, no. I wouldn't even tell my own wife!

So, now I'm putting it in print. In white on black.

Maybe because I feel like I've earned the right to be honest.

I'll never be a Fred Bear or a Chuck Adams or a Roy Roth, so shut off your hate if you're feeling it right now.

I gotta believe. Hunters compete and have egos, and that's our world. You have to be confident and tough and capable.

Everything I do in training is to be at my best on these hunts.

Yeah, but you go on the best hunts, and anybody can do that if they've got the chances you've gotten.

Really? So, if anybody can do what I do, how come nobody ever has? Answer that.

Nobody's killed five good, wild bulls in a year with a bow ever in the history of man.

So, if anybody can do it, how come it's never happened until now?

To anybody who doubts me, keep it up, because that fuels me. But don't be mistaken: I'm not doing it for you. Grinding is just what I do.

I put in the work every day. Poser or not, imposter or not, and that mindset has gotten me this far.

I've still got a long way to go.

CHAPTER 7

SMASH THE GAS PEDAL DOWN

TENACITY:

The quality displayed by someone who just won't quit—who keeps trying until they reach their goal

"I WAS BORN FOR THE STORM, AND A CALM DOES NOT SUIT ME."

—*Andrew Jackson (1767–1845),
seventh president of the United States*

"What drives man beyond?"

This was the question I asked at the start of an Under Armour boots commercial I filmed years ago. It featured me and a wolf, doing the same thing, as we hunted in the woods.

"For some, there's an instinct to defy the civilized world," I narrated. "In the wild, that instinct is not enough. Nature's hungrier."

The commercial ended with me carrying the rack of a bull elk on my back, while the wolf came up, saw me, and snarled. I shot him a look that said simply, *I won*.

When we finished shooting, I told the filmmakers that the best ending would have been if I could have arrowed that wolf. The commercial inferred that I had won, but killing the wolf would have told the story right there.

The animal they used for that shoot was a real trained wolf. It was somewhat of a celebrity that had been in the *Twilight* movies. I had brought some elk steak to give to the wolf after filming. In order to make the wolf mad and snarl like it did in the commercial, they had to give it meat and then take it away and keep doing that several times. The trainer warned me about what would happen next.

"We can make the wolf mad and snarl like you need for the commercial, but once we do that, we're done, because it's going to be pissed off for the whole rest of the day."

It's amazing to think that this wolf, which had been trained since it was 5 weeks old and was now 11 years old, still had that

SMASH THE GAS PEDAL DOWN

wildness in him. At his core, he was still a wolf. He still had that tenacious heart beating inside of him.

I've spent a lot of time around wolves like that.

"I'll just go, go, go, go, go 'til I redline and pass out. That's kind of how I'm wired."

It's one thing to "go, go, go, go, go" when you're running an ultra or you're hunting elk in the backcountry, but for "Iron" Michael Chandler, the MMA and UFC great, going until you redline and pass out can be a brutal and bloody thing.

Michael was the first outlier to officially take part in a Lift Run Shoot. I've had the chance to train with a lot of beasts over the years, and Chandler's one of the biggest. Since competing in his first mixed martial arts fight in 2009 and winning it by a first-round TKO (technical knockout), he hasn't looked back. He has won multiple world titles and has been nominated for numerous Fight of the Year matches.

If you want an example of tenacity in action, it's Chandler. His highlight reel shows what one man can do inside a cage. In one fight, he's ending it with over 30 unanswered shots to his opponent's side of the head. Another is a lightning strike and then multiple punches with both hands. There are takedowns and matches ending with a desperate tap while he's got his left arm clamped around a fighter's neck. He drives one man back and taking him down before pummeling him. Another he gives a guillotine, doing a chokehold from the front and lifting his opponent off the ground. In the Octagon, Michael Chandler resembles a rabid animal able to strike you in any way from any direction. So, who better than Chandler to launch my podcast probing the mindset of outliers? The surprise during his visit was to hear just how far of a journey he's come with his mindset.

When Chandler visited, we ended up getting a marathon done that day. He had never run over 11 miles in his life. Michael said he came up to Oregon champing at the bit to do something that he knew was going to be hard. We had said, "Let's finish this marathon off," so we ended up doing exactly that in the dark as we summited Mount Pisgah.

Before becoming one of the great UFC fighters and learning how to be a tenacious competitor, Chandler first needed to truly believe in himself.

"I was a walk-on at the University of Missouri, meaning I didn't have a scholarship, but I could essentially try out for a spot on the wrestling team. I was the hardest worker

My life behind the bow has led me to some of the most incredible hunting country in the world like the San Carlos Apache Reservation where this photo was captured. Revered land of giant bull elk.

in the room. Coach's favorite wrestler. Team captain. I did every single thing right. God blessed me with some amazing abilities. I could have been a multiple-time all-American. Maybe even a national champion. Who knows? But I didn't give myself permission to win. I didn't give myself permission to be the best. Because between my ears, I didn't think that I truly deserved it. I would tell the media, I would tell the coaches, I would tell you, 'I'm going to be a national champ. I want to be an all-American.' But I didn't truly believe it. I had this cognitive dissonance of my actual belief not matching up with the reality of what I truly believed."

Chandler recalled the moment after he came in fifth place as a senior when he was taking his wrestling singlet off for the last time.

"I realized I'd underperformed so badly over those last five years because I didn't truly believe that I could have been successful like that," Chandler said. "I should have been an all-American. And in that moment, I made a promise to myself."

He was planning to move into mixed martial arts, so Michael vowed to never let this happen again. He had fallen short because of his failure to believe in himself. He says he got shot out of a cannon into the Bellator MMA world, the American mixed martial arts organization. He ended up 12–0, with 9 first round finishes. In 2011 he beat Eddie Alvarez for the world championship, but then suffered his first defeat in a 2013 rematch by split decision.

"I wasn't ready to lose at all," Chandler said, looking back. "I was not built up enough in my mind to lose."

After two more losses, Chandler had gone 688 days without winning a fight. He said he had been doing all the work building up his body and training, but he still needed to do the mental work.

"I had just been building up a bigger, faster, stronger, yet subpar version of me because I didn't truly believe it," Chandler told me. "I just underbelieved."

If anybody deserved to believe in himself, it was Michael Chandler. He had an incredible work ethic. His coaches believed in him, and vice versa: if a coach told him to run through a brick wall, he would have done it. He left everybody else in the dust. Why, then, the doubts, for someone who outwardly seemed to excel at everything?

"It's just the mindset part of things and falling short based on your self-image," Chandler explained. "It's a such a tough thing to get over. But it can be done. It can be conquered."

There were mentors who were big brothers to him, like UFC champion Tyron Woodley and MMA fighter Ben Askren, both of whom told him he could do this. Chandler's response was always, "Oh yeah, for sure," but his mind said something else: *No, you can't. Who do you think you are? You're a little guy from a little town who was taught to do little things.*

"I'm still battling that guy," Chandler admitted. "And it's okay for me to continue to battle him and never slay him. I worked with a mindset coach named Jim Hensel. He said that sometimes we slay a dragon, and sometimes we just get really good at pushing him into a corner."

I noted that Chandler has done a good job embracing this sort of mentality, especially when he's wearing a sweatshirt that says "Walk On." It's almost as if he's challenging this mindset.

"People would look at you and think that you're bulletproof," I said to him. "They'd say, 'Oh my God, why can't I be more like that guy?' So, to hear that you're like us, you just overcome it and fight it and embrace it—I think that's pretty powerful."

Chandler expanded on his perspective. "Everybody has something that they need to work on. Everybody has these doubts and fears and insecurities. And to have things is

One of the greatest rewards of my life has been sharing my love of archery with others, such as UFC superstar Michael Chandler.

to be human. We are prone to wander, and there are different seasons in life. There are seasons where you will feel bulletproof, and everything is firing on all cylinders, and you have your breakthroughs, and everything's going great. Then all of a sudden a couple things happen, and you're down in the dumps, and you need to be pulled out of them. You have to reach back and remember those practices that you had and remember those things that you did for yourself. What did I do in those six hundred eighty-eight days? What did I do during this time of my life? How did I feel in that greatest moment of regret when I was taking those steps? You look back at your life in the mental highlight reel and the chapters of your story to continue to remind yourself that you can continue to get better and continue to grow."

Even though we've heard the expression a thousand times before, Chandler said, we have to get back up on that horse. We have to move past those disappointments and failures until we find our next success. We can surprise ourselves in how quickly we are able to forget about those losses. That's just part of competition and doing something you love, as Chandler explained.

"If you're pursuing anything worthwhile whatsoever, if you're trying to be a man or a woman of impact, if you're trying to do something that wells up something inside you that, in turn, other people can see, and it wells up something inside them—you're leaving yourself open to not just criticism, but also to loss and to the trials and the tragedies and the valleys. You're putting yourself out there, and ultimately, what else is life if you're not doing that? That's why I've always said that mixed martial arts and fighting is a metaphor for life. Those fights, where we're inside an octagon in some arena in some city on any given Saturday night, are metaphors for the fights that we're all going through in our lives. The way that we watch people overcome the odds, or we watch somebody be extremely dominant, or we watch a nice, crazy, back-and-forth battle, it's a metaphor for all the things that we're going through in life."

The moment Katie Knight takes off up the steep part of Spencer Butte, I can tell she's fucking grinding.

Oh my God—I'm so screwed today.

I knew this wasn't going to be easy running alongside this multifaceted powerhouse.

Katie is an ultramarathoner, World's Toughest Mudder Champion, and gym beast. A long run for her is nothing new. At the summit of our first hill, she grins and doesn't even seem out of breath.

"What do you think?" I ask her.

"Pretty fun," she replies. "Oregon's beautiful."

Not everybody who hammers up a mountain like we just did is calmly taking in the sights. We run around 13.5 miles on a 90-degree day, some of it running on scorching asphalt. We reach a couple summits. Katie Knight is everything she appears to be online and more. There's one simple reason why she's in such good shape, as she told me the next day.

"Hard work."

I asked her if she trains daily.

"Every day, twice a day, six days a week. Sundays, completely off. Rest day. I walk the dog. I was born, bred, and corn-fed in Iowa with that hardworking mentality. Those people there—that's what they do all day. I grew up like that. Grew up in sports. There's no excuses. You work hard, and you get it done."

During high school, Katie was an all-American in hockey for the American team, and in college she went all in on CrossFit. Since then, she has mastered both endurance sports and strength disciplines, from ultras to extreme triathlons. In only her second time running it, Katie won World's Toughest Mudder in 2021, and in 2022 she claimed the championship in the GORUCK Games, an invitation-only, two-day competition featuring a variety of activities, including an obstacle course, rucking, and weighted challenges. Combining her strength background with endurance and obstacle course racing was the perfect mix for her.

I asked her why she liked these long races, or adventures like the 42-mile Rim to Rim to Rim in the Grand Canyon. "Is it just the suffering and the pushing?"

"I like to push," she replied. "Every endurance race I try, I like to see what my mind and body can do. I was like, *Hey, I've never run more than a half-marathon, let's go and try to climb in the Grand Canyon*. So, it was definitely the suffering. And then just the beauty, the scenery. Never seen the Grand Canyon before. When I was in the bottom of it, that's when the sun comes up, and I was like, *Wow, this is magnificent. You can't beat this*. And being able to run out on the trails, it's like you get to see that beauty every day. So, it's worth it. It's worth the suffering."

How, then, is Katie able to win? What gives her that edge?

"Just mental grit," she said. "The ability just to keep going. Keep pushing. Anything

Don't let the beauty fool you: Katie Knight is also a beast. An athlete and just recently a successful hunter as I took her on her first deer hunt and she tagged a great buck.

in a race—especially one that's twenty-four hours—can go wrong. It's not a matter of *if* something's gonna go wrong, it's *what*. So: What in this race is going to hold you back from wanting to keep going or wanting to quit? Because twelve hours in is when they say the race really starts."

Katie not only has to endure 24 hours of running, but these races also include obstacles like crawling over barriers, heavy carries, and lots of other challenges they throw at you. The World's Toughest Mudder has water obstacles, which makes it even harder.

"They're just trying to make you miserable," I said.

"Oh yeah. What can go wrong? As I was saying, it's just that willingness to keep going and keep pushing, because things *have* gone wrong. I've gotten hypothermia, like I did last year at World's Toughest. I've lost toenails during the race. So, yeah, I would say just that mental grit."

Competition is in Katie's veins, so she's always motivated to win.

"There's no better feeling than winning," she said. "Having all that hard work you've done for the past year pay off, being on that podium just feels good."

I know she loves the grind, so I asked Katie if she thinks of winning when she's doing her regular training every day at the gym.

"It's just part of my life. Essentially it's my full-time job. It's putting in that work every day, all day, twice a day, and then letting those results pay off."

That tenacity and willingness to suffer comes back to the same thing Michael Chandler spoke about: the mindset.

"As long as there's no broken bones, your body will do what you tell it to do," Katie explained. "It's usually the mind that goes first. If you can keep that strong, you can just keep going. You're going to pass out before you die, so I keep that in mind."

This was something we had laughed about the night before.

"How many people have you seen pass out?" I asked her.

"I don't think any," she said. "Humans quit way before that happens. I worry about Courtney Dauwalter sometimes—she pushes so hard—but in general, nobody's pushing that much."

Katie feels that everybody in life needs both strength and endurance. When we were lifting the night before, and she was pushing me to do just a few more reps, it wasn't until those last ones when it finally felt good to me.

"I loved it," I told her. "I love pushing to failure. It just feels good. What's that saying you have?"

"'No one cares what you can do fresh. That was the same for GORUCK Games. And it's true. Anybody, when they're fresh—mentally, physically—can do a lot. It's when you get past that point where things start to go, the body starts to get fatigued, the mind starts to feel weak, *that's* when it matters. That's for anything in life: a competition or just day-to-day stuff you have to deal with."

That's what tenacity will do for you. Everybody else will do what everybody usually does. A moderate run—3 sets of 10—or whatever exercise they're working on. But usually, at the end of a standard run or 3 sets of 10 is when you're *just* starting to feel it. You're *just* starting to push your body, so why are you quitting now?

Training with people like Katie inspires me, and it makes me ache the following day.

People love to talk. They love to say they're going to do crazy things like run an ultra. Only a small set of people actually say they're going to win one. That's because for most people, merely finishing the race is enough. For undeniable people, simply finishing just doesn't work.

Ken Rideout is one of those people who puts it all out there. In 2023 Rideout decided to run his first ultra—the Gobi March, a seven-day, 155-mile race across the Gobi Desert in Mongolia. He couldn't imagine anybody training as hard as he had the last two years—short of Olympic or professional runners, and he doubted they would be going to this race all the way in Mongolia—so he told all his sponsors beforehand that he was going to win. Sure enough, Ken won the Gobi March. When he came back to the States, one sponsor said he couldn't believe Ken had won. Part of Ken thought, *What do you mean you can't believe it?*

"I told you I was going to win," he said to the guy.

"Do you know how many people call us and tell us they're going to do things and never, ever do it? Don't even come close?"

Ken couldn't even imagine this happening.

"I would have died trying," he told me. "I would have come back injured, or I would have been like, 'Okay, I came in third, but I'm getting them next year.'"

"People are too afraid to put their goals out there, including when that goal is 'I'm going to win,'" I said to Ken. "Most people avoid that because then you look like you failed when you don't win. Or you're embarrassed."

Ken agreed. "I would have been all those things. And that's why I said it."

"That's what sets you apart."

Ken wasn't being arrogant when he predicted that he would win the Gobi March. Instead, he said it for accountability.

"I'm creating accountability and pressure for myself so that I need to keep working," he explained. "By saying I thought I could win and asking these brands to work with me, I've created pressure like a professional athlete. These brands I got on there, they're going to live and die with my success. I cannot go in there and not empty the tank. I have to either win or come back dead."

Another badass who always did what he said he would do is UFC legend Donald "Cowboy" Cerrone. The Hall of Fame fighter is known as a guy who would never turn down a fight. He carried that anytime-anywhere mindset during his 11-year UFC career. You always knew that a Cowboy fight was going to be something to watch.

"That was my whole mantra: whenever, wherever," Cowboy told me. "They would ask me, 'What's your plan?' Man, I don't care! I just wanted to know that when they announced the Cowboy fight, someone would be like, "Oh, Cowboy! We've *got* to go to a bar, or anywhere we can, to watch it, 'cause my man's *going*. He's throwing down! Win or lose, he's bringing it.' That was what I always wanted my legacy to be."

I asked the fighter from Denver where he got this anytime-anywhere mentality. He didn't have a rough childhood. Cerrone grew up in a wealthy family, with a grandmother and a grandfather who were doctors. As a youth, he was street fighting all the time, and when a buddy suggested that he try kickboxing, he fell in love with it.

"The work ethic is what I think is the most important," Cowboy explained. "That was taught to me by my grandparents, because they owned their own practice. And my grandmother would work. She would raise all those grandkids, and she would practice medicine eighty hours a week. I mean, talk about a hardworking lady. She would just teach me all the ways of life growing up and what to do and what not to do. I like this way of life, because typical challenges never bother me ever."

Cowboy's grandmother always told him that there were worse things in life than what might be happening to him on a bad day.

"She'd always kind of check me and give me perspective on what 'bad' really is," he recalled fondly. "And that's kind of what I always based my life on. Same thing with working hard. She would always tell me, 'If you say you're going to do something, you do it. Don't half-ass it. You do it. So, if you say you're going to be there, Cowboy, you be there.' Whenever we start a project, we do it and work hard. And my friends can't ever keep up with me. They actually hang out with me in shifts because they can't maintain the pace that I play at and have fun at. It's just my work ethic."

When Cowboy showed up for the Lift Run Shoot, he didn't even bring running shoes but instead ran in slippers. At first, I thought he was playing a bit of possum on the run, so I wasn't sure how it was going to go, but then he killed it.

"Not making excuses, but I got surgery on my groin because I pulled a muscle off the bone," Cowboy said. "It hurts."

"I would hate to see you at one hundred percent if that was a chink in your armor with a torn-up groin," I told him. "You just crushed that hill. I got a glimpse into what makes Cowboy Cowboy right there."

Groin injury or not, Cowboy said he was going to do it. So he did. It comes down to whether you really have that internal tenacity.

"It's funny to me to see these guys that promote greatness and how they want to be that person and fake their life until they *are* that person," Cowboy said. "Sometimes, if you fake it long enough, you find it. So, I'm not totally mad at him. He preached it. Preach it, preacher. Preach. You keep preaching it long enough, you might become that guy you're trying to be. But it's a lot of hard work, you know? I mean, you run two hundred fifty miles. You couldn't fucking make me do that. There's no way."

"You could do it," I told him. "It's just a mindset. But I know what you're saying about guys who want to shortcut. They want to say, 'Hey, look at me. I'm this leader. I'm setting the tone.' But it's like, well, no. Your work isn't showing that. There are a lot of online 'experts' out there."

Cowboy agreed. "*Total* 'experts.' They only want to post a quote and take a picture in the gym. But are you really the guy in the gym? Are you really the guy when it's freezing cold outside, and you don't care? You put your beanie on in the blizzard, and you still go run? And you still get it done before you have to be to work, and you gotta take your kids and pack the lunch for your boys and drop them off at the school bus. Did you get up at three in the morning and go do all that before you got to be ready, before you go and work your twelve-hour day, and then go home and do everything

"Anytime, Anyplace" is a catchphrase of UFC legend Donald "Cowboy" Cerrone and it's fitting . . . he's a wild man.

that needs to be done before you go to bed? Are you that guy? Or are you the guy that doesn't really work, and you're living in your mom's basement, and the only thing you have to do today is go to the gym, so you make it look easy on social media? Is that you, or are you the real guy? Are you the motherfucker?"

One person who is "the real guy" and the motherfucker is three-time Olympian Matthew Centrowitz Jr. I've watched his epic 1,500-meter final in the 2016 Summer Olympics many times. He was the first American to win the gold in that event since 1908. His father, Matthew Centrowitz Sr., also went to the Olympics twice and was a four-time US champion in distance running. Centrowitz Sr. attended the University of Oregon and broke Steve Prefontaine's 1,500-meter school record while running there.

Having grown up just outside of Eugene, a city nicknamed TrackTown USA, with a father who was a legendary track guy, I had always been interested in running and watching track meets, so being able to run with Matt and then talk to him was exciting for me. The first thing I wanted to know was what does it take to become an Olympic champion.

"It takes a lot," Matt said candidly. "You could be prepared mentally and physically, and you still need that one or two percent of luck. You still need things to go right on that given day. I think that's what makes the Olympics so special compared with any other sporting event, in my opinion. Like the professional soccer World Cup, it comes every four years. It's not something like the National Basketball Association, where you have a best-of-seven series. That's the one shot you got until the next four years. And usually in this sport, those chances don't come often."

I summed up his gold-medal win in Rio de Janeiro, Brazil: "On that day, for whatever reason, all the stars aligned, and you came across the line first. So incredible."

It's hard to imagine always being known as an Olympian champion. To be called an Olympic gold medalist. Even if somebody hasn't heard of you, they know that you have climbed to the highest rung of the sports ladder. To do it in an unforgiving sport such as track, Matt told me, you always have to be on your A game.

"I will say that in running, specifically, when you go to all the professional groups around the world, and you see all of the athletes that are lined up in the Olympic finals, we all work our asses off to get there," Matt explained. "Basically, everyone's elite. When it comes down to that day, what separates first place from fifth place from twelfth place is the mental part."

He said that over the years, he's received a lot of shit because that Olympic race was super tactical and much slower than most. A "pedestrian pace," as one announcer called it. But Matt revealed to me something that I had never heard before: their 1,500-meter Olympic race that evening had been delayed because an Olympic soccer final went into overtime, and NBC TV continued to show those extra minutes. The race was supposed to start at eight o'clock, so Matt and the other runners were already warmed up. Then they were told to hold on.

"So, we've been ready to go for what felt like an hour, an hour and a half, which was probably more like ten or fifteen minutes. You could see guys looking around, panicking. They're asking officials, 'What are we waiting for?' And I remember thinking to myself, *Whatever they tell us we're waiting for, that's not going to change anything. We're still going off. Whenever those gates open for us to go out there and do one stride and get on the line, you got to be ready for it.* The mental preparation: I'm still thinking of the race like other people

"I CAN'T EXPECT ANYBODY TO BE ABLE TO RELATE TO MY SCREWED-UP MIND, BUT SOMETIMES I CAN GO RUN 15 MILES, GET A GOOD WORKOUT, GO HOME, AND AN HOUR LATER, I'M THINKING I COULD HAVE DONE MORE. IT'S HARD TO BE SATISFIED."

—*Cam Hanes*

One of my favorite athletes of all time because of his confidence and big personality, Olympic gold medalist Matthew Centrowitz Jr.

were ten and fifteen minutes ago, but now the others are just like, 'What the fuck?' 'I need to do another stride right now.' 'I'm getting cold.' Yeah, but guess what? We're all getting cold. Part of the reason why it was so tactical is that they held us so long, we were not warmed up, so no one could get off the line and want to run a fast pace because we were just cooling off."

Even for runners that are warmed up, there are times where everybody will go out slowly, knowing it's a tactical race. Nobody wants to be the pacemaker. In that Olympic final, Matt went out in front of the pack and stayed there, setting the slow pace. I remember the announcers saying that ultimately it was going to come down to a one-lap sprint, and with one lap left, Matt found himself boxed in.

"I was actually in a pretty shitty spot," he recalled. "I'd been in the best spot all race, and the kick is about to start, and then this guy bodychecks me and gets around me, and I'm like, *Fuck!* I'd run a perfect race up to this point. I'm not panicking yet, but I'm definitely trying to get out. But you know what? I can't. Like, there's too many bodies. Everyone's there. And I just went back on the inside, looked, and I knew he was going to drift out just enough for me to just squeeze by, as long as I'm not putting my arm out and I'm not impeding anyone. I just dropped my elbow down and made one quick sidestep on the inside. I didn't think twice. I just kept that momentum. I was like, *This is my bid for home.*"

According to Matt, if the other runner hadn't gotten in front of him, he didn't know when he would have started to wind it up. He admitted that he wasn't the fastest guy in the field, so for him to get that jump was everything in a race that came down to milliseconds. He ended up leading the race 1,450 out of the 1,500 meters to win. But naturally, there were critics of the slow pace.

"There's seldom ever world records set at the Olympics in middle-distance races because people are tactical," I pointed out. "Nobody wants to make that move early. And so, it doesn't really matter about the time. It's a fucking gold medal."

Matt is used to getting shit from others over the years. He has received hate ever since he won the outdoor 1,500-meter final at the 2011 NCAA championship and made a throat-slitting gesture after crossing the finish line. He explained that thinking of postrace celebrations like this helped take his mind off the race.

"But also, it's a different level of confidence," Matt added. "It's not like, *Am I going to win or not?* It's like, *When I win, this is what I want to do.* Some people call it arrogant, some people call it confident. And I think there is a difference between the two."

After the race, Matt actually worried that he was going to be disqualified for having made the gesture. But even more than that, he worried about his father's reaction.

"I respected my dad so much, and he was such a big mentor to me and someone I looked up to. I thought, he's going to yell or he's gonna be pissed. I remember talking to him because a lot of people were like, 'What the fuck was that?' Like, friends of his or just people in the stands. And my dad goes—and he told me this me, too—he goes, 'As long as he's winning, I don't care what the hell he does.' And I was like, 'That's it. I'm good with that.'

This tenacious attitude has followed Matt throughout his career. He's someone who loves to talk shit and play mind games with his opponents before races. Even during and after races, Matt has been known to smirk at someone he's beaten or even say a word or two. He knows this can make other people start to wonder what he said.

"You can spin it from there," Matt shared with me. "Was there an f-bomb in there?"

"I love it because track doesn't have that, usually," I said.

He respects the guys he competes against, so he never intends to show disrespect. Even with rivals. He just loves the good banter. Yet his only goal is to win.

"I mean, that's what you're there to do. I'm not there to make friends."

Like any elite athlete, Matt knows he has plenty of supporters in his corner, but there will also be haters, no matter what he does or says. I asked him if he thinks that maybe most people do give him credit and appreciate his accomplishments, but he's focusing on the shit talkers just to get that self-motivating chip on his shoulder?

"You want me to really be a thousand percent honest?" he replied with a grin. "I hate to admit it but, yes, you're a hundred percent right."

Matt tries to find those things that he can build up just a little bit more to give him that competitive edge. The things that some people have said about him—Matt said those words will be with him until the day he dies. As a competitor in any sport, he is willing to play the part he's been given, even if he's always the bad guy.

"I'll take that role!" he said. "I love it! I'd rather be the bad guy, but you know, deep inside, I am a good guy."

Sometimes there's nothing you can do to change a narrative when people think something about you. Matt doesn't care.

"Every movie needs a villain. Every story needs a villain. If I fit that story, and I've got to be that guy, I'll be that guy."

Let's pause briefly as Kanye West sings, "Let's have a toast for the douchebags," from his song "Runaway."

Yes, let's celebrate those haters. All those "Must be nice" guys.

I'll let NFL star Derek Wolfe share some of his thoughts on this:

"'Must be nice.' I fucking hate that," he said intensely. "People say to me, 'Must be nice.' I'm like, 'Fuck you. Must be nice to sit around and just make excuses your whole life and never accomplish anything and be a hater.' Because you know what? I've never met a hater that was doing better than I was. If somebody's hating on you, look where they're at."

"Ray Lewis said this in a speech he was giving." Lewis, a ferocious linebacker for 17 seasons in the NFL, all of them spent with the Baltimore Ravens, was inducted into the Pro Football Hall of Fame, in Canton, Ohio, in 2018. "He said, 'You think that an eagle likes it when it sees another bird at the same altitude as him? The other bird thinks it's an eagle, because no other bird flies that high.' So, fly with the eagles. Don't fly down there with the fucking crows cawing all the time. 'Caw, caw, caw.'"

Derek Wolfe continued. "Why do the eagles get to eat the deer first? Because they're the eagle. Be the alpha. Be the eagle. Don't be the whiny little bitch that cries and whines because you don't have what you want. You don't have it because you didn't work for it."

Well spoken, my friend.

There are a lot of synonyms for *tenacious*. Persistent. Stubborn. Resolute. Dogged. Perseverant. Steadfast. Unyielding. Unwilling to let go. Unwavering.

If only one person came to mind when I see that list, it's Courtney Dauwalter. I wrote about her in chapter four on consistency, but she can easily be highlighted in any of these chapters. Her ability to sacrifice for her sport is unrivaled. She brings a quiet, dogged dedication to being an elite ultra runner.

"When you talk to her, she seems so normal," Joe Rogan once remarked about Courtney. "There's no demon there. I'm waiting to meet a demon. I'm like, 'Where's your demon? How are you getting through that?' Her demon's a quiet demon. It's there, though. It has to be."

I'm not sure if she's carrying a demon, but I do know that Courtney does carry a lot of humility with her. It's not always easy getting her to talk about her incredible abilities and talents, but I was able to peek into her mindset when she came to Lift Run Shoot with me. I asked how she looked at her sport and her role in it.

"One of the cool parts of ultra running is that really no one's in it for the fanfare," Courtney said. "No one gives a hoot if anyone knows about something they did. It's about huge days out in the mountains, seeing what your body is capable of, and seeing then how your brain can help your body do even more."

I asked her about her competitive nature and that clichéd question of whether she hated to lose more than she loved to win.

"I dislike if I finish something and know that I could have done better," Courtney answered thoughtfully. "It's not loving to win or hating to lose. I think it's more like, if I'm going to do this, I want to do it all the way, all in, and see what's possible. To keep learning and growing from that. Where that lands me in the results is where it lands me."

With an answer like that, one might think that Courtney isn't competitive at all. I still will never forget the first time I ever heard her name. It was when I ran the annual Moab 240 in Utah in 2017, and "Dauwalter obliterated the competition" as *The New York Times* put it so eloquently. We've talked about this before, but when I first heard how much she was leading the race by, I was in disbelief, assuming that she had unwittingly run the wrong way! She really did it; she crushed it.

"You won by maybe ten hours," I said. "You've talked about it a million times, but it is just incredible how much you won by. You could have easily coasted in. You could have won by two hours. So, tell me: Were you still pushing?"

"Yeah. Absolutely."

I asked Courtney if perhaps she was sending a message to all the other racers. (In my mind, I hoped she was, because that would have been a cool contrast to her nice, easygoing personality.) Or was she just trying to push herself?

"It was like, let's smash the gas pedal down and see, because why not? You can make them like targets as things unfold. I think at that point my husband was pacing me, and we had chosen a time we're trying to beat just to have something to help keep the gas pedal pushed down."

That's with nobody ahead of her she's pushing to pass and nobody closing in on her that she had to keep ahead of herself. Just pure mind over body.

So, in a sport where everybody is in shape because they have to be, what separates Courtney from the rest? Everybody is dealing with pain. How can she keep going? Does the pain ever become too much?

"I have learned the lesson that I'm not made of titanium," Courtney admitted. "I'm not invincible. So, there is a line there. Over the years, I've been trying to get better at just reading the signals my body is giving me. The warning signs. I'm actually listening to them instead of just blowing right past them, thinking that I'm better than those warning signs."

Courtney learned this after having to drop out of the Western States 100-Mile Endurance Run with a hip injury in 2019 after having won it the year before.

"I think what happened that year is I had done Western States the year before. I knew the areas I wanted to get better in, and I knew there was space for improvement on that course. I just ramped it all up. I'm going to do more climbing, I'm going to do a faster pace. I'm going to do more miles, and everything went up, except no recovery or extra body maintenance was added to it. I just asked too much without giving anything back to myself, and it led to an injury."

I'm sure that for someone like Courtney, who gives *everything,* it's really hard to truly listen to her body when she asks so much from it.

"Sometimes I still make those mistakes, and I don't listen perfectly, but I think our bodies are really good at telling us what they need," she explained. "They can give us those signals if we are paying attention and distinguishing between those warning signs."

Courtney said it's key to know when your body just wants you to go sit on the couch because that sounds much more comfortable versus when you've really overdone it, and you need to pump the brakes a little.

Before that hip injury, Courtney had wondered to herself if she would know when there was a real serious issue telling her to slow down. Would she know how to actually preserve herself when the warning sign became serious?

"I wondered if I could do it because I love pushing," Courtney said. "I love that feeling of digging really deep and getting to a finish line. I wasn't sure that I would have the capacity or maturity, or whatever the word is, to actually listen. When that happened during the race, and those flags were going up and I ended up dropping, it actually felt like a big step of trusting myself afterward. I was like, 'Okay, you do have the capacity to listen if the flags are important.' So, I felt like I was learning even better how to read the signals."

That must have come as a relief, I remarked. It was, said Courtney. Kind of.

"I'm not trying to run myself into a wall and never be able to run again," she emphasized. "I want to run my whole life."

I understood. None of us are immortal, but if you have that invincible attitude, it gives you that edge.

"You push so hard, and it's so unique," I told her. "I saw you on the Colorado Trail, and you're going for that record. This is never anything humans have to worry about, but a dog or a horse can push so hard that they'll die. They just will give everything. In some ways, I admire that. Imagine if one pushed so hard they died? There's kind of a romantic part to that because for most people, a *little* bit of pain and they're like, 'I'm out. I can't do this.' I've always said that you push harder than anyone I've ever seen. When I ran with you on the Colorado Trail, I couldn't believe how hard you're pushing and struggling. It also makes me worry that you push too much."

I asked her about the line of distinction between listening to her body and pushing it. Luckily, she said, she is surrounded by people who can make those smarter choices for her in those instances. They can see the signals better than she can. No matter what happens, Courtney is always pushing herself to be better.

When we were talking, in April 2023, I asked her to name her long-standing dream or biggest goal that she wanted to achieve running. Her answer was typical Courtney Dauwalter:

"I don't have one thing. I think it's to just keep finding out what's possible."

I decided to run with this idea, no pun intended. I posed a question to her and said that if she was feeling good mentally, and if she was physically killing it, then hypothetically she could maybe win both the Western States 100 *and* the Hardrock Hundred Mile Endurance Run. Did she like that idea?

Courtney only laughed.

"That sounds like a good goal, right?" I said. "I think that would be sick."

"I'm going to try my best," she replied.

"And then the UTMB is after that. What if . . . ?"

The UTMB is the 172-kilometer Ultra-Tour du Mont-Blanc in Chamonix, France.

"Could that ever happen?" I asked. "Could one person win all three of those?"

"In one summer?"

"Yeah," I said.

Courtney didn't hesitate to answer.

"Absolutely someone could."

"Think so?"

"Yeah."

"Could you?" I asked.

"I don't know, but I'd be willing to try," she said, laughing.

I could already picture it. "Yeah, that'd be awesome. You've won them all separately, right?"

She nodded. "Yeah."

"I wonder what it would take to have a summer of wins of the most prestigious ultras in history?"

"*A lot* of cheeseburgers," Courtney joked.

I was being serious.

"Now, that's my goal for you," I said. "I just came up with it."

"Okay. I like it. I'm in for it. If it sounds crazy, I think it's a fantastic idea. And I think something like that *is* possible if you can figure out the balance of the training and preparation, but also making sure you're keeping your body happy, because you can get too excited, do a little too much, and then you're just breaking yourself down, and then it's not going to get any better."

During a 10-week span in the summer of 2023, Courtney Dauwalter ran those three ultras and won every one, a feat that had never been accomplished before.

Three 100-mile races. The Triple Crown of ultras. She broke records in the first two.

Courtney is a beast after my own heart. Always moving the goalposts. Always setting her sights on something else. Always doing epic things. Always doing something nobody else has ever done before.

DON'T STOP

There is one person I always want to beat.

Myself.

I don't do what I do for anybody else. I do it just for me.
      I need to do this.
           I like pushing my limits.

If I had listened to all the people telling me what I should do or shouldn't do or could do or couldn't do, I wouldn't have done hardly anything in my life.

I don't care what anybody says, because I'm not battling anybody. I'm battling my own body.

This is what I do.

I want to find my absolute limit and see how much I can withstand.

I don't know what I would be like without the challenges that I take on. Part of me feels like if I didn't do this, I would be a shell of myself as far as living up to my ability.

If I am able to do it, I need to attempt it. I need to try. I need to make it happen. People need to live up to their full potential. That's what I'm doing. Or at least that's what I continue to try to do every damn day.

Yes, I believe that life is all about competition, and I believe that a man needs to prove that he's better than me. But my archrival is the man I see in the mirror every fucking morning. By nighttime, I want to make sure I beat him. Or at least beat up on him.

This is what I want to show others. This is what I want to say to you.

Doubters can't stop you.
Weather can't stop you.
Heartaches can't stop you.
Only you can stop you.

Obstacles can't stop you.
Circumstances can't stop you.
Failures can't stop you.

The struggle never ends.

It's a lifelong war, but each day is a battle that can be won.

The questions you have to ask yourself are the following:

Do I want to be half of myself, living in a shell? Or do I live out my full potential?

The choice is up to you.

CHAPTER 8

SPEND TIME DOING SOMETHING YOU LOVE

PASSION: *Intense, driving, or overpowering feeling or conviction*

"NOTHING HAPPENS WITHOUT DESIRE AND PASSION. OTHERWISE, NOTHING ELSE FALLS IN PLACE. IT'S VERY HARD TO FIND SOMEONE WHO'S SUCCESSFUL AND DISLIKES WHAT THEY DO." [9]

—*Malcolm Gladwell in a roundtable discussion with* Business Insider

When I was an editor for *Eastmans' Bowhunting Journal,* I quoted Joe Rogan in an article I wrote long before I met him. Titled "Finding Your Way—Train Hard, Hunt Easy," here are the opening two paragraphs:

During a UFC Pay-Per-View some years ago, commentator Joe Rogan used a reference that caught my attention. In quoting Miyamoto Musashi, a famous Japanese samurai who wrote The Book of Five Rings, a classic book of strategy and life, he said, "Once you understand the way broadly, you can see it in all things." I was struck by this quote, which in plain English means, "Once you find the path to success, in whatever it may be, success comes easier in all things."

Sounds simple, doesn't it? But think about it. Over the years, I have met a ton of guys who've been successful in rifle hunting, decided to switch over from the gun to the bow, and true to form, they're just as successful with archery equipment. Natural-born killers, it seems. I've known great athletes who are seemingly good at everything they try: football, basketball, baseball, track, etc. Then to top it off, this group of people are usually smart, earn good jobs, and seem to get all the breaks. I am sure you know individuals who fit this mold. Musashi's quote seems applicable. These guys or gals found the way to success in the woods with the rifle or bow, on the field or court, or in the business world—everything. In short, they "see it in all things."

I've always said I wish I believed in myself as much as Joe believes in me. He's helped me so much in business, life, and as a dear friend, and it's not just me he's helped. His podcast has literally changed the world in some respects. The term "Powerful" Joe Rogan couldn't be more accurate.

If you could attribute Joe's success to just one thing it would have to be his passion for martial arts. He told me that from the time he was 15 years old to age 22, all he did was compete in martial arts. It not only gave him confidence, but, as he once said in an interview, it also was "the first thing that ever gave me hope that I wasn't going to be a loser.[10]" He won the US Open Championship taekwondo tournament when he was 19 and was the Massachusetts state champion 4 years in the row. This experience in fighting has given him authentic knowledge in order to be one of the commentators for the UFC. It also showed him he could do something really hard—something that terrified him—and do it well.

The first time I was on his show, Joe shared with me his mentality back when he was 19 and competing in taekwondo matches.

"I had this thing that I would do in the morning," Joe told me. "The alarm clock goes off, and I would get up like my life depended on it. I'd just fucking jump out of bed like my house was on fire, because I was, like, that's the way to do it. Because anything else is weak."

At the time, Joe viewed any sort of pleasure as a weakness. That included anything from enjoying good food to having sex with his then girlfriend. He said he would wake up angry and urgent and put on his shoes to run or go train. This attitude drove his girlfriend crazy.

"She's overreacting," I joked to Joe.

"It wasn't that she was overreacting," Joe said with a laugh. "I was fucking crazy. I wouldn't have wanted to hang out with me when I was nineteen. I was a fucking maniac, but, you know, that's probably better than hitting that fucking snooze button ten times in a row. Developing the discipline, the muscle of discipline. I get that through inspiration."

I told Joe that there's always an excuse, and he fully agreed. Then Joe added, "But when you get through it, you realize life is a lot of times not about doing what you want to do. Life is about doing what you're supposed to do or what you should do, and then knowing that when you want to do it, it'll be even easier."

Even before I got to know Joe personally, I knew that he was inspired by people with a passion. That's why he likes to have so many unique guests on his program. Most podcasters go with the most popular people they can get, but Joe talks to people who he sees as having a passion for life in whatever they do. For me, it was bowhunting, and that's how he found me. He started watching my YouTube videos, and he could see my passion. He knew what I was trying to do: be the best I could be.

Whenever somebody has an intense passion, people are drawn to them. It doesn't matter in what arena. For me, hunting has given me all sorts of opportunities just because of my passion for it. This is what I want to do. The same can go for you or anybody. It doesn't matter what you do. It can be any field or any pursuit. If you have passion for it, that's going to stand out, and that's going to impact people, just by believing in it and chasing it with all you've got. Do that, and who knows what can happen?

One Thursday night at the University of Oregon, I witnessed firsthand how passion draws in people. Over 500 people had come to pack a hall and listen to a *neuroscientist*? Wait, what? Other than Taylor Swift, who could bring in a bunch of young college kids on a weekday evening?

Rock-star scientist Dr. Andrew Huberman.

The associate professor of neurobiology and ophthalmology at Stanford University School of Medicine has been a celebrity since launching the *Huberman Lab* podcast in January 2021 and watching it explode in popularity. His live appearances are sold out, and he has paid premium content for subscribers. People recognize him on the street and ask to take selfies with him.

Huberman's dad was a physicist, so he grew up knowing what science was. For part of his childhood, he and his older sister had a pretty traditional upbringing. The family had dinner around the table every night. The television was off. It was a pretty wholesome environment, for the most part, one in which Andrew's passion for learning began.

"My parents were worried about me because I was obsessive about learning," Huberman told me. "When I was six, I spent all my time in pet stores cataloging all the fish. I was obsessed with medieval weapons. Then I would go to class, and I would ask if I could give lectures in class. This was when I was seven or eight. And they let me do it because otherwise I wouldn't have shown up. And my voice back then was very deep, almost like it is now. My nickname was Froggy when I was a kid. I have a mutation that affects my adrenals glands. Actually, I had hair on my Adam's apple when I was a little kid, so I was like this little man professing."

I asked Huberman if the other kids made fun of him.

"Yeah, I got teased. I was obsessive about Legos, and I was obsessive about fish, and I was obsessive about biology and learning. I loved the encyclopedia and *The Guinness Book of World Records*, and I would just be talking about them all the time."

Cam with Andrew Huberman

Ultimately, Huberman's passion was learning, and he couldn't help himself from sharing that information. That was a big part of his childhood. Then, when he was 13 years old, his parents divorced, and his life changed. Suddenly his dad was out of the picture, his sister was already out of the house, and his mom was struggling with the whole change in their family structure. At the time, Huberman was becoming really interested in skateboarding, a sport where typically parents weren't around.

Andrew Huberman

"From about thirteen to eighteen, it was super dark," Huberman said. "I mean, there were times where I'd go home, and I was just completely alone."

Huberman barely managed to finish high school and spent a month in a youth detention center before he graduated. He followed his girlfriend to UC Santa Barbara, and by the time he was 19 years old, he realized where his life was headed. He had screwed up the opportunity to get a college education after making all Ds his first year.

He and his girlfriend had split up. He had a job delivering bagels, and he didn't like his boss.

"I had a bad attitude," Huberman said. "I realized, like, 'I'm officially a loser.'"

"But did you *accept* that you're a loser?" I asked him. "Did you think that you were capable of so much more? What was your mindset?"

Huberman explained that he was bitter about what had happened in his family life. "I think I was angry, to be honest, that I wasn't good at anything. I had the victim mentality. I knew I had a strong drive and a capacity to do things. But I kept thinking, *Who's going to be the great teacher that's going to get me excited about a subject?* Then I actually wrote a two-page letter to my mom. I still have it. I said, 'This is it. I'm turning it around. I don't care if the teachers are good. I'm going to just do the work.'"

I suggested that even though the letter was to his mother, in essence it was really to himself. Huberman agreed.

"It was like, *Hey, listen: Whatever has gone on in your past, it's going to mean nothing to the world unless you clean your act up now.* So, I moved home, and I went to Foothill College, a community college."

He began to pour himself into his classes with the intensity of an athlete in training. "I started working really hard memorizing my textbooks," Huberman said. "I'd go to the gym. I always reacted well to the weights, and my body could grow quickly. I could go running, lifting. I started studying for real, and I was like, *Okay, I'm pretty good at this.*"

With his newfound dedication, Andrew quickly became a straight-A student, which enabled him to reenroll at UC Santa Barbara. Huberman ended up earning a bachelor's degree in psychology.

"I decided I didn't care who the teacher was or how much they annoyed me, I was going to be in the front row and was going to use these classes," Huberman recalled. "I became kind of a beast. An academic beast. I just put everything I had into getting the top score."

Once Huberman got his life in order at 19, he wrote down his future goals: to earn his Ph.D. by the time he was 30, to obtain a faculty position by age 35, and to get tenure by the time he turned 40. After working in a lab for an ex-navy guy who had become a physiologist, Huberman was told he was really good at this sort of work and that he should go to graduate school. He earned a master's in neurobiology and behavior at UC Berkeley and then went on to earn his Ph.D. in neuroscience at UC Davis. In 2016 Huberman joined the faculty at Stanford, where he is a professor in the Department of Neurobiology.

When working on his Ph.D., he found the ideal situation for a researcher studying neural development: a lab that he would go to at five o'clock in the afternoon, lock the door, crank punk music, and then conduct nonstop experiments on ferrets. Why ferrets? As Huberman told me, they have pretty complex brains and they're highly visual. He also did experiments on monkeys. These involved injecting small amounts of tracer dyes into specific areas of the animals' brains and then examining them. From this work, he was discovering both how binocular vision develops and also discovering the sort of genetics and molecules that allow our brain to wire up so precisely.

By the time he had finished his Ph.D., Huberman had really turned his life around.

"I was like, 'Okay, I did it right,'" he said. "'I have a path.'"

This path, which could be called his passion, resulted in him doing a five-year postdoctoral program at Stanford. This is similar to a residency, where you're not taking classes but just doing experiments. I couldn't believe how long he did this.

"For five years?" I said in shock.

"For five years," Huberman replied.

"So, how long had you been in school at this point?"

He began calculating the math out loud. "I left high school when I was seventeen because my birthday's in September. Did five years as an undergrad because I took the time. Two years as a master's, four-year Ph.D., five-year postdoc, five years as a junior professor, twelve years as a tenured professor."

It goes without saying that Dr. Huberman isn't some overnight success. Like anybody who has made a lifetime out of his passion, he has been working at it for *decades*. His journey was not unlike mine, in that I, too, was on my own a lot of the time after my parents divorced. The pain of my childhood ended up shaping me into the man I eventually became. That's why, when I choose to endure pain of any kind, I always know that it's only temporary. I shared this thought with Huberman.

"Even though it sucks carrying the rock up the mountain, that's going to be over," I said. "That shit's not lasting more than an hour. When you've been through real pain, you can compartmentalize and say, 'This is temporary. I'm good.' It's going back to the realization that 'Yeah, I've hurt. I've been in pain. I've been lonely, and this isn't that. I can get through this long run or this race. It's over in three days, worst case. Even if there's two hundred miles or more to cover, it's not that bad.'"

Huberman agreed. "I think one of the most important things for everybody to be able to say to themselves, knowing they're being completely honest, is: 'I can do hard things.

If it gets tough, I *know* I can do it because I've done it.' You can't ask the two-year-old to say that to himself or a ten-year-old. If I had my way, everyone would have the gift of a near-perfect childhood. But if I had my way also, everyone would be able to experience something hopefully not so damaging that they're permanently scarred and dissolved into a puddle of their own tears, but they could say, 'I can do hard things.' And I know that to be a fact, not just a mantra, because I've done hard things. Or in your case, you can say, 'I do hard things every day.'"

The hardships and losses we experience, Huberman said, make the good times way better. Our sense of appreciation deepens. These events also shape us and make us who we are.

"I do think having a little bit of a pebble in your shoe sometimes can keep you working harder and really persevering," Andrew said.

One of the most common questions Dr. Huberman gets is how can someone build confidence?

"The way you build confidence is by doing hard, really challenging things," he stated. Huberman recalled working so hard in a neural development class and only earning a B-plus. At the time, he considered anything other than an A to be a failure because he didn't want to backslide and become that 19-year-old loser once again. Now he sees it as the finest grade he's ever earned.

"I worked so hard, and I saw that this B-plus is my favorite course, my favorite grade, because it reminds me that it was the hardest class. He was such a difficult professor. The material was postdoc level, super difficult, and I just thought, *I can do hard things*. It's that simple. It's a short sentence, but it's one that if you can state it to yourself honestly, then you can get through anything. That's confidence."

Some outliers, such as Andrew Huberman, find their passion early in life. You might be one of them. Or perhaps you had a passion, but decided to put it on the shelf.

"I think a lot of the passions that we have as a kid come back around to meet the things that we want to do as an adult," Chris Williamson told me. "And for me, a lot of it was audiobooks. I'd listen to them in my room. You roll the clock forward by twenty years, and what's the 2023 equivalent of an audiobook? A podcast."

What is that one thing that you dearly loved during your childhood? Do you still love it?

For Levi Morgan, imagining that he would turn his childhood passion into a successful career was unimaginable. "If ten-year-old Levi could have seen into the future, he would have passed out," he told me. "I just shot a bow because I loved it. I just happened to do it, and I loved it so much that I just was obsessed with it and did it and wanted to learn every little piece of it. I've been incredibly blessed."

I'm old enough now to know how fast this journey goes and how precious life is. I don't give advice, but the following quote from Leo Buscaglia, resonates deeply with me:

"A life without passion is really no life at all. It's merely existence."

Some people never find their true passion in their lifetime. Thankfully, I was 20 years old when I first found success in bowhunting and subsequently discovered my calling. Suddenly I had a passion I could focus my energy on.

That passion hasn't dimmed. In fact, I've never been more passionate about bowhunting than I am today.

We have been given the gift of life, so it's our responsibility to get out there and *live* with passion.

What is that thing that is going to define you? What is a real passion to fuel your fire?

Sometimes a passion can come on like a sudden storm or an unexpected discovery. For Evan Hafer, the founder and executive chairman of Black Rifle Coffee Company, he was 20 years old when the moment arrived.

"I'll tell you exactly the month and date that espresso changed my life," Evan explained to me. "It was November 1997 in Capitol Hill in Seattle. The coffee shop is called Vivace Coffee, and it's still there. It was the single greatest shot of espresso I've ever had in my life. And it was life changing. So, there's not too many people that can say, 'I know when, the date, and the time.'"

Evan went out and got a book on espresso and fell in love with it. But his plans at the moment were to join the Green Berets, so coffee would have to wait.

Coming from a family of loggers and raised in a small town in northern Idaho with a population of around 800, Evan grew up knowing the value of hard work.

Black Rifle Coffee CEO Evan Hafer is a born leader. From special operations in the military to running a company that went public on the NYSE valued at $1.7 billion, I've learned a lot from Evan about life and business.

Both his grandfather and father owned their own businesses, so he watched how they managed those. Serving in the military was a given, considering that so many in his family had served.

At the time, Evan expected to serve his country for only a few years, then find work back in his small town. Instead, after spending several years as a Green Beret, including deployment during the invasion of Iraq, he became a direct contractor for the US Central Intelligence Agency. In all, Evan was assigned to more than 40 different three-to-five-month rotations to Iraq and Afghanistan. By 2014, however, he was psychologically burnt out and wanted to make a change.

"I met my wife, who had a coffee shop for several years in Denver, in 2014," he recalled. "I had been roasting thousands and thousands of pounds of coffee. I was like, 'Shit, we can put these two things together.'"

Evan decided to build his own thing. He didn't have any money and didn't get a check from anybody. When he left the CIA, he had a little money saved, a 450-square-foot house in the mountains of Colorado, a Toyota Tacoma truck, and a condo he had bought in Seattle. That was it.

"I didn't come from money. I didn't have anything. I had a coffee roaster in my garage I had been using recreationally, and my wife knew how to serve coffee. I was like, 'I'm going to figure it out. You know why? Because I can't work for anybody else. Got to do it. And I got to build a culture of people that also allows me to be me.'"

Evan knew he couldn't conform to corporate life, so he started his own coffee business. He emphasizes that actions speak louder than words, so he found something he was really passionate about and fulfilled by and decided to build a team around that.

"So, nobody wrote you a check," I said to him. "You had a little coffee roaster and now it's Black Rifle, which is freaking iconic. How did that happen? How have you done that? I hear what you're saying about finding your passion, but that's hard."

Evan agreed. I told him how many people have asked me how I knew that bowhunting was my passion. Some people hate when they're told to go find their passion. They think, *What the fuck does that mean?* Anybody can understand that trying out things is good, and that in order to succeed you have to be dedicated. But how did he go from having a passion for coffee to building America's leading veteran-owned and -operated premium, small-batch coffee roastery worth nearly $900 million?

Evan's number one reason? "I kill fear. Fear is a cancer."

"So," I asked, "if people said, 'No, this wouldn't work' or 'You can't do this'?"

"Fuck them," Evan replied. "There's part luck, but most of it is just the fact that I'm stubborn. I'm one hundred percent committed. A lot of people don't have the ability to just endure. This is a grind, man. People look at it, and they think how 'lucky' I am. I've never in my life thought about quitting anything I've done. Not one thing. I've never been close. I'm never gonna *quit*. Never been like that. The quitting mindset isn't in my DNA."

The only time those type of thoughts have ever snuck inside his head has been in the last 10 years of running this massive business, when he feels like he's just getting beat to shit on the ropes day after day.

"In the last ten years, this has pushed me to places physically and psychologically I'd never been before," Evan reflected. "Four and a half, five hours of sleep, if not less, every night. Not being able to pay your bills. The first two years of this company, I sold everything I owned. I didn't have anything left I could sell. I had a brand-new kid, a brand-new wife at home, a rental house that I was missing payments on. I leveraged all my credit cards to the fucking hilt. And that was easy. *Whatever, we'll get it done. I'll figure it out.* Then you grow. We have nine hundred employees now."

The pressure was turned on when Black Rifle Coffee Company was publicly "traded." All of a sudden he was looking at the stock price and dealing with a board of directors, and there were all these complex challenges that he encountered. Like having product in tens of thousands of convenience stores and sitting on $100 million of inventory.

"You can't have a queasy gut looking at a hundred million dollars of inventory," Evan said. "Suck it up, buttercup. It's time to go."

In the midst of growing a gargantuan business and having to weather the tides of the financial markets and interest rates and all of that, Evan knows the value of taking care of your physical and mental health.

"When you're grinding yourself into moondust after four or five hours of sleep at night, you're rewriting your playbook, you're trying to figure out the problem. Dude: You can't go out on Friday night and have a couple beers. You just can't. Because you know why? You're not cognitively functioning enough the next day to make decisions."

Evan hates the stupid saying that when you find something you're passionate about, you'll never work another day in your life.

"That's so stupid. It's like, find something you're passionate about to *grind* away at for a decade. And find something you're passionate about so that when things are fucking so difficult that you don't feel like you can take another step, you'll be able to dig deep and grab onto it and pull it forward to take the next step. That's what it means. It's not like, 'Oh,

I'm going to buy a camera and be a photographer and take pictures of the Eiffel Tower.' Okay, if that means you can sell everything and live off dog food to take pictures, that might be enough to get you through, dude. Maybe."

For Evan, passion is only the starting point, and like so many of the outliers I've met, he doesn't ascribe his success to his exceptional abilities or talent.

"In ten years, I took a company that was in my garage with no outside capital to the New York Stock Exchange where at the time was a $1.7 billion value. And I'm not the brightest bulb on the team, dude. There are smarter, better, more driven men than me in my generation. If I can do it, they can do it.

"I lived paycheck to paycheck. I missed my rent payments. The difference is, I sucked it up and I pushed through the really fucking hard times. I didn't let self-doubt creep in. I took fear for a ride, because it's scary. Scares the shit out of people, man. And that's why you have to have an iron gut, but beyond that, you also have to look back at it and go, 'Okay, let's get it on.'"

I love hunting magazines. I love the feel and smell of them, the photos and the words. I have framed magazine articles and have filled albums with cutout articles. I have full collections of hunting magazines—stacks that drive my wife, Tracey, crazy—that I could never dream of getting rid of. To me, they are an indelible part of history; my bowhunting heritage, if you will.

For me, hunting magazines are never going to die. I prefer them to their online counterparts because they are real. You can touch them. The Internet spawns so much fake stuff that I find myself looking at everything with an untrusting eye. While magazine photos can be doctored, they just seem different in a magazine. The writing seems more legit as well, because for a print magazine to exist, the paper has to be bought, advertisements paid for, and subscriptions sold. Then writers have to put their hearts and souls into words, editors have to pore over that text, and designers have to assemble inspiring graphics. To me, all of this means something. It means everything. Online, none of that has to happen. Anybody can whip up something as fast as writing an email, post it on the Web, and instantly become known internationally, even if the writing isn't worth a hill of beans. That's why magazines have more substance.

When I discovered my passion for bowhunting, I discovered a complementary passion: writing about my bowhunting adventures. After 10 years of bowhunting, I decided to write and self-publish my first book in 1999, titled *Bowhunting Trophy Blacktail*. I shared in *Endure* how it was so expensive to publish that I had to borrow money and barely broke even in the end, but I didn't care. After I published it, I worked hard to sell it with the help of the Bow Rack.

Was *Bowhunting Trophy Blacktail* a failure? Probably. That said, it got the attention of the Eastmans, validating me a little bit to Mike Eastman, which isn't easy. That led to a writing gig with *Eastmans' Hunting Journal*, which brought about a job as editor of the *Eastmans' Bowhunting Journal* magazine and host of the *EBJ* episodes of their TV show. That in turn led to still more opportunities, including more books.

My second book, *Backcountry Bowhunting,* ended up inspiring one of the outliers I was able to have do a Lift Run Shoot with me. Remi Warren is a world-renowned hunter who has been on Outdoor Channel shows like *Apex Predator* and *Solo Hunters.* His podcast, *Live Wild with Remi Warren,* is Joe Rogan's favorite hunting podcast.

"*Backcountry Bowhunting* really spoke to me," Remi told me. "I read that book cover to cover nine hundred times. I would bring it out hunting. I read that book constantly."

It was gratifying to hear that my passion for writing had helped inspire someone like Remi. He is one of the most successful and experienced hunters in the world. I had to ask him the inevitable question that so many want to ask:

"How did you get to be the best?"

"I don't know if I'm the best, but I've put in a lot of time," Remi said. "There are years in the past, before I had family, I would be out in the field—my biggest year—three hundred twenty-three days in one year."

For over 20 years, the hunter who grew up in Nevada has been professionally guiding others and spending time hunting in the mountains and learning the animals.

"It's just like anything," Remi shared. "Thousands of repetitions, and you start to figure it out in a way. And, honestly? Making a lot of mistakes."

Remi said that he has failed at certain things 1,000 times essentially, but then it's number 1,001 when he finally figures it out, and the formula works. It's constantly learning and failing and relearning. For him, he has simply loved to hunt.

Remi said, "When I was a kid, if I would go out on a hunt—let's say we had five days to hunt—and a good buck stepped out on day one, I would never shoot that buck. I would shoot a deer on the last evening of the last day because I loved hunting so much, I didn't

I have a lot of respect for Western hunter Remi Warren. In the hunting industry he's referred to as "the real deal." Couldn't agree more.

want to go home. That's the part of my brain that allowed me to go hunting three hundred twenty-three days."

Another thing that has made Remi so great is that he gravitates toward difficult hunts, where the chance of success can be really low. Those hunts have naturally allowed him to hunt longer. He calls this a weird formula.

"I'm continually pushing the bar for myself," Remi said. "And I think that lent itself to me having a lot of failures, which led to a lot of experience, which led to a lot of success."

Like me, Remi loved reading hunting magazines and watching hunting DVDs. He learned a lot from reading articles like the kind I wrote. Before I wrote about backcountry bowhunting, he thought he and his father were the only two people who'd ever backpack

Cam with Remi Warren

hunted. Nobody else they knew did that or even talked about it. Another thing he enjoyed reading about in my book was about solo hunting.

"I loved to hunt alone, but, at the time, people didn't talk about hunting alone," he explained. "Hunter safety is, like, number one: go hunting with a buddy. And I'm like, *This is bullshit. I want to go hunting when I want to go hunting.* So, to just hear the voice of somebody else doing it was very inspiring."

Just like anything, whether it's spending a decade earning a Ph.D. or building a billion-dollar business, Remi discovered that you have to develop a skill set where you can rely on yourself when you're in the wilderness. As he told me, "Building up that skill set was the intimidating portion of it in a way that asks, *Do I have what it takes?*"

For Remi, what he's doing these days is a dream come true. He can't believe how cool it is to see the positive impact he's having on people. They don't see the hard work and the intention behind things, but that doesn't matter to Remi.

"For me, the coolest part is when I talk to people and they're inspired to do something that maybe they wouldn't have done, or they've learned something, or they've found success because of something that I did that that helped them in some way. Like I've always said, I feel very fortunate to get to spend so much time doing what I love. I *love* hunting. I'm not doing this for any other reason than the fact that I love hunting, and that's just me personally, right? I've made a business and other things, but it's because I love hunting, and it helps me hunt."

Remi now loves sharing all the hunting information and knowledge he has learned.

"If you love hunting, but maybe you get only a week to hunt or a couple weekends here and there, how can I make your time more successful, more impactful, more valuable? That's where I put my focus."

A lifetime of wise decisions has helped Remi get to the point he's at in his hunting journey. It wasn't simply saying, "I like to hunt, so I'm just going to hunt more." He had to set up his life to build and support that dream, to be that dream hunter. Any of those "Must be nice" people need to realize that it comes down to a word Remi used: *intention.*

"You have to be intentional about it," I said. "And your intention was always, 'I love to do this, so I'm going to pursue opportunities that allow me to do it more.'"

"Yeah," Remi agreed, "I was very intentional about it. I intentionally waited later in life to start a family and that kind of thing. I had to be very intentional about a lot of things and choosing the things that I was focused on. It's a lot of time and a lot of hard work and a lot of grinding, in a way, but I loved it, so it didn't feel like work. It just was something

> ## "EVEN IF YOU ARE SUCCESSFUL, 99 PERCENT OF THE TIME SPENT IN THE WILDERNESS ON THIS HUNT IS NOT FUN. THE COUNTRY IS BIG, RUGGED, AND UNFORGIVING. A GUY COULD KILL AN ANIMAL RIGHT IN CAMP, AND IT WOULD STILL BE ONE OF THE TOUGHEST PACKS YOU COULD EXPERIENCE. DESPITE ALL OF THE POTENTIAL AND REAL HARDSHIPS, THE THRILL OF THE HUNT AND THE DESIRE TO SUCCEED CONSUMES ME AND DRAWS ME BACK EVERY YEAR."
>
> —*From* Bowhunting Trophy Blacktail

that I loved, and then I gained the time and the knowledge and experience. Then through that I was able to build something else in a way."

"You've kicked ass the whole way through," I told Remi.

Twenty-five years after writing that for my first book, *Bowhunting Trophy Blacktail,* those words still apply. I still find those thrills. I still feel the desire to succeed. I'm still drawn back more than ever.

Courtney Dauwalter and I were talking about passion for running, and she shared the following with me:

"If it ever gets to the point where I'm hating it and dreading heading out the door for multiple days in a row, then it would alert me to step back and see what's going on. Because running should be fun. You know? This is fun. This is a thing that we get to choose to do with our time and our bodies. I want to keep it in that zone of this enjoyable pastime that I've chosen. And I'm choosing to sign up for these races and choosing to feel that suffering and that pain-cave feeling because that was my decision to do it. I always want to feel like that."

I agree. There are days when I have to get out and get some miles in, but then some parts of me feel like I shouldn't take this for granted. We're so lucky to be able to run mountains. It's not everybody who can just lace up shoes and go out for a long run in the mountains. Whenever I take that for granted, I feel guilty. Sometimes we all get wrapped up around issues, but when I think about it and I'm being objective, I know I really can't complain.

"Even on a bad day," I told Courtney, "we're pretty damn lucky to be able to do this."

"Really lucky," she echoed. "And maybe on those days—because I'll have them too, where it just feels like you drag your feet a little longer to get the shoes on and get out the door—I'll take a route I don't usually or stop and admire the views on those benches on the trails. Testing out every bench you go by. Like, *Why did they put the bench here? Let's test it out.* You know, just appreciating the small things you do every single day. Noticing the little stuff again."

I asked Courtney what she looks forward to the most: Races or adventures? Does she prefer exploring or competing?

"Both," she said with a chuckle. "All of it."

As I mentioned earlier in the book, it was a thrill to have Aaron Rodgers come to Lift Run Shoot. He shared with me how he had a blast and how much he appreciated the experience.

"I'm always just fascinated by other people who do things at a high level and who've figured out how to master a skill or multiple skills," Aaron told me. "When Joe gave me your information and I did a big Instagram search of you, I was so impressed by the work that you've done, your mastery of this, and your willingness to share this with other people and to have a platform to tell a great story. So, for me, I just have so much respect because I know what it takes to be great at what I do, and it's the same focus in anything else."

The legendary quarterback brought up Malcolm Gladwell's book *Outliers.*

"Like Gladwell says, it takes like ten thousand hours to master something," Aaron said. "It just gives you such a keen respect for someone who's spent the time to become a master at something. And I think there's something just beautiful about that life. We all have that inside of us in some way. I think in some people, it's just untapped—giving up on a dream or getting caught in the rat race. But to be able to meet you and to see what you're passionate about—when someone's passionate about something, that's so inspiring."

I mentioned to Aaron what I always say. I can't compare myself to an NFL great like him or any of these incredible people I meet, but the passion we share is similar. I feel like I can learn from any outlier who stands out in their field. It doesn't matter what form their passion takes. It's just how they've poured themselves into it. It's how they're running with their passion.

That's exactly how Joe found me. He was following his passion of hunting and came across this crazy man carrying a rock up this mountain. Joe initially thought, *What the fuck is wrong with this guy?* But then he realized what I was doing and why I was doing it. He reached out with a tweet, and then suddenly I blinked and I'm talking to Aaron Rodgers.

It's still mind-boggling to think of the sort of people I've been training with and talking to. In a recent conversation with Joe, I made the connection that probably every person I've had on my podcast and every person he's had on his share a common theme: They all have a passion for something, and they've used it for a positive endeavor. They've overcome so much, and they all have this one thing that they're obsessed with. They rode that obsession and passion to success.

Whatever you're passionate about can elevate your entire life. I'm an example of that.

The premise of Undeniable is inspiration, lessons learned from legends and what makes outliers, outliers. Along those lines, Lance Armstrong has impacted my life for decades. Watching him dominate the Tour de France, then running with him in the 2008 Boston Marathon, then recently when he came and ran a 10K that I hosted in Austin, Texas, Lance has been the shiny object I've chased in my mind when training, when dealing with detractors, and overall just embracing that chip on my shoulder in an attempt to prove the critics wrong. Say what you want about Lance, the man, but to me he's an icon and one of the greatest competitors to ever walk the earth.

CHASE YOUR PASSION

What is next?
    What bigger adventure can you take?
        How long can this ride last?
            How deeply do you believe in this dream?
Expect a lot of yourself, of your dream. Don't make it a pipe dream, but expect a lot and expect to achieve it.

Don't overdo it. It's easy to overtrain, overcommit, overwork. You can easily go overboard if your expectations are too much. That will lead only to feeling overwhelmed and overcome.

Just go with the flow. Success will come if your work is consistent. Enjoy the journey. The dream might take months instead of days.

It's hard to imagine running 50 miles when you can barely complete a 10K. But just keep running. Just keep your eye on the prize, whatever that might be.

When I was a warehouse supervisor for the Springfield Utility Board, could I dare to imagine the life I have now? No, I couldn't, but I did have a dream to dedicate myself to bowhunting and writing of my adventures. The warehouse supervisor job led to a better job that allowed me to envision unrealistic opportunities and chase them.

If I can chase my passion in a niche like bowhunting and turn it into a story that people care about, anybody can use their own passion to change their life's trajectory.

So: What is your passion and purpose? How far and wide can you dream?

The world is going to want you to doubt yourself. At times it will humble you for lifting your eyes up to the horizon. It will beat you down for running toward your dreams. The world will block you from shooting for success. But you can't stop.

Keep lifting.   Keep running.   Keep shooting.

The world will love you on the way up because you remind them of their dreams. They will hate you when you get to the top because your journey reminds them that they gave up.

Yes, far too many people give up on their passions and their dreams. They look too big and too unrealistic. Stick with them. Be the person who never quits.

Undeniable people are always dreaming bigger, always chasing their passion. To change the world, you must first change the lens through which you see your own.

CHAPTER 9

FACE REALITY

ROY TOUGH:

*Unable to be broken;
able to endure hardships
and misery for a reward*

"THE THOUSAND TIMES THAT HE HAD PROVED IT MEANT NOTHING. NOW HE WAS PROVING IT AGAIN. EACH TIME WAS A NEW TIME, AND HE NEVER THOUGHT ABOUT THE PAST WHEN HE WAS DOING IT."[11]

—*Ernest Hemingway,* The Old Man and the Sea

"No matter where you go, I will always be around . . ."

Roy gently sang the classic Badfinger song next to me in our base camp tent on Kodiak Island. We had completed 12 days of hunting. He had arrowed three buck, two being Pope & Young class, and I had harvested two Pope & Young–caliber buck myself. As we finished off the remainders of our bland camp food and waited to be picked up by our pilot in a couple hours, all we could do was talk about what we were going to eat when we were out of the bush and back to civilization.

"I want an extra-large pizza with as many toppings as possible," I said. "And lots of extra cheese."

"And some double bacon cheeseburgers," Roy added.

We had survived another hunt on Alaska's largest island. Roy and I experienced the wilds of Kodiak Island a number of times over the years. It was always a logistical challenge to hunt remote; you never knew what the harsh weather of early November might bring. Big Sitka blacktail bucks always kept us hungry for our next trip to the island. We lived for hard hunts like these.

Just as I was swallowing the last bite of camp food, Roy stopped humming and rose to his feet.

"I just realized I still have a deer tag," he said.

"Really?" I asked him.

"I gotta stay. I'm not leaving for a hamburger."

He told me to tell the pilot to come back in three days, weather permitting. Never mind that his wife and kids were expecting him home later that night. Our pilot wasn't planning on coming back and may have had plans of ferrying other hunters somewhere else on the island. Of course, I needed to get back home to my job at the Springfield Utility Board; otherwise, I would have stayed with him.

Roy was committed to *more* success and willing to stay in the wilds of Kodiak Island alone to achieve it. The next day Roy ended up arrowing his biggest buck.

This was no surprise. After Roy moved up to Alaska, he had become a legend. For those of you who don't know, there are different types of hunting. There's lower 48 hunting, which can be hard, especially when you're hunting rugged wilderness like the Eagle Cap

On this remote moose hunt in 2007, Roy and I called this moose in but noticed its antlers weren't wide enough for me as a nonresident of Alaska to kill it legally. It needed to be 50 inches wide, and we didn't think it was. So I asked Roy, "Do you want to arrow it with my bow?" For him, as an Alaska resident, it was legal. We had shot each other's bows so much over the decades we'd hunted together I could take his bow and kill an animal (I did just that on POW Island when I killed a black bear with his bow) and he could take my bow and do the same. As the moose was coming in, I handed him my bow and release and he made a perfect shot on the bull, putting it down quickly. Then the work began.

on your own. There are wild, unforgiving places that hold grizzlies and wolves and lions and bears, so the lower 48 can be intimidating for people, but it's not Alaska. Up in Alaska, it's another level of hunting.

In 2015 I went up to Alaska and spoke as the keynote at the Alaskan Bowhunters Association banquet, and all I could think was: *Why am I talking to these guys?* I might be decent down in the lower 48, but these guys are tip of the spear with regard to hunting. They're so frickin' tough, so capable. What could I possibly tell them about bowhunting that they didn't already know? A lot of people in Alaska are tough just because it's tough

to live there. The conditions are hard, and it makes for hearty men and women. They love the challenge of the mountains. Sure, there are some very famous bowhunters in Alaska, but most of them are just grinders who love to hunt and provide for their families. They don't need to get a bunch of attention for it; they're just badasses in the mountains, and they get it done. They're tough, tough bowhunters that any other hunter should look up to.

This was the culture that Roy moved into. I know that it can be hard for an outsider from the lower 48 to earn respect up there, so to get the opportunity to speak at this event twice was incredible. Most of the time, what I wanted to talk about was Roy. In general, I hunt only with a small group of people who are badasses, but Roy was the biggest badass of anyone I knew. After he went up to Alaska and began to earn respect from the most accomplished hunters there, it gave me great pride. Everybody was learning or hearing or telling stories about this bowhunter from Wasilla named Roy Roth.

If there is any trait that an undeniable person carries, it's being tough. Roy set the bar for toughness.

"THERE'S A RACE OF MEN THAT DON'T FIT IN, A RACE THAT CAN'T STAY STILL; SO THEY BREAK THE HEARTS OF KITH AND KIN, AND THEY ROAM THE WORLD AT WILL."

—*Robert W. Service (1874–1958), British-born poet, "The Men That Don't Fit In"*

One of the first truly hard men I ever met in my life was my grandpa. Bob Seibold was one of the very best quarter horse trainers anywhere. He was as tough as he was talented. While he was hard, he was also fair. He was a man's man, and I learned so much from him. He was also someone who died much too young.

I was a junior in high school when I went to work at Grandpa's ranch in eastern Oregon. There was no babying at all. He taught me what hard work really meant. He used to say to me, "If you can't handle it, go get some sugar tit from your mom. Cry to her, and she can baby you. We don't cry here."

He was tough, and I'm so thankful for that grit.

Right after I fell in love with bowhunting, I began to learn about a certain breed of bowhunters who became legends to myself and Roy. People like Fred Bear, the first world-famous bowhunter. Or Chuck Adams, who redefined how bowhunting success was measured, as he has killed five official Pope & Young world-record animals. I would look at them and think, *How can I get to do what they do? How can I experience that type of life?* Their inspiration helped me set goals—*big* goals. Roy and I used these other men as measuring sticks.

Another of those measuring sticks was Bart Schleyer. He was a true legend. After Roy moved to Alaska, he began to tell me stories about Bart. Roy got to know Bart at Foster's Taxidermy in Wasilla, where he would hang out and tell stories in between hunts. Bart worked for the owner, Dan Foster. Roy told me stories of Bart building a longbow and sheep hunting with heads he had made from obsidian that he'd personally sharpened and lashed to his wood arrow. "He's a beast," Roy told me. If Roy said someone was a beast, no more questions needed to be asked. When Bart was 49 years old, he was killed and eaten by a grizzly bear while bowhunting moose on his own in the Yukon.

Like Bart, so many of these men who were legends ended up dying far too young. It seems like you won't generally live a long time in the mountains, but your life will be a rich one. Not financial wealth, but a wealth of a life well lived and full of adventure. This was the sort of life I longed for. These legends were ones that I looked up to, and I wanted to follow in their footsteps.

Paul Schafer was another of those legends. With his 85-pound recurve bow, he took down lions and Cape buffalo in Africa, brown bears in Alaska, bighorn sheep, and trophy deer. At 5'10" and 190 pounds, he was as strong as an ox. He died at the age of 45 in a tragic ski accident on a mountain. The book *Silvertip: The Life and Adventures of Paul Schafer, Master Bowhunter and Bowyer* by Robert Windauer provides an incredible account of this legendary hunter.

Roy and I knew of people who would try acting tough and, to validate this, might compare themselves with guys down the street. We knew about a different breed of men, and that's who we compared ourselves to. These men were as hardcore and hearty as they come. An average man? No comparison. They were just different, the kind of men who didn't fit in with society.

Whenever I've heard something inane from people, like, "Why do you pull that much weight with your bow? You don't need a ninety-pound draw," I've always wondered why they're so concerned about questioning my approach. It's not even truly questioning; it's trying to make what I do seem unnecessary as a way to make themselves feel better because they can't pull such a stout bow. Whereas I'm focusing on guys who pulled *more* than me because I want to mimic their approach and mindset. The guys who pulled 90

The last year Roy Roth and I hunted together, in 2015, we made the most of it. On this hunt in July, I killed this giant brown bear, which was 9-foot 6-inches, another 7-footer, and a black bear, all with one perfect arrow per bear. Then in September we had an epic moose hunt where I killed a great bull. This, our last hunt together, is captured in a film called The Tribute.

to 100 pounds with a recurve bow and were killing grizzlies? That's who I wanted to emulate. Someone might ask, "Why do you carry a seventy-pound rock up a mountain?" They ask this as a rhetorical question, as it doesn't matter why—they just want to say it seems pointless. They look for reasons to do less, while I'm looking at the guys who carried 200-pound packs of dead animals in the mountains. That's who I compare myself to. So, why are these people hung up on comparing themselves with me? I say compare yourselves with those guys and step up your game.

Roy was in the category of these legends.

Years ago, I had a television network interested in having me as part of its lineup, so I filmed and edited an amazing hunt of Roy's as a sample, or pilot, for a show we called *Beast Mode Bowhunting*. Why not feature the toughest living legend out there? Roy was an example of what beast mode meant to me, but the network didn't like it. They'd expected the pilot to have me playing the role of a larger-than-life hunting "superhero" training hard and going on extreme hunts.

"I'm no superhero," I told them. "I'm not going to start acting like one."

If they wanted to watch a true superhero, this hunt of Roy's was as extreme and intense as it gets.

"I guess we don't need to worry about the show, then," I told them.

That was that. I had already hosted TV shows like *Eastmans' Hunting TV* and *Elk Chronicles*, along with being on other hunting shows a number of times. I didn't really care, and I still don't care about doing just another show unless it's exactly what I want to do. What I wanted to do was a show with Roy. To show the rest of the world what I already knew. What it's like to follow in the footsteps of a legend. Since we couldn't come to an agreement on the show's concept, Roy and I focused on other things. No biggie to us. Nothing could stop us from doing what we loved.

I was Roy's number one fan. I believed in him just like he believed in me. In the hunting industry, talking shit is just something that happens. It's hard to earn respect, but I knew that Roy would never talk shit about me. We were like brothers. Whenever some moron would say something negative about Roy, I couldn't resist responding, "You're not Roy. He's ten times tougher than you'll ever be." I knew this because true outliers don't talk shit, and if you talk shit, you don't have what it takes and likely never will.

Even though Roy was the nicest guy in the world, it was tough to earn his respect. For example, he once took a guy into Oregon's Three Sisters Wilderness for a scouting trip lasting a couple days. I saw Roy after he got home.

"How'd that guy do?" I asked.

"He's kind of a whiner," he replied. Roy wasn't being malicious, just his bluntly honest self.

"What was he whining about?"

Roy proceeded to tell me that they didn't set up the tents very well, so when a big storm came through and started pouring rain, they got doused.

"Our sleeping bags were laying in water, and we were just soaked all night," he told me. I couldn't help laughing. "He's whining about being soaked in the tent?"

"Yeah, but what are you gonna do?" Roy said with a shrug. "You don't whine about it. It's just the way it is."

Roy had his own measure of toughness, and it was really hard for others to live up to it.

In one article that I wrote about Roy, I asked him how he was so successful on some of the toughest bowhunts in the world.

"Not one hundred percent sure what my key to success is," Roy answered. "I think it is probably a lot of little things. Above all, I always stay positive! I try to learn from people who know more than me, and I try to make my own luck by doing the extra stuff. Above all, I believe God blessed me with certain gifts to use for His glory."

Those people that Roy and I looked up to and compared ourselves with—the ones who we tried to learn so much from—all died. The truth is that you can live for only so long at this level of pushing beyond what other men have done. The mountains will never let you get away with that forever.

Bowhunters aren't the only badasses out there. Since I've been doing the Lift Run Shoot experience, I've spent many incredible days with some hardcore individuals. Each time, I've heard that same inner voice as when I was giving that speech in front of those Alaskan hunters. *What the hell am I doing talking to this undeniable person? I'm just some regular small-town bowhunter.* The good thing is that I feel like a lot of people can relate to me, so when I talk to outliers, I can be almost a translator for the rest of us who aren't.

It was quite the honor to be able to share Lift Run Shoot with former US Marine Dakota Meyer. A veteran of the war in Afghanistan, Dakota was awarded the Medal of Honor for his actions during the Battle of Ganjgal on September 8, 2009, in Kunar Province. He

Dakota Meyer, Medal of Honor recipient and a man I am honored to call friend

has devoted his life to motivating and helping veterans and civilians through his podcast *You're Human*, speaking, and writing. He's also the founder of the Own the Dash Gym in Austin, Texas, and Dash Hydrate, an energy drink. I've followed everything he's done for quite a while, so I was excited to learn more about his mindset. Dakota has the sort of mindset of a guy who starts running to get in shape, hears about a 100-mile ultra, and signs up for it. So, what was he thinking going all in for an ultra?

"I don't believe in the mindset of thinking that there's something I can't do if I want to do it," Dakota told me. "The only difference is if I want to do it or not."

Dakota ran track and played football in high school but admits he wasn't anything great. In the Marine Corps, he ran a lot, but after getting out, he followed a very typical path of drinking every day and not living a good life. He ended up at 265 pounds and decided to change his lifestyle. The 100-miler he'd signed up for ended up being canceled, but he entered the Austin Rattler 50K (31 miles) and crushed it.

"I'm not really an emotional human being, but, man, at mile twenty-six, I felt emotion," Dakota said. "Your mind just goes to a place. It was really humbling for me, because I got to this place to where I started hurting. And I just remember thinking to myself, *Why are you doing this? Nobody cares if you finish, and nobody cares if you don't. Who cares?*"

For this former US Marine, the pain and doubts were something he hadn't experienced in a long time. For a lot of the race, Dakota was on his own, without anybody watching or cheering him on or caring how much he hurt. He could have stopped at any time, but he realized that this was something he needed in his life. We both agreed that something like a 50K is a sufferfest.

"The big thing with the hundreds and the two hundreds and even a 50K, there's some peaks and valleys," I said. "If you end up in a low spot, a valley, you don't stay in the bottom of that valley forever. Most people get to that valley, and they pull the ripcord. They're out there and think, *I can't deal with it.*"

I mentioned Courtney Dauwalter once quitting a 100-mile ultra at mile 60 because she hurt so bad, and then realizing that this was just part of racing ultras: dealing with the self-doubt and the pain and being in the valleys. You'll always come out of them, but you won't if you quit. So, you just keep going.

Dakota has the same mentality that Roy and I had: If anybody else has done something, why can't he do it? They've gotten through this, so he can, too.

"Resiliency is nothing more than the ability to stay in suffering so that you can learn more of the lesson," Dakota said. "Because you don't get better unless you're uncomfortable, right? You don't grow. You don't move the needle any—internally, emotionally, physically, or mentally—unless you're suffering."

Part of Dakota's mindset comes from his childhood of growing up on a farm where everything was results driven. It doesn't matter how you feel on a farm, he said, because you have all these animals relying on you to feed them and take care of them. It doesn't matter what the weather is outside; you still have a responsibility. This impacted Dakota, along with being in the Marine Corps.

Corporal Dakota Meyer was in the village of Ganjgal in Kunar Province, Afghanistan, when he and his team were ambushed by Taliban fighters. The following is an excerpt from his Medal of Honor citation:

Moving into the village, the patrol was ambushed by more than 50 enemy fighters firing rocket-propelled grenades, mortars, and machine guns from houses and fortified positions on the slopes above. Hearing over the radio that four US team members were cut off, Corporal Meyer seized the initiative. With a fellow Marine driving, Corporal Meyer took the exposed gunner's position in a gun-truck as they drove down the steeply terraced terrain in a daring attempt to disrupt the enemy attack and locate the trapped US team. Disregarding intense enemy fire now concentrated on their lone vehicle, Corporal Meyer killed a number of enemy fighters with the mounted machine guns and his rifle, some at near-point-blank range, as he and his driver made three solo trips into the ambush area. During the first two trips, he and his driver evacuated two dozen Afghan soldiers, many of whom were wounded. When one machine gun became inoperable, he directed a return to the rally point to switch to another gun-truck for a third trip into the ambush area, where his accurate fire directly supported the remaining US personnel and Afghan soldiers fighting their way out of the ambush. Despite a shrapnel wound to his arm, Corporal Meyer made two more trips into the ambush area in a third gun-truck accompanied by four other Afghan vehicles to recover more wounded Afghan soldiers and search for the missing US team members. Still under heavy enemy fire, he dismounted the vehicle on the fifth trip and moved on foot to locate and recover the bodies of his team members. Corporal Meyer's daring initiative and bold fighting spirit throughout the six-hour battle significantly disrupted the enemy's attack and inspired the members of the combined force to fight on. His unwavering courage and steadfast devotion to his US and Afghan comrades in the face of almost certain death reflected great credit

upon himself and upheld the highest traditions of the Marine Corps and the United States Naval Service.

Reflecting on the carnage of that day, Dakota recalled feeling helpless after seeing bodies everywhere and watching so many people die.

"There was nothing you could do to stop this suffering at that time," he expressed. "I was scared to death. I'm scared for the people that I cared about, and I was scared for myself. I never thought that I would ever make it home. There were guys getting hit left and right, and there's nothing you could do about it."

Like so many true warriors in the military, Dakota doesn't consider himself a hero for what he did that day.

"I truly believe this with every moral fiber of my being: What I did that day is something that every human being that walks the face of this planet is capable of doing. It's not a story of heroism. It's not a story of a badass. It's none of that. All that represents is what people are capable of if they believe in it. 'Cause it's bigger than them, and they love people more

Dakota Meyer

than they love themselves. That's it. That's what you're capable of doing when you have those two things. There was nothing awesome that I did that day. My teammates were trapped. There were good people who were suffering, and I was willing to give my life, whether it was for the Afghans in there, whether it was for my teammates. It didn't matter. They were good people, they were actively suffering, and I was in a place where I could do something about it to try to make it better, and I was going to do that."

I was surprised to hear Dakota's takeaway regarding that event:

"The truth is that day is the biggest failure of my life," he told me. "I think you can try your best. You can work hard. You can find loopholes to take off the responsibility of the failure that you had. No. I failed astronomically, but I don't want that narrative to ever change, because now that I faced it, now that I haven't tried to ignore it, now I can use it to give me the lessons of every part of my life today. It's given me the ability to help others."

I asked him about feeling the responsibility of failure even though the facts clearly showed that he wasn't in control of the events that happened and that he couldn't have saved those guys in that ambush.

"I think failing is nothing more than not getting the results you set out to get," Dakota answered. "We have gotten this mentality that if we do everything right and if we work hard and we want it bad, then we're not going to fail. But that's just not reality."

I restated what I heard Dakota saying. "So, you do the best you can. You did everything you could. And you still fail."

"Yeah, and you know what? It's awesome because it's been the biggest piece of me today. I know what losing feels like, and I'm going to do everything I can to not have to feel like that again, but if I do, I can get through it. And guess what? When other people lose and when other people are down, I have this level of empathy for them because I know what it feels like to be in their position, and now I can help them get through it. I can get on that level with them and try to help them get through that piece. And it's important. It's important to feel these things and to face this reality, because the reality is, man, if you don't face it head-on, you can't ever get past it."

We all have events in our lives that have impacted us, Dakota told me. Dates that have changed the way we think or feel about life. Moments where we have learned something, where we've been tested and where we have lost and where we have grown.

Dakota said he feels fortunate. "I got to watch the very best of human beings, and I got to watch the very worst of what humans are capable of. I got to save people. I got to kill people. I felt sad. I felt every emotion that day. I lost everything that I cared about that day. I also gained a ton from it. I got all that in one day. I was also tested. Would I be who I said I would be? I got to prove that. The most impactful thing that happened to me that day was I got to see what I'm capable of. And now that I know that, I know that no matter what the world throws at me, I'm going to figure it out. Right? I was fortunate to have that moment that day, because most people go their whole life wondering, and I don't have to."

I got to see what I was capable of on October 4, 2015.

I was bowhunting with Kip Fulks and Marc Womack in Colorado trying to get a deer killed in wide-open country. It was a little early in the rut (deer breeding season, when the males get distracted and are easier to get within bow range of), so it was going to be tough. I couldn't help thinking of Roy that week, knowing he was headed up to Pioneer Peak to go sheep hunting. Early on, I'd blown it on a big mule deer. I had gotten in close but just couldn't get it done. That's what's hard about bowhunting. Everything happens in light speed, and then it's over, leaving you with the aftermath.

There are always challenges with every bowhunt—that's what makes them so exciting. I'm used to the mountains, used to using contour as a tool, and I have the ability to climb up to big vantage points in order to see a large expanse. Eastern Colorado is pretty flat, so you have to take advantage of any small rise you can. Nothing happens quickly out there. This type of hunt demands that you put the pieces of a puzzle together and try taking advantage of opportunity. When you get one chance, you have to make good on it.

After missing my shot with the big mule deer, there seemed to be no others left to find. With only two days to go after a week of grinding, I began to hear voices of doubt in my head.

Was that the deer I was meant to kill?

Did I make a mistake?

Am I really not that good after all?

I knew that perfection was the only thing that was going to make this happen. I knew it was crunch time. That day around dusk, I shot a great whitetail from 60 yards. I wasn't certain if the buck had been mortally wounded, but we decided to wait until morning to go get on blood and trail him. Let the arrow's broadhead do its job.

That night, Tracey called me and told me that Roy had fallen to his death off Pioneer Peak.

Suddenly I was faced with the reality that Dakota Meyer was talking about. One of those monumental moments that was going to change my life forever. One of those events that was going to test me and show me whether I was truly tough or not.

Roy died doing the thing he dearly loved, and I ended up hearing about it while I was doing the very same thing.

In my life, there have been only two men that I looked up to. My dad was my hero, and my mentor was Roy Roth. If there's one man who I thought the mountain would never beat, it was Roy.

How does one really know their limits unless they push them to the max? I always say bowhunting is the ultimate test, but now this hunt had become an even more difficult task. I didn't sleep that night, and it took everything for me to simply get moving and head out the door to blood-trail my whitetail. With the guys looking alongside me, I couldn't help thinking of Roy's loss and what this meant for his family and community. What it meant for me.

In the open expanse of Colorado, I could hear Roy's invitation that would change my life when I was only 18 years old:

"Dude, you need to bowhunt."

A hundred memories walked with me. Hunting in pouring rain or snowy mountains or scorching heat. Hard and miserable and rewarding times when we achieved success where not many people would have, and we achieved it together.

We're not going to be able to share the "us against the world" mentality on anything ever again, I thought.

We had so much we wanted to do, so much we talked about doing, so many dreams to chase in the mountains. I had put Roy on a pedestal, and even though I knew that the mountains could always win, and I knew that nobody is immortal, I still thought he was almost indestructible in some way because Roy had taken on every challenge. He had always come home regardless of what happened—always—and it was always positive. It always worked out. It always did.

As I covered the miles looking for the deer, wiping away the tears and feeling completely out of it, I finally heard Kip's voice in the near distance.

"Hey, Cam, we got 'im!"

When I reached Kip, I saw the buck. It was a stud of a whitetail, one I called Roy's Buck. I knew that bowhunting was never going to be the same for me. Any hunting memories without Roy would be different. I no longer had my friend to share them with after the fact, either on the phone or in person.

You can't replace somebody like Roy.

I had gone up to Alaska and hunted with Roy around 30 times on some of the most adventurous, wild hunts anyone could do. Charging brown bears, wounded black bears, majestic sheep, rugged sheep country, everything. *Everything.* The biggest adventures anybody could go on, and I was privileged to share them with a different breed of man. With Roy.

It's never going to be the same. Any trek into the deep wilderness. Any kill I have. Anything.

These memories I have since his death are watered down and muted. They are great, but it's just not the same. The past glories are all marked with pain.

I knew that any future trips to Alaska—if there would be any—would never be the same for me.

Life is competition. No matter what you do in life, there are challenges to overcome. Sometimes we forget this because we can get by in life without dignity. I spoke about this with CrossFit great Rich Froning. He agreed that too many people get soft.

The truth is if you want to rise to the top in anything, it's going to be a dogfight.

"Yeah, and you need to seek out challenges," Rich told me. "There are things that are going to come, but we face them and head through them. All good things come from hard work and through adversity. Nobody gets better just sitting still and being stagnant."

I had a choice after losing Roy. I could stand still in my grief, or I could do what he would have wanted me to do and carry on. So, that's what I've done. It doesn't mean it hasn't been a struggle.

Any compelling story is full of struggle, failure, and self-doubt. Those are the stories we learn from, either when they happen to us or when we hear others share them.

I guess if I were to write a parenting book, this would be the theme. A saga of a young man fucking up as a first-time father. A tale of two boys, one girl, and 10,000 mistakes. I always wanted to be a good dad to them but had no idea what that meant. At first, I tried to rule with an iron fist, but after that failed, I took the approach of, "For fuck sakes, I'll just show you." And that sort of worked because action always speaks louder than words. I had the boys running half-marathons at seven years old and brought them on tough hunts. Somehow—thanks mostly to their mom, no doubt—Tanner, Truett, and Taryn have blown me away with their accomplishments, brains, and pure hearts. I'm lucky to be the dad of three amazing humans who have given my life meaning.

I always wanted my kids to be prepared for everything we go through in life. I wanted them to understand that life's a competition. I might not have taught them a lot of things, but I did show them what it means to be tough. I wanted them to know what they're capable of. The truth is I know they're more talented than I ever was. They're better kids. I was hard on them, especially my sons, and I never cut them slack, but they knew I loved them.

Did I push my kids too hard? Yes. I wanted to expose my kids to adventure at a young age, and since there was no minimum hunting age in Alaska, I brought them up there when they were young. I wanted them to spend time around Roy, for obvious reasons. I thought it was important to get kids away from civilization and the ease of normal life. Did I jump the gun and do this too soon? Some will say yes, and they might be right. Others will say no. I'm no child-raising expert, but I learned over and over what not to do and what doesn't work. I was so focused on the competition of life, and that to succeed you need to be tougher, more hardened, and more willing to sacrifice than everyone else. I preached discipline and taught this through running. So, when I look at my kids, I guess it took the pushing of a too-demanding father and the nurturing and unconditional love of a mother for them to prosper. Their mom, Tracey, is the true unsung hero of their lives. She's the glue that held it all together after I'd tried (unintentionally) to fuck it up. Now the boys are better than me at pretty much everything, and my daughter is the smartest (over a 4.0 GPA at her university as a second-year math major) and sweetest person I know. (That's 100 percent because of her mom.) Again, I feel lucky to be their dad.

I invited Truett on the podcast to share his compelling story of failure and triumph with the world in his journey to set a world record in pull-ups. Hearing him share his hunting journey with me was like someone holding up a mirror to my face, and I didn't necessarily like the picture I saw.

"Growing up, we would go out every single year, not by choice," Truett said. "What I always tell people is, when we were kids, we'd go out hunting with you. We didn't have a choice. And it would be the hardest thing we did all year. And I don't know if you know this about yourself, but you can be pretty intense."

"Me?" I asked with a grin.

"Yeah. Or at least while hunting. And then, for me, I just kind of didn't want to deal with it anymore. Honestly, it's pretty hard getting yelled at. I don't think I wanted to do it. The last hunt that we did for a long time was blacktail. I think I was thirteen, back in 2010, and I didn't hunt again until, I think, 2018. I took, like, an eight-year break from hunting. And it wasn't even that I was busy. I just didn't want to do it. And then when I got reintroduced to it in 2018, I killed a blacktail. That honestly felt really good to do. So, I just kind of got that fire back a little, and then from there, you know, we've been gone just about every year since then."

This part of our discussion was tough to hear. I've made excuses for how hard I was on my kids by first saying that with Tanner, I was too young to know what I was doing. Then with Truett, I'd just say, "Well, life is tough, and if you're going to make it, you'll have to be tough, too." I felt it was up to me to prepare them. Until this podcast with my son, I didn't even realize that he didn't hunt for eight years because of my intensity. That is a flaw of mine, and anyone who has hunted with me knows this. This has caused me to reflect. To me, hunting is not necessarily a sport, as some call it, or "fun," or a vacation; it's truly life and death, which weighs heavy on me. I've gotten better since being so hard on the boys when they were young.

The boys hunted backcountry Alaska for bears as their first big-game hunt; Tanner was 7 and Truett, 11. They hunted Africa and black bears in Hells Canyon in big, rugged country. Tanner killed his first bull elk deep in the backcountry after driving for nine hours and packing in miles with no sleep following his high school football game. To me, this was how it was done. Roy and I did similar things all the time, but at that point I didn't realize Roy Roth was one of the toughest mountain hunters on the planet, and I was fanatical. Subjecting my teenage boys to the types of adventures Roy and I lived for and were defined by wasn't appropriate. I know how unforgiving this world can be, so as a dad I didn't want to be too easy on them, especially my sons. I believed that weak-spirited men feel entitled and exhibit a victim mentality because life's not "fair" or too hard. But I knew that being too hard on my kids would push them away. Parenting in between the extremes with indifference meant bare-minimum

Cam with Truett Hanes and Ed Kinsey

expectations, which often means average results. I see "average" effort every day and that's not what I wanted for my kids. I wanted to raise winners. Young men with no air of entitlement who would make those around them better. You get what you earn and nothing more.

Truett's attempt at the pull-up record began when we met David Goggins back in 2018 and did a 50K with him. After the race, we went to the gym to work out for an hour, and after the workout, Goggins did 100 pull-ups to finish. Truett described this to me.

"He would do five, walk to the other side of the gym, walk back, do five, and he just kept doing that until one hundred. And then I was like, 'Dang, that actually looks pretty cool.' And then I started to do that."

Five years earlier, in 2013, Goggins had broken the Guinness World Record for most pull-ups in a 24-hour period. He did 4,030 pull-ups in 17 hours, 16 minutes. After meeting Goggins, Truett started doing 100 pull-ups a day. Then Goggins sent Truett a video to encourage him.

"You're looking to be a savage," Goggins told Truett in the video. "I see out of Oregon there your dad has a farm, and all that comes out of it is savages. You've joined the ranks, my friend of the savages. Remember that video of 'Who's gonna carry the boats?' You're carrying it, my friend. Stay hard and carrying it proud. Stay savage."

Those words of encouragement and belief ignited Truett. In 2022, after a few years of training, he set out to beat Goggins's record and do 4,100 pull-ups in less time. He was a beast and accomplished his goal. Then he set his sights on another goal: a world record for the most pull-ups in 24 hours. He needed to beat 8,008 pull-ups.

On his first attempt on April 22, 2023, Truett failed to reach his goal.

"I definitely didn't train hard enough, and I found that out on game day, when I got the cameraman to come out and flew people out," Truett said. "Then obviously I failed. I got half of what I was supposed to do, and I was absolutely done. I told myself I am never doing that again because it's miserable, and physically, I probably just couldn't do it. But then I didn't realize how much training actually pays off. I just had to find a different level of dedication."

Truett had texted me to see what I thought. "Do you think I'm a failure if I don't try for the pull-up record again?" he asked. I told him I thought he just needed to take a break. As long as he was working toward something, that was all that mattered. Soon Truett decided to go for it again. He wanted to see this thing through, to see if he could actually do this. So, for the next six months, he trained and focused on breaking the record.

There's a lot of anticipation and anxiety in setting a big goal and knowing that everybody is paying attention and you're putting yourself out there. No matter how strong you are, you can't just pretend that failure is not an option. It could definitely happen.

By the time he had done over 6,600 pull-ups, there was a feeling in the room that things weren't going well. It was obvious that Truett was slowing down. I shared with him the story about Courtney Dauwalter's first 100-mile race, when she reached 60 miles and then quit due to pain. She hadn't realized that pain was a big part of the race and that you had to just push past it.

"So, you told me that's what separates winners and losers," Truett explained. "Winners, when it hurts, they're able to push past it, and that's what makes them great. Whereas other people, they feel pain and then they quit. Then you were like, 'Did you think this was going to be easy?' and 'You're the one who brought this upon yourself.' You never really know what's going to get through to someone when they're just going through hell. But those words stuck with me."

Seeing his wife in tears and feeling the support around him, Truett kept going. There was a moment he shared that he went to the bathroom and looked at himself in the mirror.

"I was like, 'You have more in you,'" Truett said. "'You can do this. You just need to find a different gear.' I went back out, and then I kind of decided I'm going to go ahead and try to do this instead of just feeling sorry for myself and scared of how bad it's going to hurt. I'm just going to try. The worst that's going to happen is I'm going to end up failing, but at least I'll have given it my all."

With the music pounding and all of us cheering him on, Truett kept going and didn't quit. He broke the record and set a new one with 8,100 pull-ups in 24 hours.

As Roy and I used to ask, "Has it ever been done before?" And in this case, it hadn't—until now.

I was proud to see Truett dedicating so much time and effort and mental and physical energy to this accomplishment.

"I don't think people realize how mental a lot of their life is," Truett shared. He had reached that point where he was done mentally, but his body still had more to give. The only thing ultimately that switched was his own belief that he could finish this.

During our conversation, Truett brought up something I used to always say to my kids: "You'll thank me eventually."

All parents probably say that to their kids at one point.

"I guess that's actually true, looking back," Truett admitted. "I'm like, 'Geez, I could have been so soft as a kid.' Like the fact that you just wouldn't really allow it or you wouldn't even entertain the idea of us just being able to do whatever we wanted to do, like just being lazy and playing video games. That's carried over to my adult life and made quite the impression."

"So . . . don't you have something to say to me?" I asked him coyly.

"Thank you, I guess?"

I had to laugh. "Just kidding."

The truth of the matter is that I have to thank God for how blessed I am. Our family is healthy, and we love one another. I have so much. Personally, I feel I don't deserve to be where I'm at. Truett and Tanner have worked their asses off pretty much their whole lives. So, Truett truly earned that world record. He showed just how tough he really is.

Whenever I see our three kids having any kind of success, it does give me a little encouragement that maybe I wasn't a complete failure as a father. It's validation that this mentality does work. You work your ass off, there are rewards. That's all I've tried to really show them. And it seems like they got it, because they're all very hardworking young men.

Destiny defined. That is how I see the wild.

Out in the wilderness, I feel like you can fulfill destiny more than anywhere else. When your arrow flies true, the animal dies. That's destiny because that was meant to happen. If it doesn't happen—if something goes awry and the bear survives—maybe you die? Then that was meant to be, too. In the wilderness, we're fulfilling our destiny. In town, with everything else that's going on, I think your destiny can be interrupted. It can be altered, but out here, I think what's meant to happen will happen. It's pure.

In 2021 I found myself back in the wilds of Alaska, and I felt like I had something to prove. Not to the public and not to myself, but to Roy. I needed this hunt to live up to his memory. Here in this rugged and raw country, you find out who you really are and what you're really about. The outside world can mask who you are and hide different things about your life, but out here all of that is stripped away. Out here all that matters is finding bears, making a good shot, getting food and water, and catching some sleep when you can. That is it. Anything else is a waste of time and mental energy.

It took me years before I wanted to go back to Alaska after Roy's death. I didn't know if I'd ever go back after he fell in the sheep mountains and passed away nearly six years earlier. For 20 years Roy had called the Last Frontier home; without him everything felt different.

Kip Fulks, my former adversary at Under Armour, invited me to join him on a spring grizzly hunt. Over the years, he had become more than a friend and was now a bowhunting blood brother. I thought long and hard before deciding I was ready to chase my bowhunting dreams in Alaska once again. My only goal was to perform in the mountains in a manner that would make Roy proud. This trip was about honoring him. I wanted him to watch down on us and be entertained.

Despite my best efforts, however, I fell short of the standard I expect of myself. Part of me thinks that Roy likely enjoyed watching down on me working hard, helping others with a common goal, failing, owning it, wanting to clean up the mess myself, and then ultimately owning my mistakes. He no doubt watched me make what I thought was a nearly perfect shot at 50 yards on a big grizzly after a long stalk. The arrow hit hard, my razor-sharp three-blade-fixed broadhead lead arrow passing through the grizzly like a hot knife through butter, then burying in the tundra on the far side. It was awesome as the wind held and the bear cooperated. After my shot, I bet Roy watched us follow the heavy, steady blood trail into the thick brush after a couple hundred yards of what I thought was a death sprint. It was a longer trail than I would have liked, but I felt my arrow was only a couple inches left of perfect. These animals are tough and hearty, but I reasoned the bear was no doubt dead after such massive blood loss.

I led the way on the blood trail. After side hilling, the bear took a hard pitch straight down the hill and through the alders.

Last-gasp death sprint, I thought.

Our guide, John Rydeen, followed me with his Remington .300 Ultra Magnum rifle cartridge, and not far back was Koby Fulks, Kip's brother, with a heavy-duty bear gun. Kip and filmmaker Branlin Shockey—yes, Jim Shockey's son—trailed the group, capturing it all on camera. Much earlier in the day, I'd insisted a number of times that I didn't want guns involved in my hunt. Yes, using guns was absolutely legal, as this hunt gives the sportsman an "any weapon" option. I wanted my destiny fulfilled by my arrow only. Either I killed the bear, or there would be some other less desirable outcome, whatever it might be. Either way, I wanted to control the hunt's fate. Fortunately, or unfortunately, depending on your perspective, a grizzly hunt by a nonresident of Alaska requires a guide, and a hunting guide's job is to keep their hunter safe if possible. So, with John being the consummate professional he is, I'd be silly to expect him to do any less than his best. After all, he's been in the business for 21 years and has guided 94 successful grizzly/brown bear hunts. He's a credit to his craft. Experience helps, but nothing is guaranteed in the mountains, and surely not when the bowhunter is pursuing a grizzly. I've killed three Alaskan brown bears with three arrows in years past, and while reading this blood trail across the snow and tundra, I felt sure that I had just killed a grizzly with a single arrow to follow suit. Pushing through the brush while following blood, I heard John behind me say, "Dead bear." I had an arrow nocked, just in case a follow-up shot was needed. John's keen eyes saw the grizzly lying motionless in the brush with its head down. I moved closer to within about 5 to 10 yards, and the bear lifted its head weakly.

"Hold up," John said. "Bear isn't dead."

As it laid its head back down, I eased to my right trying to find a shooting lane.

"Don't shoot," I whispered to the guys toting guns as I moved a little closer. I'm a bowhunter only, and as a romantic of the tradition, having rifles involved in my hunt isn't something I'll ever agree to if asked. I don't want it to sound egotistical, because it's not. It's just a measure of how much bowhunting means to me. There's a line I won't cross. I don't judge others for the weapons they choose to hunt with and don't care about anyone else. I know what's important to me and my purpose: death by arrow or nothing. The bear raised its head once again, and this time its haze had cleared some as we locked eyes. This is always a key moment when hunting true predators. I came to full draw but all I had for a shot was the grizzly's head, which is notoriously made of thick bone and has caused even bullets to ricochet off the skull. In other words, not a high-percentage bowshot. Holding at full draw, I dropped to one knee.

At that moment, I was four yards from the bear.

The difference between a grizzly and a deer or elk is that a prey animal will burst from its last bed and run away from its pursuer, likely dying after a short burst. Grizzlies are not prey animals. They are predators, and they survive in this country by being aggressive and keeping their spot at the top of the food chain, unchallenged.

Sure enough, my bear exploded from its bed and charged me. It was weakened and had to try to fight through thick alders to get to me. Still at full draw, I released my arrow, striking the grizzly in the chest as it lunged toward me. John fired his rifle from the left of me and Koby fired his from a little behind John, also to my left. A bullet hit my bear in the

hip, diverting it from its path toward me and taking its feet out from under it. John shot once more through the top of its back to neutralize the threat.

"Fuck," I cussed. "Fuck!"

I wasn't rattled at all, but I was certainly frustrated that I couldn't get an arrow off before the bear charged. Frustrated that I even needed to shoot another arrow at all. But, most of all, frustrated that others had to weigh in on my destiny, especially with guns. All those feelings came to a crescendo and had me pissed. I gathered myself, approached the fallen bear, and silently offered my respect. Then I thanked John and Koby for being so unflappable under a stressful circumstance. Kip, Branlin, Koby, John, and I succeeded on this hunt together. I consider this a team effort—to say otherwise would be lying.

It makes me sick when an animal suffers more than I think it should in dying from my arrow, and, for whatever reason, this bear hadn't died from what I felt was a mortal wound. My other brown bears died in seconds, and that was, of course, my goal on this and all my hunts. I dedicate my life to being a merciful bowhunter, which is why this experience leaves a pit in my stomach. I'll second-guess myself forever. Should I have given the arrow more time to do its job? The bear would have bled out in just a few more minutes, I guess, but who really knows? It was late, and maybe my desire to recover my first-ever grizzly pushed me, when I should have suggested we be more patient and let the bear die without one last adrenaline surge. I needed to be more disciplined. I wasn't, and that's disappointing.

I wasn't upset with my partners. In fact, just the opposite. I am bonded to them for life through this hunt and this experience. Pursuing incredible animals in truly magnificent and wild country with the best of men is something every bowhunter dreams of. No matter what, I'll never take it for granted. While I caused this bear's death, I can't ever consider it a true bow kill, since a rifle was involved. I also can't say it won't mean just as much as a bow kill to me because of the memories this bear's life and death has etched in our collective minds. As I've said many times, the hunt is more than the kill. The kill is but a part of the journey. Yes, I let myself down by not making a perfect shot and causing this bear to suffer longer than it should have, but in my heart, I hope that Roy knows I tried my best. Even though I'm not an infallible bowhunter, I'll own my errors, then work harder and sacrifice more to improve upon them. I believe destiny best defines hunting in the wilds of Alaska, because it's only here that your fate lies in your hands. Your ability, your decisions, the outside world, and all sorts of other factors beyond your control weigh in, but here, my arrow either kills a grizzly or wounds a grizzly. If all the outside circumstances are removed, the grizzly either dies or attacks me. That's the way I like it. That's what I see as a fitting end.

This didn't end that way.

In this case, other people were part of the equation, which is just the way it goes. My destiny was interrupted. I did get an arrow off, hitting the bear in the chest as it charged. Would that have killed it before it could have killed me? I don't know. My destiny was removed from 100 percent of my actions. If given a choice, I always prefer hunting and blood-trailing alone because I know that the mountains always give us the truth.

The test we seek is not to kill an animal. It is to test ourselves. To rise up in the face of a great challenge and either fail or succeed. To live to hunt another day.

As I packed out the bear, reservations aside, I couldn't have been more grateful for

Roy Roth and I on our last hunt together for moose in remote Alaska

sharing this hunt with these men in this special, magical country. I also couldn't help being overcome with emotions.

I remembered the legend who used to walk in this country. The toughest and best woodsman I had ever known. If you put a bow in Roy Roth's hands, something was going to die. He was also the most optimistic person you have ever come across. I've been bowhunting for 35 years and hunted with some amazing people—some very capable, incredible bowhunters themselves—but none of them were like Roy.

My mind drifted to our last hunt together, miles deep in the wilds of Alaska. We were four miles back and up over this big ridge and got this bull moose killed. I could still picture Roy breaking down that bull around midnight while he sang. He was always singing and always loved the work part. He always loved being miserable.

I remember that night as we lay in our tent, soaking wet. Everything was wet because it had been snowing. We were eating all our food because we were getting out of there, so we were stuffing our faces with as much candy and treats as we could. Wrappers were littered around us. We were just having the best time of our lives singing and reading stories. That was something Roy loved having me do. I'd pack magazines for the hunt, and I would just read him stories at night. I love to read, so anytime I was reading something and Roy was around, he wanted me to read it out loud to him. When we were at hunting camp, I'd read hunting articles; we would just lay there in the tent, and I'd read while he listened. Camp life with Roy was always great.

I didn't think I could come back to Alaska, but destiny had called. As Roy once told me about having success while hunting, it was just all about being out there. "If you're out there, anything can happen," he said.

I had to be tough and suck it up and come back to this place to honor my best friend.

This incredible hunt was something he surely watched down on and enjoyed. We lived for these moments: charging grizzlies, big boars, incredible country, and hard work.

Thanks for still guiding me from above, Big Roy. I miss you. Man, you would have loved this adventure. It was the wild bowhunting roller coaster we dreamt of incessantly.

"This is for you," I told Roy. "Miss you, but we're still getting it done. 'Til we meet again." Somewhere in the distance, I could hear Roy singing.

WRITE YOUR STORY

What story are you writing with your life? Have you even begun to put the pen to paper yet?

It's important to share stories like the kind that are in this book. Stories of incredible men and women. We should celebrate what it means to be tough. We should spotlight those who are determined and focused. We should praise all of those outliers who are passionate and live a life with purpose.

Are you one of those? Then keep going.
  Let's keep setting the standard.
    Let's keep pushing the envelope.
      Let's keep sharing legendary stories.
        And let's make our own stories ones that
        people might read in the future.

So, get out there. Be different and daring.

Become immersed in your passion.

Revere and respect the greats who have come before you.

Embrace the daunting challenges that come your way. The environment, the odds, the unforgiving setbacks. When things get tough, keep going. That's what makes a great story. That's a great opportunity to overcome. To believe in yourself, to get it done.

Life is competition, and there are many arenas. If you're going to compete, you'd better be prepared. Winning is the easy part. Getting up and forging onward when you get knocked down is all that matters when chasing audacious goals.

When you've lived through the toughest conditions in your arena, then you get out in the regular world, and it's a cakewalk. You get to come home to share your story with others, and that's a beautiful thing. People love to hear stories of greatness. How great can you make yours?

We all still have a story left to tell. What page are you going to write today?

CHAPTER 10

MAKE THE MOST IMPACT

PURPOSE:
*The reason for which
something is done or
created or for which
something exists*

"WHAT DO YOU WANT TO BE KNOWN AS?
I THINK ABOUT THAT ALL THE TIME. WHEN
YOU'RE GONE, WHAT DO YOU WANT TO BE
KNOWN FOR? I WANT TO BE KNOWN
FOR BEING A FUCKING SAVAGE KILLER
MOUNTAIN MAN. THAT'S IT."

—*Kip Fulks, in the film* Once We Were Wolves

Find your purpose.

I found my purpose when I discovered bowhunting. I've spent a life pursuing that purpose and sharing that journey with others.

Does your purpose have to be bowhunting? Of course not. Your purpose doesn't have to even be physical. Running, fighting, competing—those are all activities that will make your life better, that will make you stronger. Maybe you were meant for a different purpose.

As many of you know, the story I shared in the last chapter about going back to Alaska for the first time after Roy's death was documented in the incredible film *Once We Were Wolves*. To date, the video has a million and a half views. It's an epic story full of adventure and meaning that truly honors Roy Roth. The creator of the film was filmmaker Branlin Shockey, a man who has spent decades perfecting his craft of telling hunting adventures through film with a goal of igniting the ancestral human spirit. He has such an incredible ability to capture things with the camera that other people wouldn't see or think to capture and then to turn it into a story.

The irony of Branlin's career is that hunting seemed like the natural path he was meant to go down. He is son of Jim Shockey, the ultimate hunting badass. Jim has had awesome adventures with his muzzleloader all over the world. As an impressionable youth, I wanted to be a bowhunting Jim Shockey. My first step was to rock a bandana around my neck like Jim did. Over the years, I've continued to be a huge fan. He's had such an impact on me as a hardworking hunter and for his talents as a writer.

Jim Shockey isn't the only hunting icon in the family. Jim and Louise Shockey had two children: Branlin and his sister, Eva. I think of Eva as the Princess Diana of hunting. Not only has she been a trailblazer in the hunting industry, but she's also a savvy entrepreneur and a dedicated mother. I hosted Eva for an incredible Lift Run Shoot, during which we talked about everything from long-range bow shooting, professional jealousy, and living up to your personal brand.

Coming from a family like that, it's surprising that Branlin didn't share his father's and sister's passion for the hunt.

"I was not a hunter," Branlin told me. "If I did some hunting, I wasn't hunting first. I don't watch hunting movies or films, and if I do, I don't look at them in terms of how big that elk was."

He went to a university as a business major, thinking he wanted to go into finance or marketing, but his father persuaded him to come film a hunting series, something Branlin admitted he knew nothing about. For the next six months, he learned all he could about video editing. The result has been a career as a filmmaker. He feels honored to be in the position that he's in. For him, it all comes down to hearing stories that affect him.

"I try to be as creative as possible," Branlin told me. "But I believe—I truly believe—that we tell ourselves stories in order to live. The writer Joan Didion said that. I want to tell great stories, and I want to impact other people's lives. Obviously, my family and my kids aside, that's all I want to do. I want people to look at something I've done and be like, 'Holy shit! There's something there that he gets.' And then I want to positively impact as many people as possible. That's it. Through whatever creative medium."

Branlin believes that you can tell stories in any medium you want, whether it's telling big production stories in the theater, telling stories on Instagram, telling them around the campfire or over the phone. For him, the central theme of those stories involves the outdoors and inspiring people to do more.

"I truly believe that there's a disconnection that we are not even close to addressing or figuring out," Branlin said. "I think that there are millions of people that are not living their best life because they don't understand what that really means. They understand necessities—providing for your family however you can. But I'm talking about what you do on the weekends. I'm talking about why you haven't called your buddy up from high school and done anything cool like you did in the old days. We used to build forts, used to go adventure in the forest, and it was all fun. What happened to that? I just think there's more out there for everybody, from the most successful people on the

Film producer Branlin Shockey put together the film Once We Were Wolves, *which chronicled my return to Alaska six years after Roy Roth passed away. My goal was to hunt in a way that would make Roy proud.*

planet to just the average everyday men and women living their lives. I just want to be part of that."

Someone once said, "Success is measured by the number of stories a man has." Branlin is indeed a success story himself. I'm grateful and humbled that we're working together and that we can shine a different light on hunting.

Embrace your purpose.

An inspiring example of someone doing this is Tulsi Gabbard, an American politician, military veteran, and onetime presidential candidate who broke barriers in the political landscape. Having served as the US representative for Hawaii's Second Congressional District from 2013 to 2021, Tulsi was a 2020 presidential candidate and still serves in the Army Reserves. She's a rare mix of wit and charisma. I have a lot of respect for Tulsi and was honored to have her come for a Lift Run Shoot.

Midway up the mountain for a run, we stopped so that Tulsi could hoist the rock onto her shoulder.

"The mountain never lies," I said to Tulsi. "You can convince yourself you're in good shape. You can do this or that. But the mountain will be like, 'Well, we'll find out!' I've never made the mountain quit. It's tested me, though."

"That's one thing I appreciate about remaining in the military," Tulsi replied. "Whether it's a rock or a run or whatever, I don't care who you are, what your rank is, or who you think you are. It keeps you honest."

Tulsi was a beast. Not many men or women have put that rock on their shoulder and hustled up the steep part of my mountain like she did. She's an example of a tough political leader, the sort we desperately need in our day and age. Someone not only smart, of course, but also strong and capable. I wasn't surprised to see her strength, but I was still totally impressed.

So, how did this girl growing up in Hawaii end up becoming such a political superstar? For Tulsi, it began with a mindset that was formed partly by the tropical paradise she lived in.

"I first learned how to swim," she explained. "The swimming lessons were out in the ocean. I surfed a lot and just really grew up appreciating nature. And so, as a teenager, there were different things I was involved with around the protection of water and clean water."

When a businessman wanted to come in and build a landfill over one of the largest water aquifers on the island that she grew up on, Oahu, Tulsi got involved with a group that was trying to stop it. Even as a teenager, she knew that building a landfill was a bad idea, because once that water aquifer became contaminated—whether in a year or 20 years—Hawaii didn't have the option like other states to have water trucked in or funneled in any other way. Once that source was gone, it was gone for lifetimes.

"We started gathering signatures and trying to figure out how do we stop this thing and lift the voices of the people up," Tulsi told me. "There was a powerful person in the state senate at that time who was greasing the wheels for his buddy, the landfill operator." When the citizens' anti-landfill movement prevailed, she recalled, "It was an incredible experience for me as a teenager to see, 'Wow, so this is how we can make change.'"

After cofounding a nonprofit organization that would clean up trash off beaches on the weekends, Tulsi grew frustrated at how futile their work seemed to be. Every weekend that she and the other volunteers came back, there would be more trash to remove. This got her thinking of how to change things on a broader scale, so Tulsi came up with a fun educational program that they presented to elementary school kids across the state.

As Tulsi explained, "We were just teaching them that when you throw your soda can out the window, and it gets down into a storm drain, it ends up out in the ocean where you like to go surfing every weekend. The first, second, and third graders were just sitting there watching with bright eyes. It was so cool for me to see them connect the dots, like, 'Oh, okay, so there are consequences to my actions.'"

When Tulsi was 21, a seat opened up in the Hawaii statehouse. She was at a juncture in her life where she could either go to school and "study political science and earn my bachelor's degree, or I could go and offer to serve and do it. Don't talk about change, *be* the change. That's what drove me to first run for office in Hawaii."

The candidate herself went canvassing from home to home. Many of the people who opened their doors expressed surprise at how young she was, but Tulsi had a brilliant response.

"My answer to them," she recalled, "was, 'Don't you want young people to go and work hard for you, bringing fresh ideas and a new perspective to the challenges that we face? Or do you want a whole bunch of people who've already lived their lives, who have retired and are kind of kicking back and taking it easy a little bit?'"

Tulsi won, although she never had any aspirations for a political career. For her, that was a foreign concept, but her journey began out of her core purpose.

Tulsi Gabbard is a political superstar, serves in the military, and is a complete badass in my book.

"The thing that has been the common thread throughout my life is how and where can I best be of service to God and be of service to others? How and where can I make the most impact? And it has taken me into politics. It has taken me out of politics. It's taken me to a lot of different places. But that's the constant internal introspection and prayer that I have. And what I'm seeking to do with my life."

I asked her how that 21-year-old woman went from local politics to running for president of the United States. Where did that confidence come from?

"When I was twenty-one years old, I was going and knocking on people's doors," Tulsi reflected. "I was super shy and an introvert. It was very, very hard for me to summon up the courage to knock on a total stranger's door, not knowing who was going to be behind it, not knowing what they were going to say to me. What were they going to ask me? Would I be able to answer the question? All of these fears and things running through my head, right? But the thing that kept me going door after door after door—I knocked on thousands during that campaign—was my sense of purpose. And my mission. And never once did I think, *I can't do this because I'm twenty-one,* or *I can't do this because I don't have a bachelor's degree,* or *I can't do this for any number of reasons that other people probably thought why I shouldn't do it.*"

Tulsi is undeniable because she is someone who learned her purpose at a young age and has decided to live it out. She said that politics has become such a game to a lot of politicians, especially during election times, where the races are treated like horse races and fantasy football, and where too many people lose sight that this is about real people. Tulsi knows firsthand that if you're not happy with the way things are, the only way to change it is by voting.

For her, it comes down to making the most impact and asking herself how she can best be of service. I asked her how her faith impacted her decisions and her daily life.

"It's everything. I draw strength and clarity and courage. It's what I pray for every day, asking God every day to please let me be of service. And having faith in Him that even though I don't know what the outcome may be or I may not know where the next ten steps lead, as long as I'm doing my best in that mission and that goal to serve, I have faith that that things will work out."

Drawing her strength and her happiness from doing the best she can to be of service to God is what keeps her grounded and focused, Tulsi told me. She doesn't care what people say about her, because she's not trying to win any popularity contest. She's heard it all—every kind of attack one could imagine.

"I don't draw my validation from what people in Washington say about me," Tulsi shared. "I wake up happy because I have an opportunity with my life to try to serve. I'm far from perfect; I'm a highly flawed individual. But I know that that so long as I continue to try to do my best, that is where my happiness comes from. It comes from within. It comes from God. And knowing that no matter what happens, His unconditional love is there for me, for every one of us."

Share your purpose.

Who is to say that your passion and your purpose can't impact people? Look at me.

How the hell can somebody like me end up with a story that inspires others? I came from nothing, and nobody believed in me. I was this regular guy destined for an average life, at best. I had a chip on my shoulder and spent years working hard. Now, looking back, I've achieved far more than I deserve. So, my message continues to be that if I can do this, other people can do it. There is greatness in all of us. And that greatness can impact others.

Look at Nedd Brockmann, the young electrician from Australia who ended up running 50 marathons in 50 days and who ran across his country. He, too, found his purpose at a young age. Nedd knows that you might be able to amass all the wealth in the world, but you can't take it with you when you pass away. All of that means nothing when you die.

"What we do leave is a legacy and the impact we have," Nedd told me. "At the end of the day, I much prefer to leave the world knowing that I left a lasting impact."

He said that too many people worry about themselves and are concerned about how their day looks. They don't look around at their world, but instead simply focus on themselves, and so many spend their days miserable.

"I just get frustrated when people are wasting their lives, but that's fine," Nedd said. "That's on them, but for me, I can't live knowing I didn't live up to my potential. My potential is making that impact."

Nedd believes that his running inspires others to go do something. To help with something. To be a part of something.

"I guess you're saying it starts with that first toss of the pebble in the water," I said.

"So, I do this. It might be ten people. Those ten people then go, 'What can I do?' And then those ten people, another ten people, and all of a sudden you've got this thing that's building upon itself."

All it takes is that one person who decides to make a change, to go live their life and do something they've always wanted to do, and in doing that, knowing that there's a ripple effect that eventually will have an impact on others.

Former US Marine Dakota Meyer is another person who sees the value of making a positive impact in such a negative world. He said to me, "We're messing up because we're just telling people what we're against, but we don't even know what the hell we're for." Dakota is someone who cares about people and wants to help them. He wants people to believe in themselves again. And he wants to provide hope, so the only way to do this is by saying things that provide hope.

"I don't care how you do it," Dakota said. "Are you making the world a better place? Are you having an impact on people? Are you helping people look in the mirror and believe in themselves again? I mean, that's all I care about. Whether you're doing it Jocko's way, David Goggins's way, or Tony Robbins's way. Whoever, whatever it is, are you having an impact on good? That's what matters."

As I wrote earlier, I saw firsthand the impact that neuroscientist Dr. Andrew Huberman is having on the world when I saw him speak at the University of Oregon. Andrew believes that in order to make an impact, you have to be willing to share wisdom and insight with others.

"When you share widely, people are grateful," he told me. "When you share widely, you suddenly have friends that are teaching you new things that you didn't know. And I realized this is the key. Don't hold everything close to your chest. You give it away. I had a revelation: I was like, 'Wow, there's a whole other way of doing science, where you share.' And I became known for what I'm doing now and for being extremely generous with these resources. When I started my own lab, I started working on neural regeneration. I always wanted to work on this. I want to have an impact on the world."

Impact doesn't have to affect millions of people, however. Recently, when I visited a prison to speak to around 100 incarcerated men, I shared with them how when I started to bowhunt, I had an impact on a small amount of people. But now I've been given the opportunity to impact a large group. Yet that doesn't mean my actions should change. I'm doing the same thing that I was doing years ago. I encouraged them to do the same. Even though they didn't have the opportunity to impact a large group of people, each of them could still have a positive impact on the incarcerated men next to them. It's all about that positive impact.

> **"THE PURPOSE OF LIFE IS TO DISCOVER YOUR GIFT. THE WORK OF LIFE IS TO DEVELOP IT. THE MEANING OF LIFE IS TO GIVE YOUR GIFT AWAY."** [12]
>
> —*David Viscott,* Finding Your Strength in Difficult Times: A Book of Meditations

If you're not making a positive impact in your life, what's your point? What are you doing? I want to make a positive impact on people every day. That's why I love social media and sharing what I do. I love to see people inspired. Hopefully, I can inspire others to do more. They don't have to enter a 200-mile race or run 10 miles a day or do any of this, but maybe they'll run 1 mile. Maybe they'll do something more in their life today by seeing what I do.

For Evan Hafer, founder and executive chairman of Black Rifle Coffee Company, he has chosen to ignore the hate that any impactful person will get these days.

"I've said this to lots of people," he told me. "Putting positivity in the world is awesome. It's inspiring people to be better. And there's always going to be negative information, negative people, and what they're doing is putting toxic fuel out into the world. I'm not doing that. I don't broker in that bullshit. I'm only in the game of putting fucking positive fuel back in the world. Guys like you, guys like Joe, guys like Goggins, and Jocko, and all these guys—you guys are putting positive fuel in the tanks of hundreds of thousands of people every day. And, man, we need an *army* of people like that. We need an army of people that are willing to go out, be in the public eye, and just accept it for what it is and go, 'You know what? I'm putting positive fuel into the world. I don't really give a shit what other people are gonna say.'"

I agree with Evan 100 percent. It's too easy to release toxic fuel into the world. Everybody has negative shit in their lives. I could easily share negativity all day long. I'm overcoming all sorts of hurdles all the time, but what's the point in spreading that? I want to be positive, and I want to inspire. I'm constantly amazed to go to places and meet the number of people who sometimes wait in a long line just to come up to me and share their stories about, say, losing weight, or some success they've had, or their bowhunting journey. This always makes me wonder, *How can a bowhunter make this much of an impact?* I have no idea, but it happened.

So, I'll ask you again: What's your calling in life? And if you know what it is, how are you using it to make a positive impact on this world?

Love your purpose.

One definition for passion is boundless enthusiasm. That perfectly sums up professional mountain and ultra runner Sally McRae. I wrote about her in chapter three but wanted to share more of her story here. She is one of the happiest people I've ever seen, with her big personality and big smiles and constant laugh. After reading her book *Choose Strong: The Choice That Changes Everything,* it's hard to believe she can be so positive, considering everything she went through in her teens.

"I was a happy kid," Sally told me. "I was just joyful. And I think happiness and joyfulness are different things. When you're happy, happiness can be fleeting. As parents, we say that we just want our kids to be happy. But joy is something that you can feel in darkness because joy is when it comes out. It's strength. It's rooted in gratefulness and hope. It's the idea that even though it hurts so bad or this sucks, even in a race, you can be joyful in that moment because of the fact that your body is on the move, and you have this opportunity to test yourself even though it hurts so bad and things aren't going your way."

Sally was the middle child of five kids growing up in a chaotic household in Southern California. She started racing when she was seven years old and also participated in gymnastics, but playing soccer was her first love. She was always the fastest on the team and scored the most goals. By the time she reached high school, many major college soccer programs began recruiting her, including Stanford, Berkeley, and Dartmouth. But everything in her life took a back seat when her mother was diagnosed with breast cancer.

Sally was only 14. Diane Moffett was brave in her battle with the disease, but ultimately passed away four weeks after Sally's seventeenth birthday.

Her mother had been the encouraging parent who told Sally she could do anything. Her father, however, was emotionally and physically abusive. After her mother died, Sally was left with many questions and no parent to give her answers. She had been working her ass off trying to be the best she could be in everything, and then her mother died, her dad got sick, and then was arrested. During the year that she turned 17, there was one bad thing after another every month for Sally.

"I really started to question whether or not life was ever going to change," she told me. "Even if it was worth living. I would have these very long prayers at night with God, and I would ask, 'Why? Why is it that some people have to hurt so much?'"

Sally learned at a young age this idea of having to endure pain and hurt and holding on to hope. Her mother was very honest in the last conversation they ever shared. She told Sally that she loved her and that she was going to be fine, but she also said life was going to be hard.

"I think that that's a really powerful message that we can tell our children or friends or anyone that we love," said Sally, a mother of two. "I'm not going to lie to you and tell you that life is going to be easy. It's going to be hard. But I want to encourage you that you're strong enough to get through it because that's a part of life for all of us."

Her mother was a woman of deep faith, always telling Sally that God loved her no matter what. That love is unconditional even when we fail and make bad mistakes. Yet with a father who was harsh and cruel to her, Sally still grew up with a very rough view of who God was. As she watched the peace her mother carried in those last months of her life, Sally could see her mom knew that she was going to go somewhere better. Sally witnessed the incredible hope her mother held in her heart.

"For someone to be at the end of their life and have peace and hope—I want that," Sally told me. "That's really how I've lived my life ever since. I can't imagine my life without a faith in Jesus Christ. All my hope, my joy, my strength—that's where it is. And when I talk about going to a quiet place, when I talk about embracing pain, it's just that place of prayer."

When everything in her life was ripped away at age 17, Sally didn't fully understand the plan God had for her life, but slowly things began to change regarding her faith. Now it is the most important part of her.

"The only one who knows me at my core is the one who created me," Sally expressed.

Known as Yellow Runner on social media, Sally McRae is a beacon of light for me and many others.

"And to be able to find strength and peace and hope in that—that's all I care about. That's where I find it every single day I get out of bed, and that's where I had to find it as an eighteen-year-old."

Sally shared that the greatest, grandest dreams we might have for ourselves don't compare to the plans God has for us. She often looks back at the dreams she held for herself as a teenager versus what she is doing today and knows she could have never imagined the life she is living now. Her faith allows her not to worry about meeting other people's expectations and instead experiencing the greatest joy from trusting God's plan for her. This joy and hope she holds is her purpose, and it's how she uses her platform.

"Running is just the excuse," Sally said. "It's literally the shiny object."

Now that she's an adult, Sally realizes that it's the hurt that most often binds humans to get us where we feel the most connected. Because now we can connect and empathize. Now we can have compassion with so many people because of our hurt. This gives her an opportunity to share her shiny object with others, especially when she meets people struggling in similar dark spots that she was in. She encourages everybody to know that there is something far greater than anything you can find in this world.

As Sally said, "The grass withers, the flowers fade, and the man-made stuff will always fail. You need something stronger and greater than who you are that will unconditionally never, ever change. Unconditional love."

Most people are looking for a life that has meaning, Sally said. They just want to know if their life mattered when they reach the end. Did they make any sort of impact?

"On a very personal level, I believe we are all put here for a purpose, a very unique purpose that only you can live out," Sally stated. "But you're not going to know that unless you live."

For Sally, running is a beautiful metaphor for life. She said that's why she does it. She loves to talk about the message of life in running.

"Racing is such a gentle way to experience discomfort and pain," Sally told me. "It's gentle because you know when you hit that hundred-mile mark, you're going to be all done. But life is not like that. Sometimes all you're thinking about is, *When is this going to end?* And sometimes we lose hope, or we give up, or we stop trying too early because there is no finish line in sight for us. There is no light at the end of the tunnel."

Life is just like running, Sally explained. We have to keep going because the finish line will eventually come into view. We have to hold that hope inside of us to keep moving forward, to keep checking that map, and to keep knowing that we're on the right path. That we're going to get there.

Humans are built to be strong and resilient, Sally said. We have to understand that we were created by a creator who is so powerful, and that His strength is in us.

According to Sally, "If you want to believe that—if you're going to step in faith and believe 'I am strong because I was made by a strong creator'—it will change your life."

Sally isn't the only person to talk about a "shiny object." UFC fighter Michael Chandler spoke about this after I'd asked him what impact faith had on his life.

"Mixed martial arts is what I do, but it's not who I am," Michael explained. "Yes, I am a fighter, but ultimately it's my shiny object that gets people to look at me."

Chandler wants people to see the layers that lie underneath that shiny object. He wants to show off the layers to his existence, that there's a mission and a platform that is so much different from the punches and the kicks that he dishes out. How does he treat people or love his wife and kids?

"I think operating in gratitude for the blessings that God has given me makes me feel the most like Superman," he said. "I think we get so caught up in the ego, so caught up in the me-me-me, when really there is no *me* without God having me in the palm of His hand

Sally McRae

my entire life. Every single season, every single relationship, every single person that's come in. Even the people that have had to leave."

The key to operating in gratitude every day, Chandler said, is to realize that we are where we are because of the blessings that we have had and the people that have been put into our lives. God speaks through people or through situations during both great times and tough times. We have to remain grateful throughout whatever season of life we're in. Chandler calls his life a masterpiece that he is painting. It's one that someday his children and grandchildren will learn about through headlines and fights and stories.

"I think we were called to be so much more than just little wandering generalities and people of mediocrity on this earth," Michael said intently. "There are different seasons for different people. There are going to be times of extreme accomplishment; there are going to be times of idleness. But ultimately, it's about trying to move forward toward the man or woman that you want to become. I think ultimately accomplishing things is great. Making an impact and having a platform or making money or business is great, but ultimately it's the man that you become on the other side of it, the woman that you become on the other side of it, that you can look yourself in the mirror and say, 'Man, I'm proud of what I built, a life that I built and the person that I built.'"

Cherish your purpose.

When I was growing up, there was this guy in town named Jim Carter who used to go hunting all September. Once I started bowhunting, I began to pay attention to him. I was killing bulls, but I had never killed a 6x6 bull. Jim was killing 6x6 big bulls every fucking year. I drove myself crazy obsessing over this.

How the fuck does this guy do this every year? How can he keep doing that? I can't kill one!

I'll be honest: My ego was bruised a little bit. I was wondering if I really sucked at bowhunting or if this guy was just that much better than me. I was envious that he hunted the whole month of September. For most of my life, my dream had been to be able to hunt all September. But even when things began to explode for me as a bowhunter, I still had my full-time job. Taking off an entire month was impossible until 2010, when I'd accumulated enough paid time off each year to take off the whole month. That is if I never used any sick days. And I never did. That said, I still had the obligations of work and the mess back at the office to clean up when I returned.

In September 2023 my dream came true. It took only 55 years to arrive.

That September was the first time in my adult life that I didn't have to hustle to get back to my nine-to-five, knowing every day I was away, work was piling up and issues were unresolved. After working 26 years at the Springfield Utility Board, I retired so that I could focus full-time on hunting and podcasting. The only work I had to do now was in the wilderness. The only unresolved issues were arrowing those elk.

As September came to a bittersweet end, I found myself on the Oregon coast. My whirlwind hunting trek had started in Idaho, moved to Utah, shifted to Colorado, journeyed to San Carlos, and then finally reached my home state. After killing a big Oregon Roosevelt elk, I felt melancholy as I balanced the feelings of a goal achieved with the death of an animal. The balance is becoming harder for me these days. I think I'm softening in my old age, but I am a bowhunter, and death will always be part of the journey.

This hunt is always my hardest and most rewarding of each season. Oregon bulls in this logging country are a challenge. My first bull in 1989 was a Roosevelt on an over-the-counter tag in logging country just like this last one. Killing a bull in my home state, where I was born and have lived my whole life, means so much to me. I always thank God for one more bull.

As the reality of the special month having reached its end sank in, I knew I would be going back to my normal life of preparing for next September. All the experiences of this past month in the mountains would be cherished until my last day. All the people I shared it with have enriched my life, and I'm so grateful for their company as I live out my life's purpose as a mountain bowhunter. I was excited knowing that we had some cool footage to share with the public that would help us buy some time until the next elk season.

I know how blessed I am to live this life, to have the opportunity to live in the mountains of the West and chase my elk-hunting dreams. All I've ever wanted to do is spend all month hunting the animal I dream about hunting for the other 11 months of the year. I hope to never take these memories for granted. If I do, I'll watch the videos from that month and smile at all the incredible country and the amazing people I shared this season with. In the 34 years between my first and last bull, a lot has changed and nothing has changed. Bowhunting gave me purpose then, and it still does. In 1989 I was struggling to determine if it was even possible for me to kill a bull elk with an arrow. I'd see guys

"YOU HAVE BECOME A DIFFERENT PERSON IN THE COURSE OF THESE YEARS, FOR THIS IS WHAT THE ART OF ARCHERY MEANS: A PROFOUND AND FAR-REACHING CONTEST OF THE ARCHER WITH HIMSELF. YOU WILL SEE WITH OTHER EYES AND MEASURE WITH OTHER MEASURES. IT HAPPENS TO ALL WHO ARE TOUCHED BY THE SPIRIT OF THIS ART."[13]

—*Eugen Herrigel*, Zen in the Art of Archery

like Jim Carter killing it, and I began to doubt if I ever would. And to be honest, there are still many times I've wondered, *How have I ever done it?* Bowhunting is so hard for me sometimes that it feels impossible.

Every year, I embrace the impossible and love to challenge it.

In many ways, bowhunting defines me.

Remember your purpose.

We can never forget where greatness comes from. The great world champion archer Levi Morgan never forgets. When he visited me, Levi shared a story that most people don't know. It was early in his career, when he wasn't making any money as he was traveling and sacrificing everything to make his archery dreams possible. He had come home defeated and was still involved with a rock masonry business. As he was leaving to go to his second tournament, his wife told him that they didn't have enough money to even enter the competition. For Levi, that was confirmation that he had to let this dream go.

"I'm like, *Okay, that's it. God, I think I get it. I'm not supposed to do this. It's my dream, and I'm not going to put my family through this.* So, I call my dad because I knew it was kind of his dream too for me. And he'd sacrificed so much, along with my mom."

Levi told his father that he didn't have the money to go and then explained that he was walking away from his dream of becoming a champion archer. His dad persuaded him to go one more time.

"If you go one more time, I'm going to pay your way," his father told him. "Just one time. You just go one more."

Levi said he would and promised that he would find a way to pay back his father. At the shoot, he felt this additional weight of pressure on him. After falling behind in the competition, something came over Levi.

"So, I'm sixteen points back," he told me. "I'm so screwed. But something clicked right there, and I lost all fear of anything. It was a 'now or never, bud' kind of thing. I just started gunning. I set a world record that's still never been broken and won the entire event. And I've still never shot that high of a score to this day. It was a crazy feeling."

He called his dad, and they cried together. All the hard work and effort that Levi had put in had finally paid off. It was his first pro win, and it came right after he'd almost quit. For Levi, this wasn't about his exceptional talent. It was about God sending him a message.

"It almost felt like I had to get to the point where I had given it all that I had," Levi said, "and God was almost showing me, 'Without me, you ain't doing this.'"

I love that story. Levi has always been one to always give God the glory in all his successes and efforts, including sharing the following with me:

"I've had so many instances like that where I'm like, 'I don't have any more, I'm not feeling it this weekend. No way I can win.' And in those moments, it always seems like something clicks, and I know it's not me that does it. I've always just felt like, 'Why me? Why am I allowed to do this?' Because I don't feel like I'm that good. I don't feel like I deserve to be the one standing there when the smoke clears, but God has just allowed me to do it so many times. So, that's why I think I'm so quick to give credit to Him, because I know deep in my heart that it wasn't me. I did the work, but a lot of guys do work, and a lot of guys are great. I'm just very grateful, very thankful to have been able to do what I've done."

So am I, Levi.

Practice your purpose.

I do that every day. Lift, run, shoot. And these days, I get to do it with others.

How fucking awesome is that?

Live out your purpose.

The outliers I'm around inspire me. And they don't all have to fly into Springfield in order for me to see them. I have many outliers in my life, ones I get to see every day.

Outliers like my brother, Taylor Spike. I'm so proud of him. After everything he has been through, he is crushing life. The times we've shared together—running the brutal races—are some of my most cherished memories. Every time I see him, I always feel good.

Taylor runs with purpose. Every mile means something to my brother. Years ago, he took a step to get out of his comfort zone to do something real and scary. To become something more and to embrace life. He conquered his addictions and focused on something bigger to spend his time doing.

"You don't realize what you're doing, and you think it's okay if everybody else is doing it," Taylor told me. "But you have way more purpose than that in life. We need to do what we can to make sure that people can do better. We can make them smile or inspire them. If you can get people living their life a little bit—that's my goal. I've made a lot of bad choices, but I've made a couple good choices that have positively impacted my family and my life and then others, and I just want to keep doing that."

I always see people talking about Taylor and mentioning him to me, and every time they do, it's always in a positive light. They're always telling me how he's made a positive impact on their lives.

On my podcast I was able to express my love and appreciation for my brother.

"Whatever your goals are or whatever you've been through in life, all I know is what you're doing now, you should feel proud," I told Taylor. "You're helping people. You're pulling back the curtain on what's possible to people, and you're encouraging people, and they're seeing you, and they want to do more. So, it makes me feel very proud to be your brother."

"That's super humbling," Taylor replied. "It's good to know that. It's an honor to hear that from you."

"I'm just really proud to be your brother," I told him. "So, thank you. Thank you for how you've enriched my life and what you're doing for others. And just the example you're setting. You've learned lessons that people can maybe learn from your journey, too. That's what life's about."

Another outlier I have known most of my life who is living a life of purpose is Wayne Endicott, the owner of the Bow Rack in Springfield. Over three decades ago, Roy was Wayne's second customer at the store. Since that time, Wayne has been a friend and brother as our lives have been focused on the archery lifestyle we love. Wayne and his wife, Lisa, play a key role and have become a fan favorite on the Lift Run Shoot series.

Like so many of these men and women who have talked to me on the Keep Hammering Collective, Wayne's purpose is centered around his faith. He didn't grow up in a Christian family. His parents were good, moral people, but they didn't know God. By the time Wayne was 18, he ended up having an unbelievable experience.

"I was the rottenest kid in the whole, entire world and was following a girl to church," Wayne shared. "A youth pastor asked me, 'Wayne, if you die right now, where are you going to go?' And I'm like, 'Without a doubt, I'm going to hell.' I knew that. I knew that was written on my heart. I had a dark heart. I didn't like church. I didn't like anything about it. I didn't like anything about God. I didn't know there was a way out. I never heard the gospel."

After being honest with himself, Wayne had somebody lead him in a prayer, and for the first time in his entire life, he felt clean. But that didn't mean the rest of his life was going to be perfect. He shared a story of a time when he was hunting with Roy, and although he still had his faith, Wayne was back in a dark place. He was in a broken marriage and was living for himself. Being around Roy woke him up to what faith really looks like.

"That's why he is who he is," Wayne said about Roy. "Because he's sensitive to what God wanted for his life. And I wasn't at that time."

Wayne still grieves Roy's loss, like all of us who knew him. He sang Roy's praises while we were talking. He called Roy that "once-in-a-lifetime type of guy"—a statement I agree with completely.

"Literally the toughest, kindest, most unbelievable individual I've ever hunted with in my life," Wayne said. "And we both were super blessed and super gifted that we had that time with Roy. We are beyond imagination. He impacted us. We didn't deserve to have a guy like that. To know he's in Heaven, it comforts me because I know the Lord loved him so much. If there was a multiple choice on how you were going to go? He went the way he wanted to go."

Wayne has found a new sense of purpose in life these days. He had another life-changing event happen to him when he was contacted by a former neighbor, Carl, who wanted to see him. Carl was battling colon cancer. One night on the way home, Wayne felt God telling him to go see Carl and pray with him, but Wayne talked himself out of doing that.

"I started arguing with God," Wayne said. "'That's going to be awkward. And I heard he was doing better. Lord, I just heard he's in remission. I saw him driving the other day.' You know, making all these excuses. "'I'll do it, but I'm not going to do it tonight. I'm tired. I'm going to go home.'"

The next morning, right before heading into work, Wayne received a call and was told that Carl had passed away sometime earlier that morning.

"I was instantly on my knees, and I'm like, 'Lord, I blew it big-time.' Carl needed me. He needed me that night. He needed me there. He needed to know. And I struggled with this for the longest time."

Later, Wayne found out that two men had gone to see Carl the night before he died, and Carl ended up giving his heart and life to Christ. Wayne couldn't believe this. This news changed him. It has been like a stamp on his heart. He knows now that if he feels God telling him to do something, he has to obey. Wayne told me that he feels he has heard a clear message from God.

"The Lord is like, 'Look: If you don't obey me, there's not going to be that many more times for you. Because this life is short. I mean, you're on the other end of the hourglass, son. You might think you're nineteen, and you may try to live like you're nineteen, but you're not. You're sixty-one. None of this is coming with you. I've given you a lot of gifts and I've blessed you with a lot of things. And if you are not salt and light to this world, then you're no good. If you're not salt and light, you're nobody.'"

From that time on, Wayne has become involved with street ministry. He says it's one of the most exciting things he's ever done in his life. Sharing the gospel with strangers on a street corner and praying with them. He said it's been so rewarding and so fulfilling to see God moving into the lives of the men he meets. And it's all because he found a new sense of purpose in his life. His neighbor's passing away like that changed him. It imprinted him, and he said he will never be the same.

"In my life, I'm passionate about archery and bowhunting," Wayne said. "I want to help everybody. But with that, there has to be a message of life with it, and so incorporating that just completes the spectrum."

Leave a legacy of purpose.

I love hearing stories of people who have a definable purpose; and to be honest, I'm jealous of people who have an undeniable faith.

Sometimes I will go to church and hear a sermon and think that it all makes perfect sense, but there are times when your mind can be your biggest adversary, because you start to question everything. I wish I had that blind faith—that trusting faith—that so many I've met have. For me, it's still up and down. I love hearing stories like the kind that Wayne shared. I love hearing about the purpose behind people's lives, like Sally McRae's. It's beautiful to hear how much joy she has even though she's gone through so much pain. How can you not be impacted by that?

Roy always seemed to know his purpose. Maybe that's why he had faith in a loser like me with no purpose or direction. Maybe that's why he encouraged me to start bowhunting. As a 20-year-old greenhorn, I felt my life had purpose in the wilderness. I found my passion, a goal to strive for. I wanted to be a backcountry bowhunter, and when I became one, I wanted to be the best backcountry bowhunter that ever lived.

The truth is I was always following in that legendary bowhunter's footsteps. The irony, though, is that Roy never wanted to be the best bowhunter. The legacy he wanted to leave was bigger and better than bowhunting.

"My legacy has everything to do with hunting, but very little to do with hunting," Roy told me once. "My legacy, I believe, is that God has given me the talents that I have to affect people for the good. To impact people that otherwise I never would have been able to meet. I believe the hunting world is my mission's field. You can't just come up to a lot of people and start saying, 'Hey, this is what I believe, this is how I think you should believe,' when they have no respect for you. You've got to gain their respect for people to listen to you, for you to have an impact on them. The hunting world is a hard world that way. So, if you can gain the respect through your accomplishments, I believe that's the way. That's why God gives you those talents."

Those words have stuck with me years after he said them, especially this line:

"I believe the hunting world is my mission's field."

I believe it still is.

The world was a better place when Roy Roth was here because of the impact he had on me and many others, but I think his legacy lives on and continues to positively impact people.

These outliers I've been able to meet, and lift, run, and shoot with, and hear from their hearts are all a result of Roy having come into my life. Every time they share something positive and affirming and inspiring with listeners, they are doing that because Roy did the same with me. Anytime one of these undeniable people share their faith, they are continuing the legacy of Roy's life. The difference is that now his mission's field isn't just the hunting world. It's the whole world.

I don't know if it's my responsibility to continue Roy's legacy, but it's something I want to do. The irony is how I'm currently doing it today.

Life can be funny. Looking back on your life can provide a lot of amusement. Over the years, I've hated public speaking and podcasting and talking in general. I've never wanted to act like I know anything about anything because—well, I don't. Unless it's bowhunting and bushwhacking in the mountains. At the first seminar I ever gave, at the Eugene Sportsmen's Show 25 years ago, I had eight people in attendance. Five of them were my family. Lots of things have changed since then. I still hate getting up in front of crowds, and I don't enjoy speaking as much as writing, but it seems like I'm talking a lot these days on my podcast. I love asking questions and listening to the experts. There are so many valuable lessons that I've learned, like the ones I've written about in this book.

The truth is I never had a purpose until I met Roy, and even after I became obsessed with bowhunting, I never had the feeling that this was my purpose. It's just kind of happened over time. From the start, all I loved was shooting a bow. All I had was that shitty $189 bow that my mom got me for Christmas. That was all I needed.

In my quest to meet and train with as many outliers as I can, I've been criticized by some of my fellow hunters for bringing too many people into the cherished pastime we love. I speak of my passion for the timeless tradition of bowhunting, and naturally others want to learn more about it. I've always believed this was a good thing.

If Fred Bear, the godfather of modern archery, hadn't shared his experiences in print and video, would bowhunting still exist or would it have died out? How about Chuck Adams, who I read growing up as a young archer and who was known as the world's most recognizable bowhunter? Did these legends ruin the pursuit I love? No, they fostered its growth and acceptance. Has Courtney Dauwalter ruined trail running by excelling, sharing her journey, and becoming a household name? Of course not. She is an icon, just like Michael Jordan. Sharing what we love and what pushes us to live a purposeful life is what it means to be a healthy human. To those that question and criticize this, maybe you're just miserable burnouts and that's impacting your perception? Or maybe not. I don't know; I'm not a psychologist. I'm just a redneck bowhunter, but if what I do upsets you, buckle up. We're just getting started.

BECOME UNDENIABLE

You aren't born undeniable.

Yes, a few individuals inherit their great abilities, but most men and women who achieve greatness are born lacking it. Their refusal to accept this becomes the very thing that defines them.

We often look at the abilities of those who are undeniable as traits we can acquire. Maybe the thing that makes someone become undeniable is the act of refusing and rejecting the life and path they're on and rewriting their story.

You don't wake up undeniable. You work up to it. And the truth is you don't stop waking up and working. You do it day after day after day.

If you're truly dedicated to your craft, and you believe in your skills, there's only one person who can make your dreams a reality.

The person in the mirror.

You might be able to look yourself in the mirror and say all the right things, but if you don't believe them, it's going to be tough.

It starts with a purpose. Do you know yours?

A writer puts pen to paper. A doctor heals the sick. An artist shares their vision. A carpenter builds. You'd never expect any of them to do anything other than their calling. So, come September, don't ever expect me to do anything other than roam the mountains, bow in hand.

This is my purpose.

> **This is what I do.**

> **What about you?**

If you do have a goal and a dream, what is your bottom line? And what is your breaking point that will get you there?

How far can you take this? Really take this?

How deeply do you believe in this dream?

You've heard me say that yesterday means nothing.

You've seen the saying "Nobody cares. Work harder!"

We don't rest on our laurels. The job's not finished. It's never finished.

Those whose talents are unquestionable and indisputable are never finished.

There's a saying that man's greatest regret is unfulfilled potential. When you get to the end of this journey and you're lying there, how will you answer this sobering question:

Did I give all I had? Did I truly give all I had?

Nobody will know except you.

Maybe if tomorrow never comes, your answer to that question would be "no."

So, maybe you should start truly giving all you can today.

Today might be the greatest day you've ever known.

You can block out the noise and ignore the nonsense.

You can write out your passion and follow your purpose.

You can become tunnel-vision focused and have unwavering determination.

You have to be tenacious because it's going to suck.

You have to be disciplined because it's going to get uncomfortable.

Be confident.

    Be resilient.

       Be consistent.

          Be tough. Become ROY TOUGH.

That is how you become undeniable.

EPILOGUE: STAYING ON TOP

Everyone wants to be on top of the mountain, but no one wants to suffer to get there. Becoming undeniable resembles a hunt. When you start off, you're kind of surveying the land. You're taking into account all the conditions. Then you wonder, *Am I going to make it to the top? Am I actually going to get this kill?* Then you get a kill, and you're at the summit. It takes a lot of fucking work to get there, but in the end the reward outweighs the doubts and fears.

You can't truly appreciate or fully experience the top of the mountain without having to grind up from the bottom. That 16-year-old whose world was only 20 miles big is a lot different from this 56-year-old who has traveled all over the world hunting, running, living, and learning. There have been a lot of miles covered, a lot of sweat wiped from my brow, and a lot of blood spilled in those 40 years.

This simple man's mountain journey with bow in hand has been a long, tiring, uphill road that began four decades ago. To quote the nineteenth-century Russian novelist Fyodor Dostoyevsky, "There is only one thing that I dread: not to be worthy of my sufferings." That's why I love bowhunting. It will expose you. It will crush you. Yet conversely, it can change your life for the better, like any hard-earned achievement. The big difference with bowhunting is that a life is at stake. It's not a game; it's not a challenge like running a marathon, where pain is surface level and temporary. In bowhunting, when it hurts, it hurts deep because of the animal and the work required to kill with an arrow. When it works, it feels purposeful and as God intended. Hunter versus hunted, predator versus prey. Unlike animals that kill, man has compassion, so for the bowhunter, mercy plays a key part.

What separates the greats from the average? There's a difference between knowing the path and walking it. Many know what to do, but results show who's actually doing it.

I'll say it again for the millionth time: Talent-wise I can't compete, so I've had to rely simply on work. To be honest, without hard work, I'm nothing. However, if you're like me, and all you have to lean on is outworking the competition, many times that's enough. People really don't enjoy competing with someone who won't quit. Keep hammering, and good things will happen. That's a guarantee.

When I was talking to the always brilliant Chris Williamson, he shared something that the ancient Roman emperor Marcus Aurelius wrote in the second century AD: "Life itself is but what we deem it."

Chris calls them "the eight most profound words in all of philosophy," going on to explain, "What he means is that things are going to happen. You are going to have experiences in life. Almost all of the important impacts of how those experiences change you are going to be the story that you tell yourself about what that experience means."

According to Chris, the story that we tell ourselves and the framing we place around our present situation largely determine our experience of it.

"This is where having faith in yourself, having confidence in yourself, an undeniable stack of proof that you can deal with whatever is put in front of you, is super important," he told me.

Do you have an undeniable stack of proof in your life? I can say that I have a big stack, but that doesn't mean I'm going to sit on top of it. It means nothing if I don't keep going.

I have my own version of Marcus Aurelius's famous quote. Consider this the Cam Hanes paraphrase. It's one simple word:

"Poser."

Just as Marcus ultimately wrote those words to himself, I wrote "poser" to myself. I wrote it on the rock we carry up the mountain. Some people call me a poser, so that's the only word I need. When I see it on the rock I'm carrying, it's a reminder that some people don't think I'm shit. And half the time, I myself feel like some kind of fraud, like a poser.

Of course, on the other side of the rock, I wrote out the following Bible verse, from Isaiah 54:17:

"No weapon formed against thee shall prosper."

To me, it means that I listen to what the haters say, prove them wrong, and don't forget about it. The longer time goes by, the less I'm listening to shit talkers. Life's so good that I can focus only on the positives these days. There is power in positivity. Look at all of the outliers in this book and all the others I didn't have time and space to include. They have positive attitudes. Their lives are having a positive impact on others. That's what I want to continue doing in my life.

That means I'll wake up and run in the dark on a rainy, 37-degree morning. Those are good conditions to run in, as it keeps you honest. As in: Are you truly who you say you are? Yeah, okay, then prove it.

Do you know what else is good? Life challenges, because once you quit wallowing in self-pity, quit making excuses, put down the bottle, or keep the lid on those pills, regular life challenges come and go. Yes, you get wet and cold when it rains, but you dry out. Once you realize the world is bigger than you, when your head is up and your eyes are clear, you can do some real work. Look around, see what's going on. People need you to be strong, to lead, or to lean on. Be that person. Make a positive difference. Fight the good fight. These are critical times we live in, so any wallowing you might do is pathetic. Trust me, I know. I was that person.

Just realize that everybody hurts. The key is to keep pushing, and even though it doesn't feel like it, eventually the pain will pass, the clouds will part, your eyes will brighten, a smile will return, and the sun will shine on the mountains once again. The key word in those sentences is *will*. It was always destined, but in one's mind, the feeling of *will* is oftentimes replaced with a less definitive feeling of *hope*. Instead of "I hope tomorrow's better," change your mindset to "Tomorrow *will* be better."

That's one reason I love running long ultras. Once you get through the night and that sun starts to break on the horizon, everything changes. With the new day, you are always reenergized. As the hymn goes, "Morning by morning new mercies I see.[14]"

I've been seeing a lot of new mercies these days. I get to experience one every time I am privileged to hang out with an outlier. It's an amazing thing to suffer a little bit with someone. Once you have that connection of pain, the discussion that follows will always be more intimate and personal. There's more trust that's been built up.

That mountain isn't going anywhere. Neither is that rock. So, I'm going to keep climbing. If you're undeniable: I'm listening, I'm watching, and as always, I'm trying to learn."

Do you have what it takes to make this wall? All it takes is becoming undeniable . . . get to work.

ACKNOWLEDGMENTS

First, I am so thankful for my wife and kids. I appreciate Tracey, Tanner, Truett, and Taryn for their love and support and giving my life purpose. You all make my work, sacrifice, and accomplishments mean something. I don't tell you all enough, but, thank you. I love you.

Second, over the years I've been continually inspired by the support and passion of all of you who have followed my journey. It's easy to talk about and occasionally comment on the haters, but it's impossible to let this incredible community know how much their positive feedback has meant to me over the years. I never take your support for granted.

Last, it's been a pleasure to partner once again with Marc Resnick and the talented team at St. Martin's Press on *Endure* and now, *Undeniable*. Thanks Alicia Hanes and Emmy McCormick for reading through the manuscript and offering such great feedback. And, thanks to Travis Thrasher for being my right-hand man in this process. Travis, you're such a talent and great man.

NOTES

1 "Allen Iverson Remembers Kobe Bryant," ESPN, Facebook, last modified February 20, 2020, https://www.facebook.com/ESPN/videos/allen-iverson-remembers-kobe-bryant/612291322957696/.

2 Dwight R. Schuh, *Bowhunter's Encyclopedia: Practical, Easy-to-Find Answers to Your Bowhunting Questions* (Mechanicsburg, PA: Stackpole Books, 1987), 340.

3 Michael Jordan, *Driven from Within*, ed. Mark Vancil (New York: Atria Books, 2005), 81.

4 Saxton Pope, *Hunting with the Bow and Arrow* (New York: G. P. Putnam's Sons, 1923), 117.

5 Lee Iacocca with William Novak, *Iacocca: An Autobiography* (New York: Bantam Books, 1984, 2012), xvi.

6 John C. Maxwell, *Failing Forward: Turning Mistakes into Stepping Stones for Success* (New York: Harper-Collins, 2007), 75.

7 "The Man from Booger Bottom—A Realtree Original: Michael Waddell," Realtree online, last accessed December 2, 2024, https://realtree.com/michael-waddell.

8 "Courtney Dauwalter Wins UTMB* in Chamonix to Complete the 'Triple Crown,'" Salomon online, last modified December 1, 2023, https://www.salomon.com/en-us/courtney-dauwalter-triple-crown-2023.

9 Jenna Goudreau, "Malcolm Gladwell Shares the Single Most Important Factor of a Person's Success," *Business Insider*, last modified October 8, 2014, https://www.businessinsider.com/malcolm-gladwell-most-important-factor-of-success-2014-10

10 Thom Carnell, "Interview: Joe Rogan," January 2011. Archived from the original on February 6, 2017.

11 Ernest Hemingway, *The Old Man and the Sea* (New York: Charles Scribner's Sons, 1952).

12 David Viscott, *Finding Your Strength in Difficult Times: A Book of Meditations* (Chicago: Contemporary Books, 1993), 87.

13 Eugen Herrigel, *Zen in the Art of Archery*, trans. R. F. C. Hull (New York: Pantheon Books, 1953), 90.

14 Thomas Obediah Chisholm, "Great Is Thy Faithfulness," 1923.